THE PROPHECY
OF EZEKIEL

THE PROPHECY OF EZEKIEL

The Glory of the Lord

By

CHARLES LEE FEINBERG

MOODY PRESS

CHICAGO

To
My past and present colleagues
of
Dallas Theological Seminary
and
Talbot Theological Seminary
this volume is respectfully and
cordially dedicated

CONTENTS

PREFACE

No EXPERIENCE of a Christian, even beyond teaching and preaching the Word, leaves him more aware of shortcomings than an attempt at a written exposition of a book of prophecy. This is especially true of the prophecy of Ezekiel. But the spiritual rewards of such activity far outweigh any sense of inadequacy. Every generation of believers must interpret afresh the timeless truths of the Word to its own temporaries. Such is the justification for this work.

Over a period of years this exposition appeared serially in the missionary magazine *The Chosen People*. So many were the gracious and repeated comments of blessings received and so frequent the reiterated desire that these studies be placed in book form, that the author has acceded to these requests in the midst of a busy schedule of teaching, preaching and writing.

It is a pleasure to express thanks for the patience and encouragement of Dr. Daniel Fuchs, editor of *The Chosen People*; for the help rendered on the manuscript by my son, John; for the courtesies shown me by the Moody Press staff; and, finally, for help on the manuscript and encouragement in ways too numerous to mention, rendered by my beloved and understanding wife.

This work is thus commended to the blessing of the people of God everywhere and to the glory of the triune God.

CHARLES LEE FEINBERG

La Mirada, California

INTRODUCTION

THE PROPHET

OF THE PERSONAL HISTORY of Ezekiel we know nothing beyond what is found in his book and what is known of the times in which he lived. He is not mentioned in any other Old Testament book nor is he directly cited in the New Testament, although the imagery of the book of Revelation is clearly based on his visions. His name means "God will strengthen" or "God strengthens." He was a priest (1:3), and as the son of Buzi the priest he was of the Zadok family. There is no evidence that Ezekiel ever performed any priestly functions in Jerusalem before his deportation to Babylon. He was taken captive to Babylon with King Jehoiachin (1:2; 33:21) in the eighth year of Nebuchadnezzar (597 B.C.; see II Kings 24:14). Most of the captives deported with Ezekiel were settled at the river Chebar (1:3) which has now been identified as a royal canal of Nebuchadnezzar (cf. Ps. 137:1).

Ezekiel was deported to Babylon in 597 B.C., and if 1:1 refers to his age, he was born in 627 B.C. He was married and had his own home (8:1; 24:18) where the elders of Israel came to consult with him. His wife died during his ministry, but he was expressly forbidden to mourn (24:16-18). He began his ministry in the fifth year of Jehoiachin's captivity when he was thirty years old (1:1), and he prophesied about twenty years (1:2; 29:17). We know nothing of the end of his ministry. Ezekiel was a contemporary of Jeremiah, but nowhere does Ezekiel mention him.

The book is full of the personal experiences of the prophet. He shut himself up in his home, bound himself and was smitten dumb (3:24-26); he was charged to lie on his right side and then his left side for 430 days (4:4-8); he ate bread prepared in an unclean manner (4:12); he had to shave his head and beard (5:1); he was not permitted to mourn at the death of his wife (24:15-24); and he lost his speech (24:27). God intended Ezekiel to be a sign to Israel in the experiences of his life (24:24).

The prophet has been spoken of as suffering from a mental abnormality, even from a form of catalepsy. Such a conclusion arises from a failure to understand the nature or the purpose of Ezekiel's visions and experiences. His life and service were completely under God's appointment and he

11

became a man greatly used of God. In fact, he has been called "the father of Judaism" because of the influence he is said to have exerted on the later worship of Israel. A comparison may be made between the Apostle John on the island of Patmos and Ezekiel at Chebar—both lived in a place of isolation and oppression.

THE TIMES OF EZEKIEL

No prophet nor prophecy of the Bible can be adequately understood unless the historical background is taken into account. Along with Jeremiah and Daniel, Ezekiel was one of the three captivity prophets. While Jeremiah was ministering in Judah, Ezekiel was preaching to the Jews taken captive to Babylon in the siege of Jehoiachin (597 B.C.) and Daniel was serving at the court of Nebuchadnezzar (Dan. 1:1-7). Neither Jeremiah, who was the older prophet, nor Ezekiel mentions the other, although there is a legend that Ezekiel was Jeremiah's secretary. However, Ezekiel does mention Daniel three times (14:14, 20; 28:3). The only other period of such fullness of prophetic testimony was the time of Isaiah, Hosea, Amos and Micah in the eighth century B.C. Ezekiel shows a closer relationship in concept and message to Jeremiah than to Daniel.

Many of Ezekiel's prophecies are dated in great detail within the time of the captivity of King Jehoiachin. The date in 1:1, which has been the cause of much difference of opinion, must refer to Ezekiel's own age, the specific time when Levites entered upon their priestly duties (Num. 4:23, 30, 39, 43). At first his messages were not well received (14:1, 3; 18:19, 25), but with the passing of time his prophecies began to bear fruit, and the nation was purged of its idolatrous tendencies. Ezekiel lived in a context of spiritual declension, distress and uprooting. He saw clearly that the times called for further judgment from the Lord, which came in the third deportation from Judah. When judgment had accomplished its full work, then the need of the hour was consolation for the weary and wounded nation.

MESSAGE OF THE PROPHET

If the message of Isaiah centers about the salvation of the Lord, that of Jeremiah about the judgment of the Lord, and that of Daniel about the kingdom of the Lord, then that of Ezekiel is concerned with the glory of the Lord. Ezekiel is probably the most neglected of all the prophetic books. The difficulty which chapter 1 introduces seems to deter many from a study of the book. This is indeed unfortunate, for the message of Ezekiel is vital to the canon of Scripture and is not duplicated anywhere in the Bible. The prophet stresses primarily the divine government of the universe. Large divisions of the prophecy deal with judgment on Jerusalem and the nations before the fall of Jerusalem in 586 B.C.; after the city's capture the prophet predicts blessing and glory for the city and nation in the future. Ezekiel's denunciations against Judah's spiritual declension are more severe than those of Jeremiah. Ezekiel ministered to all twelve tribes and his purpose was twofold: (1) to remind them of the sins which had brought judgment and exile upon them; (2) to encourage and strengthen their faith by prophecies of future restoration and glory.

The figure of the Messiah is not so prominent in Ezekiel or Jeremiah as it is in Isaiah. Actually, neither the first nor the second coming of the Lord Jesus Christ, Israel's Messiah, is mentioned in this book. It is interesting, also, to notice that nothing against Babylon is stated in chapters 25-32 which are the oracles against foreign nations. The turning point in the prophet's life and ministry became apparent when news of Jerusalem's fall was brought (33:21) because it was God's confirmation of Ezekiel's previous predictions and formed the foundation upon which his later ministry was built.

The vision Ezekiel had at the time of his call never left him but influenced his thought continually. It was the knowledge of God: holy, glorious and sovereign. The prophet does not show a struggle with his feelings such as is so evident in Jeremiah's life and service. Ezekiel carefully vindicates God's justice throughout (14:23; 18:5-20; 33:10-20).

STYLE OF THE BOOK

Ezekiel uses more of symbol and allegory in his writing than any other Old Testament prophet. As many writers have vainly tried to show, the book of Ezekiel is not derived from heathen sources but has its foundation in the sanctuary of Israel and in Old Testament concepts and viewpoints. One who was prepared as a priest was eminently qualified to give the descriptions set forth in chapters 1 and 10, as well as in the extended portion of chapters 40-48. Commentators have expressed themselves on the obscurity of the beginning and end of the prophecy of Ezekiel. But it must be remembered that Ezekiel is the great mystic among the inspired writers. Because of the difficulty in interpreting his figurative and visionary prophecies, he is the most neglected of all the prophets. However, it must be kept in mind that in Ezekiel, as in all the Old Testament, the figures of the Scriptures are meant to reveal, not conceal, the truth of God.

The prophet also delivered his messages by symbolic acts. At least ten are given: 4:1-3, 9-15; 5:1-4; 3:25, 26; 4:4-6, 8, 13; 12:3-7, 17-20; 21:11-12; 24:3-5, 15-24; 37:15-17. No prophet tells so much about the manner of his inspiration as Ezekiel. God's ways were revealed to him in visions, and his visions were frequent. The glory thus conferred upon him is registered in passages that are among the most remarkable in the Scriptures. (Cf. Ezek. 1 with Rev. 4-5; Ezek. 3:3 with Rev. 10:10; Ezek. 8:3 with Rev. 13:14-15; Ezek. 9 with Rev. 7; Ezek. 10 with Rev. 8:1-5.)

Actually, the style of Ezekiel is quite varied; he uses visions, symbols, parables, prophetic discourses and allegories (chap. 23). He liked to convey his messages in as concrete form as possible. His style ranges between poetry and prose.

OUTLINE OF THE BOOK

The book is commonly divided into two parts: chapters 1-24 and 25-48. The first portion treats the moral condition of Israel under the reigns of Jehoiachin and Zedekiah, the last kings of Judah. Some commentators divide at 33:21 because of the importance of the destruction of the temple. Before that point the prophecies center on judgment; afterward, on promises and consolations. A threefold division of the book is possible: (1) chapters 1-24, prophecies before the destruction of Jerusalem with emphasis on the sin of Jerusalem and Samaria; (2) chapters 25-32, prophecies during Jerusalem's fall; and (3) chapters 33-48, prophecies after Jerusalem's fall. Others divide the book into four parts: (1) chapters 1-24, prophecies relating to Israel, exhorting them to repentance before the fall of Jerusalem; (2) chapters 25-32, prophecies against seven nations surrounding Israel; (3) chapters 33-39, Israel's spiritual condition and promises of future blessing; and (4) chapters 40-48, an extended portrayal of millennial conditions and glory. For the purposes of this study the following outline is used:

I. Prophecies of Jerusalem's Destruction (chaps. 1-24)
   A. The call of the prophet (1:1—3:21)
   B. Prophecies of the fall of the nation (3:22—7:27)
   C. The pollution of the temple (8:1—11:25)
   D. The certainty and causes of the nation's doom (12:1—19:14)
   E. Additional prophecies of Israel's judgment (20:1—24:27)

II. Prophecies Against the Nations (chaps. 25-32)
   A. Ammon, Moab, Edom and the Philistines (25:1-17)
   B. Tyre (26:1—28:19)
   C. Sidon (28:20-26)
   D. Egypt (29:1—32:32)

God Is Sovereign

From the first to the last chapter of Ezekiel one supreme thought runs throughout, that of the sovereignty and glory of the Lord God. He is sovereign in Israel and in the affairs of the nations of the world, though the loud and boisterous claims of men seem to have drowned out this truth. In His sovereign will God has purposed that we should glorify Him in life and witness to the ends of the earth. Was there ever an hour more weighed with terror and yet more opportunity than is ours? Hours of opportunity do not tarry for the convenience of man. What we do must be done quickly.

1

THE VISION OF THE GLORY

Jacob saw God at Peniel and his life was transformed from that hour. Moses went up to Mount Sinai and communed with God face to face and thereafter was marked for the rest of his life. Isaiah saw the glory of the Lord in the sanctuary and his entire ministry was suffused with the beauty of the holiness of the Lord. Paul saw the risen and glorified Redeemer on the Damascus road and was blinded from that day on to all the allurements of the world. John saw visions of the glorious unfolding of God's program for Christ, the church and all the redeemed, and as a result was unmoved by the adverse circumstances that surrounded him. Ezekiel saw visions of the glory of the Lord God of Israel and his ministry never lost the impress of it. Such is the importance for Ezekiel's life and ministry of chapter 1 of this book.

Historical Setting of the Prophecy (1:1-3)

In the early verses of chapter 1 notice the extensiveness of detail noting the time. Also of great significance are the four ways in which Ezekiel received the message of God: the opened heavens, the visions of God, the coming of the Word to the prophet, and the imposed hand of the Lord. Ezekiel is the only prophet who is said to have seen the heavens opened, probably an indication of the breadth and depth of insight granted him.

The thirtieth year referred to in the opening line of the book, which is taken to be 593 B.C., has been explained in different ways. Some assume it to be a reckoning from the time of Josiah's reforms in 621 B.C., but it is not easy to see any connection between the events in Josiah's reign and the time of this prophecy. Others understand it to be a date from the rule of Nabopolassar, the founder of the new Babylonian Empire. Still others refer the date to the year of Ezekiel's life, which appears to be the most probable explanation since the prophet is seen among the captives of Judah. Furthermore, his ministry is related chronologically with Jehoiachin's captivity (see II Kings 25:27; Jer. 52:31). The nation had had sufficient warning to repent and ample proof of the disaster of disobedience by this time. Did it avail? The answer can be found in II Chronicles 36:11-16. It is an indication of the times of the Gentiles when the Judean

17

king is in exile. The capture of Jerusalem under Zedekiah had not yet
taken place. All that is indicated is the place of Ezekiel's residence; no
reference is given to suggest that others saw the vision granted him.

Chebar, noted as the place of Ezekiel's vision, was known among the
Babylonians as the grand canal; it flowed southeast from the Euphrates at
Babylon. Canals were vital to the irrigation of the land. Along this river
the prophet made his home at the community of Tel-abib (3:15).

When it is stated that the word of the Lord came expressly to Ezekiel,
the sense of the statement must be accepted in its literal truth; it was not
merely the result of an hallucination or of an unreal imagination. This
declaration is the fullest confirmation of reality. The hand of the Lord
upon the prophet was actually a gripping which speaks of the special
influence and power the Spirit of God had on the prophets; thus they became channels for the communication of divine truth. So important and
prominent is the thought expressed here that the phrase occurs in six
other verses of Ezekiel: 3:14, 22; 8:1; 33:22; 37:1 and 40:1.

VISION OF THE FOUR CHERUBIM (1:4-14)

The remainder of chapter 1 is occupied with the vision of the glory of
the Lord according to Ezekiel himself (v. 28). This vision is referred to
again in chapters 10-11. In this inaugural vision the prophet is seeking to
picture something which far surpasses the power of any human
language to express. His picturesque representation can be compared with
Isaiah's vision (Isa. 6) because it expresses the absolute sovereignty of
God. Among the attributes of God emphasized in the vision are His
omnipresence, omniscience and omnipotence. Compare the call of Ezekiel
with that of Moses (Exodus 3), Amos (Amos 7:15), Isaiah (Isa. 6), and
Jeremiah (Jer. 1:4-10). All had an encounter with God. So did Paul in
the New Testament record.

The phenomena Ezekiel records are seen issuing from the north. It is
generally held that this direction has reference to Babylon. Actually, the
storm of God's wrath had burst upon Judah from the north and would
do so again (Jer. 1:14). The wind, cloud and fire (v. 4) are all symbols
of God's glory (see Ps. 18:8-13; Hab. 3; Jer. 4:11-13). The tongues of fire
were such that one reached to the next. The general appearance is that
of a tremendous thunderstorm seen from afar, in which the great ominous
cloud is lighted up repeatedly by flashes of lightning. The glowing metal
is amber, the electrum of the Greek Old Testament and the Vulgate, a
brilliant metallic substance compounded of silver and gold.

In the phrase "living creatures" the emphasis is on "living." They are
distinctly not "beasts." The word is found in Ezekiel and Revelation some

thirty times. In Ezekiel 10:15, 20 they are recognized as cherubim, real beings, not as mere symbols (see Rev. 4:6-9). Cherubim, wherever found in Scripture, are related to the holiness of God. They do not represent a likeness of God, which was forbidden by commandment. They are instruments of His government. The church Fathers connected the living creatures with the Gospels: the lion, Matthew; the ox, Mark; the man, Luke; the eagle, John. However, other combinations were also suggested. The feet are described as straight feet because they were without a bend as at the knee; they were ready for motion in any direction.

The hands of a man speak of the power of manipulation and a certain deftness of touch. The joining of the wings emphasizes the perfect unity of action on the part of the living creatures. Their faces are that of a man, speaking of intelligence; of a lion, standing for majesty and power; of an ox, displaying patient service; of an eagle, depicting swiftness in meting out judgment, and discernment from afar. The rabbis said of the living creatures:

> Man is exalted among creatures; the eagle is exalted among birds; the ox is exalted among domestic animals; the lion is exalted among wild beasts; and all of them have received dominion, and greatness has been given them, yet they are stationed below the chariot of the Holy One.[1]

The cherubim went straight forward, conveying to us the truth that the principles of God's sovereignty go on without deviation. It is interesting that with their wings they covered themselves and flew. Worship is first and foremost, then service (see Luke 10:38-42). The burning coals of fire point to the intensely pure and consuming justice of God that must punish sin. The fire traveled up and down, indicating the energy and vigor of God's Spirit which is unwearied and unresting (cf. Ps. 104:4; Heb. 1:7).

VISION OF THE CHARIOT (1:15-25)

The vision of verses 15-25 is part of the one described in verses 4-14. Later Jews called this the vision of the chariot (cf. I Chron. 28:18). Ezekiel saw a throne-chariot, a supernatural chariot giving the effect of great motion and irresistible progress. Wheels, it has been suggested, mean primarily and naturally the revolution of time. The wheels connect the chariot with the earth. Nothing is stationary in God's universe; all is in motion and progressing. A second wheel was inserted in each wheel at right angles. The government of God is orderly and controlled and progressing. This description has absolutely nothing to do with any modern invention or discovery.

[1]*Midrash R. Shemoth.*

The rings or fellies are the circumferences of the wheels. The eyes in the rings are symbolic of divine omniscience in the workings of nature and history (see Zech. 3:9; 4:10; Rev. 4:6; II Chron. 16:9; Prov. 15:3). Though the workings are all intricate, yet they are under the control of divine power, "spirit." When the cherubim stood, they let down their wings in reverence to listen to God's commands.

Vision of the Divine Throne (1:26-28)

Nine times in this chapter the word "likeness" is mentioned. We can only think of God by reasoning from what is highest in our thoughts of human greatness and goodness, entirely apart from their present limitations. Ezekiel did not see God Himself (John 1:18) but certain likenesses and appearances conveyed to him the character and attributes of the majestic and sovereign God. Reverent expositors find in the mention of a "man" on the throne a strong hint of the great truth of the incarnation. He who is meant is the worthy Lord Jesus Christ. If God is to be portrayed in concrete form, the highest symbol man can use is the human form. When God wanted to reveal Himself in the supreme revelation of His person, He did so in the form of the Man Christ Jesus.

The bow shows that the God of all majesty and power is also the God of promise and grace who is ever mindful of and faithful to His covenant regarding the earth. Ezekiel makes it clear that the vision concerns the appearance of the likeness of the glory of the Lord. The Talmud says there is the "large face" of God and the "small face," and man can only see the latter. The effect of the vision upon the prophet was like that upon Daniel and John (see Dan. 8:17; 10:8-9; Rev. 1:17; Isa. 6:5).

No prophet was given so strange, so complicated, nor so significant a revelation at his call as was Ezekiel. He had doubtless read and meditated on the manifestations of God (see Exodus 19:16 ff.; 24:10; I Kings 19:11; 22:19; Nahum 1:3; Ps. 18:11; 50:3; I Sam. 4:4; II Sam. 6:2; 22:11; Isaiah 6:1). In chapter 1 God has brought together in one vision the essence of all that was to occupy Ezekiel, just as is found in the initial vision of the Apostle John in Revelation. The importance of the vision of this chapter can be seen by the threefold repetition (3:22 ff.; 8:4 ff.; 43:1 ff.). Its significance was not only in the revelation that the temple and commonwealth of Israel in Jerusalem were to be summarily destroyed but in that God was still in the midst of His people and would yet consummate His earthly kingdom in a future day in spite of the fact that God's people were then in exile. The old temple was to be destroyed, but the new one was yet to be built. The repetition of the vision relates it to all his ministry whether in speaking of judgment or of mercy, showing God's resistless activity was controlling all in a spirit of holiness and justice. After the Lord's self-revelation, Ezekiel will be charged to condemn Israel's sins and to declare that judgment is soon to fall.

How Does It All Relate to Us?

When the average reader of the Scripture comes to a passage such as Ezekiel 1, he sometimes may conceive that the matters under consideration are far removed from his life and service. But the opposite is true. Just as Ezekiel was a faithful messenger for God, warning of judgment for the unbelieving, and assuring of blessing for the believing, so we today have the unparalleled privilege to call all men to the truth in Christ the Lord. If we have ever had a view of the holiness and majesty of our God, how can we fail to herald His message of urgency to the lost! If we are faithful, He has promised to call forth a remnant from all peoples. May God grant this fulfillment to be realized in our lives.

2

CALL AND COMMISSION OF EZEKIEL

GOD NEVER GRANTS VISIONS of His glory to man without a purpose. His ultimate objective is to convey to man a message of His will and program. The man who has had a vision of God's glory has a telling and potent message for man. A prophet without a vision from God would be false; a vision without a prophet to herald the Lord's message to man would be useless.

THE STRENGTHENING OF THE PROPHET (2:1-2)

The first two chapters deal with the call and commission of Ezekiel who received his call after he had fallen prostrate on his face at the vision of the glory of the Lord. The voice that spoke to him was not that of one of the cherubim for they are never authorized as commissioners to the service of God, but it was rather the One seated on the throne (1:28). Ezekiel's vision of the Lord in chapter 1 reminds us of the vision of Isaiah (Isa. 6:1), while his commission resembles that given to Jeremiah (Jer. 1:8). Ezekiel is addressed as "son of man," a phrase of great significance for him. It is found more than ninety times in this prophecy and always refers to Ezekiel. The title appears once in Daniel (8:17) but is not used of any other prophet. When used of man it points out the prophet's position as a frail creature in the sight of the majestic Creator. It is not meant so much to distinguish man from the angels and living creatures as to differentiate man from God Himself. As a phrase used to designate man it is very common in the Aramaic language. Since the prophet is identified with man, he can be expected, as no angel could, to manifest human understanding and sympathy.

A most significant use of the phrase "son of man" was that made by our Lord Jesus Christ. He alone referred to Himself under this designation, but He did so scores of times in the Gospels. When He used this expression he was pointing out His link with the lost world (Luke 19:10). So, similarly, the reference underscored the reality of Christ's manhood just as "Son of God" emphasized His deity. Christ, as the representative Man, is seen both in His lowliness and in His exaltation in His first and second comings (note Ps. 8:4-8; 144:3; Dan. 7:13-14; Matt. 16:13; 19:28; 25:31; 26:64; John 5:27; Heb. 2:5-18).

Ezekiel was commanded to stand upon his feet; the fact that he needed to be so instructed pointed up the feebleness of human instrumentality. His spirit of fear was rebuked by God. Ezekiel was so unnerved that he had to be reminded: when God called to His service, He always gave the needed wisdom and power. This enablement had been provided both on behalf of Moses (Exodus 4:10-15) and Jeremiah (Jer. 1:4-19). As God's enablings accompanied His commands, so the Spirit of God entered into Ezekiel. In fact, it was the entrance of the Spirit which formed the basis of his prophetic inspiration. This relation to the Holy Spirit can be compared to the New Testament method of describing empowerment for service. He was quickened both in mind and in body at the time of this vision. For in God's provision of revelation, the Word of God and the Spirit of God are always connected. In actuality, Ezekiel had heard and recognized the One who spoke to him. Thus overcome by the divine glory as a servant of God, Ezekiel was able to recover by the strength God provided. His vision included all of his nature: physical and spiritual were alike stirred.

CALL OF THE PROPHET (2:3-5)

In this short portion the prophet was given the conditions which accompanied his prophetic ministry—the disposition of the people's hearts, the hardships of his office as well as the encouragements, the objective of his ministry and the binding obligation upon him to perform as directed. The purpose of God is twofold: to acquaint the prophet with the difficulties of his calling and to encourage him in the execution of his office. The commission of the Prophet Ezekiel is to the children of Israel who had recently become united. Since the captivity of the northern tribes, "Israel" has been the designation for the kingdom of Judah together with those who left the northern kingdom in allegiance to the Davidic dynasty. Strangely enough, this same Israel is referred to as "a rebellious nation" (Ezek. 2:3), the last term being the very word used in the Old Testament for the Gentiles. This idea forcefully expresses the nation's alienation from God (see Hosea 1:9; John 8:39). The word "rebellious" can be understood as the key to the attitude of Israel throughout the book. Israel had forfeited their privileges and had become as the peoples around them, so completely paganized with idolatries that they had fallen to a plane of heathen morality and guilt. This was not a new development; the character of the nation had changed little since the days of their fathers and indeed since the days of Moses.

Following in the steps of their fathers, the Israelites of Ezekiel's day were marked by impudence and stubbornness: literally, they were hard of face and hard of heart. Their shamelessness resulted from these inner attitudes. According to Ezekiel 3:5-7 the difficulty was not intellectual, as it seldom is, but rather spiritual. Their wills were unsubmissive and unyielding to the extent that the feeling of shame and the inclination to repentance were ruled out (cf. Acts 7:51). Regardless of their hardened condition, Ezekiel was sent to them with a "Thus saith the Lord God"—the very mark of divine sanction and authority.

At the outset Ezekiel was warned that there would be some measure of failure in his ministry. It was always the lot of the prophet to bring a message which opposed the ungodly, a voice which the people did not welcome (e.g., Isa. 6:10; Jer. 1:17-19). Because his message would meet with so little success on the part of the majority of the nation, it was all the more necessary that Ezekiel be conscious of the presence of the Lord; he needed the enablement and attestation that his words originated with God. God's Word is still absolute regardless of the reception accorded it (see Isa. 55:11; II Cor. 2:15-16). No matter what their reaction to Ezekiel's message, Israel would never be able to plead ignorance (see 33:33; Deut. 18:21-22; Jer. 28:9). The fulfillment of his words would bring the truth of his ministry home to them. Moreover, the judgment that would surely follow the prophet's preaching would reveal that a true prophet had been among them. The statement "they . . . shall know that there hath been a prophet among them" is a counterpart of the truth that they might know that God is the Lord. These truths, reiterated so often throughout the prophecy, become evident in God's dealings with His people and the nations of earth. Over a dozen times in Ezekiel the phrase "rebellious house" (literally, "house of rebellion") is employed; instead of the "house of Israel" they had become the "house of rebellion." The greater the position of privilege, the greater the extent of disobedience.

THE CHARGE TO FEARLESSNESS (2:6-7)

The warning to Ezekiel was similar to that given Jeremiah at the beginning of a ministry which was also largely predictive of judgment. With the opposition Ezekiel was to encounter he needed just such assurance and encouragement. Briers and thorns (v. 6) proverbially represent that which is unyielding and piercing; the scorpion (v. 7) is a reptile about six inches long with a deadly sting in its tail. These three words may indicate a scale of degrees in resistance. No matter how great the opposition would be, Ezekiel was told that he would have nothing to fear. Four times over in verse 6 he is told not to be afraid. The figures are strong and suggest determined and distressing opposition from Israel to God and His messenger. Doubtless the message of Ezekiel would entail personal suffering for him.

God even revealed to Ezekiel that suffering was expected; the reason was that the prophet's countrymen, in God's predictions, were so rebellious, they were literally rebellion itself—rebellion personified, in fact. Who would undertake such a mission, except under divine compulsion? The failure of Ezekiel's mission would in no way invalidate his authority to speak for the Lord. He was called to faithfulness to the task, not to success as the world conceived it. Never too often can this principle be repeated: with stewards of the truth of God, faithfulness is the primary requisite of service, not apparent accomplishment (I Cor. 4:2). The Lord's highest commendation in the day of judgment will be for faithfulness in fulfilling His will (see Matt. 25:21, 23).

ASSIMILATING THE MESSAGE (2:8-10)

Though Israel would resist and rebel, the prophet was not to evidence the same resistance of attitude as the nation. He could not afford to be rebellious himself if he was to rebuke the rebellion of the nation; if he was to denounce their resistance to the will of God, he could not be found opposing that same will. He had to be on guard against his natural weakness to respond in kind. He would need to assimilate the message before giving it forth, as was suggested by the command for consumption of the scroll (3:3). Eating conveys the idea of receiving into the heart. Thus God's words were to become a part of his very life (cf. Jer. 15:16; John 6:53-58). This symbolical act which Ezekiel obediently performed signified his acceptance of the commission offered him. Even this transaction took place in the vision described in the opening chapters. How Ezekiel was given the scroll is not definitely indicated, although that it was offered is apparent in 3:1. The hand stretched out to Ezekiel either belonged to a cherub or to the One on the throne itself. The prophet avoided using the name of the Lord; it was customary to treat it with great fear. Indeed, the transcendence of God is evident throughout the book and nowhere more obvious than in the singularity of this command (cf. Rev. 10:8-9). Perhaps it can be better comprehended with the background in ancient times when books were written on skins sewed together, or on long strips of papyrus. Rolls of skins are still employed in Jewish synagogues for the Torah. Thus the roll was spread out before Ezekiel so he could see the extent and the nature of the contents; it had writing within and without. Usually parchments were written on one side only, but here the message of the Lord was so full of threatenings and woes that both sides

had to be utilized. It may be also that the contents of the scroll treated
truths both manifest and of a more concealed nature. The prophet saw
that the roll contained lamentations, mourning and woe. This further
revealed the extent of Israel's hardened condition. The contents may have
described the earlier part of Ezekiel's ministry up to the destruction of
Jerusalem and the temple; after chapter 33 his messages were more com-
forting and hopeful in character.

HOUSE OF REBELLION

As one reads this chapter of the prophecy he is struck by the clear
picture God gives of the hardened, rebellious condition of His people.
Some may be inclined to ask, why a prophet at all? Had the Israelites
not become the very embodiment and symbol of opposition and revolt
against God? But God's love could not let them go without another and
another, and still another, loving entreaty to flee to the refuge available
in God Himself. Is not this the basis of all missionary endeavor to Israel
today? True, they have opposed the message of the gospel and have
refused it repeatedly, but the loving heart of God would warn them again
while it is the day of His boundless grace.

Besides the local application, God still works in all the contemporary
world despite the indifference and rejection of Him which is prevalent.
May we today fortify ourselves with the same resources by which Ezekiel
was encouraged in his ministry. Futility was not then and need not be
now a barrier to service for God.

3

EZEKIEL'S PROPHETIC MINISTRY
INAUGURATED

CHAPTERS 2-3 treat the same general subject: the disclosure to Ezekiel of his prophetic office and his induction into it. The instructions and charges set before him were as specific and elaborate as those granted to any other prophet in the Old Testament.

EATING THE ROLL (3:1-3)

The roll first mentioned in chapter 2 is now presented to Ezekiel for his assimilation. The Word of God is meant specifically to be the message committed to Ezekiel. No true prophet ever chose his own message; he always followed a course of action that was given to him by God. The message had to be received and assimilated by the prophet, for he who gives forth the Word of the Lord must feed on it himself. The experience of Jeremiah (Jer. 15:16) confirmed this requirement. Furthermore, when Ezekiel ate the roll his action signified the removal of any unwillingness on his part to assume the office of prophet. Though the message was a bitter and difficult one, he had the joy of knowing he was the channel for the Lord's truth to Israel. No matter how painful the labor, there is satisfaction in finding and doing the will of God and in realizing service in fellowship with the living God.

OPPOSITION OF THE PEOPLE (3:4-11)

If the Lord had sent Ezekiel to a people of strange speech and of a hard language (literally, deep of lip and heavy of tongue), the assurance is given that they would have heeded the message. The barrier of different languages would have added materially to Ezekiel's difficulties, but such a handicap in communicating thought would have been negligible in comparison with the moral and spiritual opposition which would effectively hinder the perception of spiritual truth. Strange languages are more easily mastered than the spiritual hindrance of unbelieving hearts. This telling comparison reveals that God's people were more hardened in spirit than were their heathen neighbors. Again it must be remembered that Ezekiel was clearly warned, as was Isaiah (Isa. 6), that his work and ministry among Israel would be a failure. The future would reveal that this nation of the "hard forehead" and "stiff heart" (v. 7, ASV) was of the same disposition in the time of Christ's incarnation (see Matt. 11:21-24; Luke 4:24-29).

It is sad to observe that exile and affliction did not make the people of God more openhearted to God; rather they were the more hardened by their sufferings. God promised to make Ezekiel stronger and more unflinching than those who opposed his message. In these scriptures the word "hard" means "strong," a word-study with an evident double meaning in Ezekiel's name which means "God strengthens." Indeed, the man of God had to be endowed by the Lord with a hardness to equal or surpass his antagonists. This same divine defense was the armor of others who ministered to Israel (see Isa. 50:7; Jer. 1:18; 15:20). Since Ezekiel was evidently of an extremely sensitive nature, the Lord was to make him as adamant as the very limit of hardness would allow (Jer. 17:1; Zech. 7:12). And just because the nation would be so unwilling to hear the message of the Lord, Ezekiel himself had to be all the more diligent to hear and wholeheartedly receive any word from God. He is designated now as the prophet of the exiles.

LEADING OF THE SPIRIT (3:12-15)

If Ezekiel were to be strengthened to carry out his commission, he needed a new revelation of God's power as did Moses preparatory to his mission, in Exodus 3:15. In a condition of ecstasy the prophet was transported to the place of his ministry. Then the vision of the glory was removed. As Ezekiel was conveyed to Tel-abib, he entered into the spirit of his message, projecting himself into bitterness and intensity of spirit. He assumed the same position as God did toward their sin; like Jeremiah (6:11) he shared God's indignation against Israel. The name of Tel-abib signifies "mound of green ears"; its location is no longer known. But Ezekiel was there and he sat where they sat, showing his deep sympathy with them as they were about to receive his messages. He was himself overwhelmed by the terror of the vision and the commission to be undertaken. It is interesting that his ministry began not with speaking but with silence, which was similar to the seven days of Job 2:13 when there was a silent vigil with friends and sufferer together.

THE PROPHET A WATCHMAN (3:16-21)

A parallel passage to these verses is Ezekiel 33:1-20. Both designate a particular function of this prophet. Ezekiel is the only one among the prophets to be designated a watchman. The duties of Habakkuk (Hab. 2:1), Jeremiah (Jer. 6:17), and Isaiah (Isa. 56:10) were far more national and corporate than individual. Ezekiel realized that from that time on his would be a mission mainly to individuals. It is a matter now not of national fidelity but of individual faithfulness in the message of God as a watchman. Each man must bear his responsibility to his response after hearing the Word. A man "lives" or "dies" according to his individual righteousness or wickedness, but it was the solemn responsibility of the watchman toward others to warn of the coming judgment. The ministry of the prophet was to extend not only to the nation in general (and other nations also, as indicated in chaps. 25-32), but to individuals as well (see 14:21-23; 18:1 ff.). As a faithful pastor, Ezekiel was responsible for each man individually; the individuals within the nation, however, were personally responsible for their actions to God (chap. 18). This accountability was a new concept in Old Testament revelation and was an important step in its progressive unfolding.

The work of the watchman is vividly set forth in II Samuel 18:24-27 and II Kings 9:17-20. His function as a watchman over the city was preeminently to warn of impending disaster; the prophet as a watchman was to call to repentance and faith. Here the true prophet differed from the false; the spurious prophet would voice but one theme: "Peace, peace!" when there was no peace. The duty of the prophet extended to the giving only of the warning, not to the results. It is comparable, perhaps, to the Christian pastoral office which is responsible for the care and cure of souls. The prophet who was negligent in his duty, which was a commission from God to perform on behalf of the righteous and the wicked, became in a real sense a manslayer and was viewed as such by God. The blood of the man who had not been warned would be required at the hand of the prophet—a warning given as an evident allusion to Genesis 9:5. Paul, doubtless, had this chapter and chapter 33 in mind when he spoke the words of Acts 18:6 and 20:26.

The words of this passage in Ezekiel have been taken erroneously to teach "falling from grace." The phrase is found in Galatians 5:4 where the context makes the meaning clear. The belief in falling from grace is true of all legalists who abandon the basis of grace for works of their own. Apparently there is no difficulty in the minds of many in understanding the case of the wicked man who is warned and turns, or fails to turn, from his wicked ways. The misunderstanding appears in the interpretation of what transpires with the "righteous" man. From the context of this passage and the general teaching of Scripture, we must conclude that the "righteous" person of this chapter was not one who had the root of re-

generation, but one who was righteous in outward appearance and deed
only. His individual acts of righteousness would not be reckoned because
he was ultimately found lacking in the basic element of true righteousness. Final perseverance was the only method whereby the prophet could
know and judge. All that is meant here with regard to the characteristic
"righteous" is an outward conformity to the way of obedience and righteousness. In the Old Testament period when one truly trusted God he
manifested it by delighting in God's Word and obeying His law. Of
course, there were numerous occasions, as implied here, where conformity
to the law was not accompanied by inward grace. When it is stated that
God lays a stumbling block before the righteous, this is not to be taken
as an inducement to sin; such is absolutely impossible with God (James
1:13-14). But God does permit circumstances in each life which draw
out the governing principle of that life. Here it is the language of appearance. It is by way of permission, not of divine direction, that the
righteous was found in the condition indicated.

EZEKIEL'S ENTRANCE INTO HIS MINISTRY (3:22-27)

This conclusion of chapter 3 gives the introduction to Ezekiel's first
prophetic act and announcement. In an ecstasy from the Lord the prophet
went forth into the plain where he was to receive the final words of his
commission. He was given another vision of the glory of the Lord, as the
one he had received by the river Chebar, with the same effect. The command given to shut himself in his home indicates he was to refrain for a
time from public ministry and to perform in his own house what the Lord
charged him to do. His fellow countrymen could come to his home to
receive his messages, as so indicated in 4:12; this would signify almost
complete withdrawal from public life. The restraint would be moral
rather than physical. Likewise, the bands did not mean that he was
imprisoned, nor does it follow that anywhere in the book would the exiles
attack him in a hostile manner. By their hardness of heart and opposition
they would limit his freedom in preaching. The reference in 4:8 is different from the binding here. Some interpreters have taken verse 26 to teach
that Ezekiel suffered from a nervous disorder which hindered his speaking, but this interpretation is to misunderstand the entire intent of the
passage. God revealed that the prophet's ministry was to be a private
one, limited to those who would come to his house (8:1). It is not necessary either, as some have done, to take these words to mean that Ezekiel
was led to realize he was to be a literary prophet, as well as a preacher
of righteousness. His dumbness was not to be complete nor absolute; it
was meant as a sign to them in their rebellious condition. God restrained

Ezekiel, not by outward and temporal power, but by spiritual power. He was only to speak when God permitted him to do so; he was not to speak from any motivation of his own. His state of intermittent dumbness was with him until the day of the siege of Jerusalem, and was finally removed when word came of the capture of the city (cf. 24:27; 33:21-22).

4

SIEGE OF JERUSALEM PREDICTED

Chapters 4-24 cover the period from Ezekiel's call to the beginning of
the siege of Jerusalem. His theme is the impending judgment and destruction of the city and sanctuary. Four symbolic acts (4:1–5:4) portray
the desolation, then direct prophetic discourse is employed through chapter 7. Ezekiel is charged to use object lessons to convey God's message
to His people, the symbolical acts depicting the stringencies of the siege
of the capital city and the exile that followed. There is general, though
not complete, agreement among interpreters that these actions were carried out (see 4:3, 12). The protest of verse 14 points decidedly in this
direction.

Sign of the Tile (4:1-3)

The tile mentioned in the text was a tablet of soft clay, baked to make
it durable, such as the Babylonians used for writing purposes. On tablets
like these the Babylonians and Assyrians wrote their private contracts,
historical inscriptions and other data. These were their books, great
quantities of which have been uncovered by archaeological excavations.
Ezekiel was to portray the ground plan of the city of Jerusalem on the
tablet in order to incite the people to ask the meaning of the various signs.
While Ezekiel prophesied, the army of Nebuchadnezzar was besieging
the city of Jerusalem, though false prophets were trying to persuade the
people that the invaders would never capture the holy city and the sanctuary. To Israel the city was the heart and center of its life and spiritual
activity; its naturally strong situation above the surrounding area gave it
a prominent position. To the godly and the ungodly as well, Jerusalem
represented the glory and uniqueness of the nation Israel (see Ps. 48:2).
Every feature of an actual siege was portrayed on the tablet, with the
forts as a rampart with towers for archers and siege engines. The mound
(v. 2, ASV) was to connect the rampart with the city's walls. The camps
were filled with soldiers, and the battering rams were readied to pierce
the walls. Another siege of Jerusalem seemed most unlikely at that time
because Nebuchadnezzar had conquered the city twice within a few
years. Only another rebellion could bring on another invasion, but such
desperation seemed out of the question. But Zedekiah was guilty of lead-

ing an anarchy (cf. II Kings 24:20). The iron pan was meant to indicate the impenetrable wall of the besieging army, to show the severity of the siege, as well as the impossibility of escape. A secondary thought may be the impregnable barrier between God and them because of their sin (see Isa. 59:2). Ezekiel was enjoined to set his face against the city to reveal the determination of the invaders to capture the city. These symbolical actions were a sign of events surely to come to pass on the whole house of Israel.

SIGN OF THE PROPHET'S POSITION (4:4-8)

When Ezekiel lay on his left side, he faced north; when on his right side, south. The Oriental habit was to face eastward when indicating the points of the compass. In his actions the prophet was representing the nation; the north standing for the northern kingdom of Israel and the south for the kingdom of Judah. Since all this was commanded by God, it is wholly unnecessary to claim, as some scholars have, that Ezekiel suffered from epilepsy or catalepsy. A cataleptic patient does not act as indicated here. It is admitted by all that the exact meaning of the times mentioned in this chapter is difficult. But verse 4 makes it plain that the period must not represent the time of Israel's sinning, but the period during which the nation bears its iniquity and is punished. Observations on verses 5-6 show that, first, the longer period of captivity for Israel would indicate greater guilt before the Lord. Second, it must be remembered that Israel and Judah bore the penalty for their sin for part of the time simultaneously. The end of the period was the same for both. Third, no suggestion advanced makes the calculations come out exactly correct numerically, as we shall see. Fourth, with such great diversity of opinion among students of the prophecy it would be foolhardy to be dogmatic. Wherever the numbers begin, they do point out the patience of God with the sins of Israel and that the long-suffering of God was coming to an end.

Many believe that the Greek Old Testament is probably correct in giving 190 days (representing years) in verses 5 and 9 instead of 390. Ezekiel would then have been on his left side 150 days and on his right side 40 days. The period from the deportation under Tiglath-pileser in 734 B.C. (II Kings 15:29) to the fall of Jerusalem in 586 B.C. was 148 years, or about 150 years. The forty years (about a generation) for Judah correspond approximately to the period from 586-536 B.C., the time of Judah's exile in Babylon. According to this reckoning there can be no exactness in the numbers; round numbers are the most that can be hoped for. Another view holds that, since there is no question as to the numbers in the Hebrew text, the longer period must be reckoned from the disruption of the kingdom under Rehoboam, son of Solomon (I Kings 11:31). According to the chronology of the book of Kings the period from Rehoboam to 586 B.C. was 394½ years. The figures can hardly refer to the duration of the northern kingdom apart from Judah nor even to Judah itself, because the kingdom of Israel continued from about 930-722 B.C., while the kingdom of Judah went on about 136 years after the fall of Samaria. The 40 years for Judah are assigned as those of the reign of Solomon.

Other interpreters take the 430 years (390 years plus 40 years) to be symbolic. They see the figures as a representation of the future in the terms of the past, specifically a reminiscence of the 430 years Israel spent in Egypt and of the 40 years in the wilderness. Thus no exact period is in view by the prophet. Obviously, no completely satisfactory solution has been found as to the number, though the general concepts are clear enough.

It is not necessary to assume that Ezekiel was in the prone position day and night. It was doubtless part of each day, if he were to prepare his food as stated later in the chapter. Lying before the people, Ezekiel was to set his face with a steadfastness of purpose (15:7; 20:46). The uncovered arm showed readiness for battle when withdrawn from the flowing sleeve of the robe (cf. Isa. 52:10). In order to show the restricting and confining nature of the exile, the Lord was said to lay bands on the prophet to hinder his movement from one side to the other until he had completed the allotted time for each part of the nation.

SIGN OF THE POLLUTED BREAD (4:9-17)

Scarcity of food in the siege especially made necessary the mixing of all kinds of grain for bread. This was not forbidden by the law of Moses, for the rules of Leviticus 19:19 and Deuteronomy 22:9 are not applicable here. The portions stated were daily rations given in an orderly manner, not when hunger dictated. The twenty shekels of measurement indicated would be a little over nine ounces, while the sixth part of a hin would be about a quart or less.

Some have wholly misunderstood the command of verse 12 which relates only to the fuel to prepare the food and not to the making of the food itself. Barley bread was prepared on hot stones (I Kings 19:6), which were here to be heated by human excrement because of the lack of ordinary fuel. The whole procedure was polluting as well as repulsive (cf. Deut. 23:12-14; this was in violation of Deut. 14:3). For the moment the ceremonial is overridden to bring a moral point. As a punishment Israel was to be placed on the level with the heathen (see Hosea 9:3-4 for the meaning of this transaction). The purpose of the sign was to show how Israel's position as a separate, sanctified people would be destroyed. The horrors of the siege and exile could not be more vividly depicted. The state of exile itself was defiling, as seen in Amos 7:17. God wanted to impress them with the pollution and uncleanness of idolatrous worship and practices. Idolatry is so vile in God's sight that nothing could be too polluted to portray its essential nature before a thrice holy God.

As a priest's son Ezekiel had always kept the dietary laws (44:31). His sensibilities reacted against this pollution, even though commanded by the Lord for a purpose (cf. Peter in Acts 10:14). The godly prophet was more concerned with that which offended his conscience than that which displeased his taste. That which died a natural death was forbidden in Leviticus 7:24; 22:8; and Deuteronomy 14:21. That which was torn of beasts was prohibited because the blood was not thoroughly drained (cf. Exodus 22:31; Lev. 17:11-16; Deut. 12:16). Abominable flesh has reference to sacrificial meat three days old, as in Leviticus 7:18 and 19:7. With his priestly background Ezekiel had these injunctions of the law, especially in Leviticus, before him continually.

The Lord graciously conceded to Ezekiel's ingrained scruples. Cow's dung is still used as fuel by Palestinian peasants, but not for baking. Now the meaning of the symbolism is told forth plainly. God intended to remove the staff of bread, upon which life is said to depend, so that food and drink would be rationed out as in famine conditions. Indeed, they were soon to have neither bread nor water in any amount. The threat just pronounced was sufficient to instill dismay in the stoutest heart among them. They would pine away for their iniquity (see Lev. 26:26, 39). In summary, the purpose of all the acts in symbolic form was to impress the people with the coming famine during the siege of Jerusalem and the people's subsequent pollution in exile among the heathen.

ALWAYS GRACE BEFORE JUDGMENT

In Scripture God repeatedly extends words of warning and admonition in grace before He unleashes forces of destruction in judgment. Thank God, the same procedure is true today. God has prepared a message of grace for Jew and Gentile before the day of His wrath appears.

5

JUDGMENT ON ABUSED PRIVILEGE

THE SERIES OF SYMBOLIC ACTS begun in chapter 4 is concluded in this chapter. The theme of threatening doom over Jerusalem and her people is carried over, and is enforced by direct and powerful prose discourse. No man who suffers the judgment of God at any time can complain that he has had insufficient warning of the issues involved in disobedience.

THE SIGN OF THE SWORD (5:1-4)

The figure employed was intended to convey the truth of the expulsion of the inhabitants of Judah from their country. The prophet was commanded to take a sharp sword, not a knife, to be used as a barber's razor for the shaving of his head and beard. Here the sword was a symbol of the king of Babylon as it was of the king of Assyria in Isaiah 7:20. He was the agent for the execution of God's wrath on His people. In this command of God to the prophet another departure occurs from the ceremonial, but only on the ground of God's authority. Such shaving was forbidden to a priest like Ezekiel and ordinarily meant the loss of priestly status and position. The hair of the priest was a mark of his consecration to God's service (see Lev. 21:5; 19:27). Shaving all the hair was a sign of humiliation (II Sam. 10:4-5), catastrophe (Jer. 41:5) and mourning (Job 1:20; Isa. 22:12; Jer. 7:29). The balances showed that the judgment was a discriminating one. God's justice is accurate (Jer. 15:2).

The treatment accorded the hair indicated the fate in store for those still residing in Jerusalem, namely, fire, sword and scattering. Some would die by fire in the siege (for a similar prophecy of a much later time see Zech. 13:8-9); others would be slain by the sword and still others would be scattered to the wind, the latter being a fulfillment of the prophecy of Moses (Lev. 26:33) and Jeremiah (9:16). But God never leaves Himself without a godly witness. There are some who deny the doctrine of the remnant to Ezekiel, but this is scarcely tenable in view of verse 3. One of the important subjects of Old Testament prophecy (and it is to be found in the New Testament as well) is the remnant in Israel who are faithful to God in the midst of the unbelieving majority (for a careful study of this theme notice a few of the many passages in II Kings 25:22;

Isa. 6:13; 10:22; Jer. 23:3; Ezek. 6:8-10; 9:8; 11:13; Zech. 13:8-9). After the fall of Jerusalem this teaching becomes the dominant note of the prophecy.

But even the remnant was to undergo further trial and ordeal. In Jeremiah 40-44 can be found their trials in the land which took place even after the destruction of the city and the sanctuary; in this category are the difficulties after the assassination of Gedaliah by Ishmael and the descent into Egypt under Johanan. In short, the judgment reached the entire nation. What Ezekiel had done to his hair, God would do to the inhabitant of Jerusalem and Judah.

JUDGMENT ON JERUSALEM (5:5-12)

The four symbols found in chapters 4-5 are now explained directly and forcefully. The Lord declares that He has placed Jerusalem in the midst of the nations. This divine strategy is here stated for the first time, although it is important to remember the word in Deuteronomy 32:8. Ezekiel reiterates the truth in 38:12, and it is found later in rabbinic and Christian literature (especially of the Middle Ages). It has been suggested that the intention is not a geographical notation nor a typical one, but that the text is to be understood in a historical or redemptive sense as in Isaiah 2:1-4 and Micah 4:1-3. But the geographical implications cannot be ruled out. God intended for Israel to be the great monotheistic missionary to the nations of the ancient world—Egypt and Ethiopia on the south; the Hittites, Syrians and Assyrians toward the north; the Philistines and Phoenicians on the coast; the Ishmaelites, Ammonites and Moabites of the desert to the east and south; and even the peoples of India in the time of Solomon.

But instead of being a witness to the heathen nations about her, Israel excelled them in idolatrous practices. It has been denied that God's people were actually worse than the pagans about them, but reckoning must be in proportion to spiritual knowledge and privileges enjoyed. The judgments of God are always relative to light and privilege granted. The servant who knew little was beaten with few stripes, whereas the one who knew much and disobeyed in unbelief was beaten with many stripes. The Latins have a pointed saying: *Corruptio optimi pessima* ("The corruption of the best issues in the worst"). How those with high and ample privilege in spiritual matters need to take these words to heart! Israel, endowed with position and privilege, became turbulent; they raged in their opposition against God. The verb is not the same as in Psalm 2:1, but the concept is similar. Repeatedly Ezekiel states that God's visitation upon Israel will take place in the sight of the nations for an example, and to vindicate God's nature and ways before the world (cf. 20:9, 14, 22, 41; 22:16; 28:25; 38:23; 39:27; Amos 3:2). It is no circumscribed tribal or national God who speaks, but the Lord God of the nations of the earth. God's honor must be and will be vindicated throughout.

Since Ezekiel's people were unique in their disobedience, they were to be outstanding in their punishment. Some understand this to refer to the destruction of Jerusalem by the Romans in A.D. 70, as well as the invasion in 586 B.C. by Nebuchadnezzar. The account by Josephus, the Jewish historian, parallels the broad outlines given here. But still others extend the reference to the final confederacy under the Roman beast and the Antichrist (Zech 13:8-9; 14:2; Matt. 24:21). It is not needful to go beyond the day of the Prophet Ezekiel to find the sad fulfillment of these dire threatenings. The book of Lamentations (4:10) reveals how literally these predictions were realized, when parents ate their children, the conditions of siege driving them to cannibalism. And the added word was given that the sons would eat their fathers. Human plight can know no greater depths. Down the centuries came thundering the mighty threats uttered by Moses in Leviticus 26:29 and Deuteronomy 28:53, to be taken up by Jeremiah (Jer. 19:9; Lam. 2:20), and sealed in the life of the wayward nation. Even the remnant would suffer wide scattering.

The declaration in verse 11 is prefaced by the clause "as I live," a most solemn oath pledging the very existence of God for the carrying out of the prophecy. It is found fourteen times in this book, more often than in any other prophet. The greatest sin Israel committed was the defiling of the Lord's sanctuary. The detestable things are elaborated on in chapter 8, and refer to their rites and images borrowed from foreign cults. When the worship of man is polluted and corrupted, then all of life is affected. Since they had diminished the word God had commanded them (Deut. 4:2), He would diminish them and not pity. The four well-known judgments—pestilence, famine, sword and scattering—would be their ultimate portion. The loss of Jerusalem meant for them no place to offer the atoning blood to God. For Jerusalem to be cast off meant the nation was left to bear the full punishment for their sins. When the temple stood, they would not engage in the proper worship of God; now they would not be able to do so.

ISRAEL A REPROACH (5:13-17)

Ezekiel's purpose here was to impress on Israel's conscience God's intense hatred of idolatry. The judgments would not end with the destruction of Jerusalem. Three times in verse 13 is the wrath of God pointed out. The verb "comforted" is used either of the feeling of compassion, or of consoling oneself by taking vengeance (Isa. 1:24), probably the latter here. God's honor, flouted by the people in the sight of the nations, had to be vindicated before the eyes of those very nations. The prophet stressed zeal or jealousy as a determining motive in God's action: to punish His people in order to reveal to them that He could not tolerate sin (16:38, 42), and to restore them so that the nations would not doubt His power (36:5; 38:19; 39:25-29). Then Israel would know by bitter experience that it was the Lord indeed who had spoken. They would have ample time to contemplate it when they became the taunt, reproach and instruction of all the nations. Israel, suffering for her sins under God's righteous wrath, would be an object lesson to the nations. The heathen would be amazed because they had not seen a national deity so deal with a people who professed his worship (cf. Deut. 28:37). The evil arrows of famine (Deut. 32:23-24) were hail, rain, mice, locusts and mildew. The four scourges of Leviticus 26—famine, evil beasts (as in Samaria, II Kings 17:25), pestilence and the sword—would overtake the nation under God's judgment. And the entire tale of woe and sorrow was closed with the strongest assurance that the Lord Himself had spoken these things and vouched for them.

"I, THE LORD, HAVE SPOKEN"

Three times in the last division of this chapter Ezekiel stressed that the Lord Himself had spoken. Whatever the message contains, it can be relied upon when God has spoken it. He has made known that only through faith in the Redeemer can any know blessing and eternal life. He has spoken that we should go and bear the message glorious, whether to our neighbor or across the seas. He has spoken. How have we responded?

6

DESOLATION OF THE LAND

THE PROPHECIES in chapters 6-7 are related in that they elaborate on the symbolism of chapter 5. However, each chapter has its distinct message and emphasis. With denunciation after denunciation Ezekiel strove to move the heart of the nation to the Lord. Whether they would hear or refuse, they had to know there was a prophet in Israel as the mouthpiece of the Lord.

DESTRUCTION DECREED UPON THE LAND (6:1-7)

Ezekiel was commanded to set his face in opposition toward (i.e., against) the mountains of the land, action which speaks of a recurring position assumed by the prophet (see 13:17; 20:46; 21:2). The mountains were mentioned, not because they were a poetic expression for the people of Israel, as some maintain, but because they were the places where Israel practiced idolatry (cf. Lev. 26:30-33; Isa. 65:7; Jer. 3:6; Hosea 4:13). The mountains of Israel were in sharp contrast with the plains of Babylonia. The judgment would extend from Jerusalem to include all the high places on the mountains of Israel. The mountains were addressed as though the people were incurable. So it was with the prophet in I Kings 13 who did not address Jeroboam the king, but rather spoke to the altar. The words of this text parallel the truth of Micah 6:2. By way of contrast and bright promise, Ezekiel in 36:1-15 set forth an extended prediction of restoration for the mountains of the land.

The high places were places of worship which were polluted by the Canaanites in the rites of their cult. Hezekiah in the eighth century B.C. and Josiah in the seventh century removed the high places, but their reformations were temporary in character. After the deaths of these godly kings the people reverted to their old practices (II Kings 18:4; 23:5). All parts of the land witnessed the abominations of idolatry; even the watercourses (literally, ravines) were used for the rites and worship of Molech (see Isa. 57:5; Jer. 2:23; 7:31-32). The sword with which God threatened them was that of the invading forces of Nebuchadnezzar and his army which would put an end to the high places and their worship.

The sun-images (v. 4, ASV) referred to by Ezekiel were objects sacred to the worship of the sun (cf. II Chron. 34:4, ASV) probably formed in the shape of an obelisk placed beside the altars, intended for the worship of Baal-hamman. Worship of the sun was an ancient form of idolatry which was highly developed in the Amun worship of Egypt where it dominated the entire national life. The term for idols in verse 4 is one of contempt; it may have been coined by Ezekiel who uses it thirty-nine times. It probably means "block-gods." The slain of Israel were to be cast down before their idols. Contact with a dead body was defiling in the extreme (Num. 9:6-10; II Kings 23:14, 16). Because the land had been defiled by idols, the idols themselves would now be defiled by the corpses of the worshipers, a retribution in kind. This would be the height of desecration, replacing the fragrance of incense with the odor of putre-faction. The thought is repeated when Ezekiel warned that the bones of the dead in Israel would be scattered round about their altars. They would not even be accorded the dignity of a burial. They had dishonored God by their idolatries; He would honor them neither in life nor in death.

In verse 6 Ezekiel addressed the people themselves, not the mountains. In several threatening predictions Israel was informed that judgment awaited their cities, high places, altars, idols, sun-images and works. Their works, a comprehensive term, would be abolished (literally, blotted out). God had commanded that this should be done to the Canaanites who were in the land before them. Since Israel had disobeyed, their own works patterned after those of the surrounding nations would be com-pletely obliterated. Because of the visitation of the Lord the people would realize that God, not their idols, is the Lord. The last clause recurs in verses 10, 13-14 of this chapter and sixty times elsewhere; it represents a characteristic of this prophecy and shows the motivation in all God's acts. He must be acknowledged as the only God.

A REMNANT SPARED (6:8-10)

Those who complain loudly of the severity of the dealings of God in the Old Testament period fail to take into sufficient account how the doctrine of the remnant underlines the mercy of God in spite of man's failure. The presence of a remnant indicates an easing of the dire punishment so amply deserved by the nation. The mass of people is rejected, but mercy and grace are extended to a godly nucleus in the nation. There never has been, nor will there ever be, a complete end made of Israel through the judgment of God. From the comprehensive wording of the passage ("among the nations" and "through the countries") it is clear that Ezekiel was looking beyond the time of the Babylonian exile. Nor is there need to restrict the reference to those in Israel who were faithful to the Lord.

between the Babylonian captivity and the rejection of Christ. The doctrine of the remnant may be studied from such passages as Isaiah 1:9; 10:20; Jeremiah 43:5; Zephaniah 2:7; 3:13; Zechariah 10:9 and Romans 9:6-13; 11:5.

The translation in verse 9, "I am broken," may better read "I have broken." God breaks the heart to bring the sinner to true repentance with the calamities He brings upon him. The heart is mentioned because it was their inward motives which were all wrong. But both eyes and heart were involved in their departure from the Lord, their eyes alluring them from steadfastness in the Lord toward ungodliness and idolatry. Theirs would be true repentance and contrition, for they would remember the Lord. Once they had gazed upon the Lord again and beheld His holiness, they would loathe themselves for all the abominable idolatrous practices they had committed. Such godly repentance is not to be repented of (see Job 42:5-6). And when they abhorred themselves (see 20:43; 36:31), the Lord would declare to them that He did not abhor them (Lev. 26:44). The idols after whom they had gone were referred to with utter contempt as literally "dung-gods." When the idolaters would be moved to loathe themselves and be constrained to trust the Lord, it would be evidence that the Lord had not spoken in vain. The lesson of their chastisement would not have been lost on them. Blessed is the reproving of the Lord when it has such a salutary effect.

LAMENTATION OVER THE DESOLATION (6:11-14)

Since smiting with the hand and stamping with the foot (v. 11) are not elaborated upon, there has been a wide divergence of opinion as to the meaning of these gestures. They have been interpreted as expressions of exultation (25:6), scorn, joy, vigorous denunciation to stir their dull consciences, triumph, horror, recognition of the extent of the calamity, indignation, sorrow, ill will and even evil satisfaction. Needless to say, it is useless to be dogmatic here, but the context would seem to point to the gestures as expressing great earnestness in view of the vehemence of the impending judgment. One completely misunderstands the heart of the prophet to believe that he looked with satisfaction at the judgment to fall upon his people, because he so hated their evil practices. This idea reveals a woeful misreading of the motivation and intent of the man of God. The main concern of Ezekiel was the vindication of God's honor and name, but this did not move him to delight in the affliction of God's people. Rather, because he loved the truth of God and the people of God, he would all the more earnestly impress upon them the dire consequences of their godless ways. Emphatic warning was directed to them in the light of the three dread calamities predicted: sword, famine and pestilence. There would be no escape when these somber horsemen began their ride of death. Notice also that distance would make no difference. Whether near or far, wherever they were, the judgments would find and overtake them. The wrath of God would be inexorable and relentless. It always has been a fearful thing to fall into the hands of the living God (Heb. 10:31). In their own wisdom and their own devices there was no way for the ungodly to escape the penalty for their sins.

When these judgments had overwhelmed them, they would realize God's holiness and sole claim to underived deity. Ezekiel enumerated the different localities where they carried on their idolatrous practices, purposely mentioning them all to underscore the wholesale manner in which they had entered into their godless worship. The sweet savor referred to is literally "smell of rest," used with respect to sacrifices to indicate the pleasure and satisfaction given either to God (Gen. 8:21) or to idols, as here, by the offerer and his worship.

The desolation of the land would be thorough, from the wilderness toward Diblah (v. 6, ASV). Because the name Diblah does not occur elsewhere in the Scriptures, it has been suggested that it refers to Diblathaim (Num. 33:46-47; Jer. 48:22, ASV) on the eastern border of Moab. The wilderness near the city would then be meant. As early as Jerome a change from Diblah to Riblah was suggested and, although most modern commentators favor this revision, none of the old versions supports it. If Riblah is chosen, the place was north at the entrance to Hamath on the Orontes River (see II Kings 23:33; 25:6-7; Jer. 52:9, 27). From the wilderness to Riblah would thus be equivalent to the distance from Dan to Beersheba. Ezekiel would appear to be including with one sweep all the land from the south to the north. Throughout the land and in all their habitations the overflowing scourge would sweep all before it.

"Then Shall Ye Know That I Am the Lord"

Here is what has well been called the holy and royal monogram. When this seal is attached, God Himself vouches for the truth of what has been declared. This is so not only with words of judgment, but with precious promises of grace as well. The same unchangeable God who has announced that all have sinned has provided a blessed salvation for all through faith in Christ. As we bear the message of loving favor in Christ, men can know of a surety that our God is the Lord Himself. What better credentials could be provided? As we desire the lost to obey the call of salvation, let us heed the call to witness, and we too shall know in a higher sense that God is the Lord.

7

FINALITY OF THE JUDGMENT

THIS CHAPTER, actually in the form of a lamentation, concludes the first extended message of the book. The frequent repetitions, which have puzzled some interpreters and self-styled emenders of the text, are intentional and emphasize the certainty of the coming calamity. The sentences are filled with deep emotion, and a note of finality runs through the entire passage.

DOOM OF THE LAND (7:1-9)

Because the pleas of God had fallen on deaf ears, Ezekiel was charged to declare that the entire land of Israel was ripe for judgment. The time of God's patience had run out, and punishment could no longer be averted (see also vv. 3 and 6 and the similar wording in Amos 8:2). No part of the land would be exempt from the stroke of God. The thought of the end was repeated for emphasis and to underscore the truth that there was no further hope. All was meant to express the inevitable nature of the approaching catastrophe. The historic event which the prophet had in view in this passage was doubtless the taking of Jerusalem by the army of Nebuchadnezzar of Babylon.

Verses 3-4 are repeated in verses 8-9 with but slight modifications as a sort of refrain. The causes of the coming calamity were stated clearly and repeatedly: their wicked ways and their abominations, that is, their idols. Their extreme departure from the will of the Lord would be manifest to all, even in the midst of them. When the Lord stated that He would not pity and His eye would not spare, the thought is not the lack of love for His chosen people, but rather that His actions would be carried out according to the dictates of His holiness.

Once more it was proclaimed that evil was definitely on the way. It was to be an unrelieved calamity, an unprecedented and unparalleled adversity, unique in character. In a beautiful play on words, impossible to reproduce in English, Ezekiel pictured the end as though it had been quiescent or asleep, but would be awakened and aroused to come against the people of the land of Israel. The word translated "doom" in verse 7 (ASV) is of doubtful meaning. It occurs in Isaiah 28:5 where it means

44

"crown," but that rendering is not suitable here. The sense here seems to be that of "turn" as of the revolution of a wheel. Sin had run its course and judgment alone remained. The day would be one of terror and tumult, far removed from the joyous cry of the vintage (Isa. 16:10; Jer. 25:30) and of the harvest season. Because verses 5-7 have a comprehensive sweep about them, some have thought the day of the Lord is in view. However, the context favors the position that the great calamity of the dissolution of the monarchy in Israel and the destruction of the land was the primary intent of Ezekiel's words, even though history is so integrated that every judgment is one in a chain leading to the ultimate and final one.

The repetition of truth and warning in verses 8-9 shows the monotonous character of their sins. It is remarkable how soon even threatening messages are forgotten by the hearers. There was a need to enforce and reinforce the heart of the message so that when the blow did fall, they would realize that the Lord is a God of judgment, and that the visitation had proceeded from Him.

NEARNESS OF THE CALAMITY (7:10-16)

Again Ezekiel declared that the day of visitation was at hand, and the doom of the wicked in Israel was a foregone conclusion. The rod of verse 10 has been understood in two different ways. The rabbis interpret it as a reference to Babylon, that agent whereby Israel was to be chastised. They adduce in proof such passages as Isaiah 10:5 (spoken of Assyria) and Jeremiah 51:20-24. Thus, Nebuchadnezzar would be the agent of God's visitation upon them. Others explain the passage as referring to Israel, especially their rulers, with a possible allusion to the rods of the tribes mentioned in Numbers 17:8. It is true that pride was manifest in Israel and that their rulers were blameworthy in the coming calamity, but the first explanation which understands the subject to be Babylon is preferable in the light of the entire chapter. Since the sin of the people was fully grown and manifest, the chastening rod was already prepared for the day of reckoning.

But it is poor interpretation to make the rod of verse 11 the same as that of verse 10. The second reference points rather to a wicked ruler in Israel, or the ungodly in the nation in general. How corroding sin can be is evident from the fact that neither people nor wealth would remain after the blow of the enemy had accomplished its work. Instead of "eminency" in verse 11 (ASV) a better translation is "lamentation" or "wailing" (AV). So great would be the slaughter that no one would survive to lament the dead.

When a land is shortly to be overrun by the hordes of the enemy, of what use are buying and selling? There is no profit in commerce then. For the buyer to rejoice at the good purchase he has transacted is entirely pointless; similarly, the seller has no cause to lament the necessity which caused him to sell. Because of the devastation, all property rights would cease. By the Mosaic law real property reverted to the original owner in the year of jubilee (see Lev. 25:13-16). For Israel in Ezekiel's day no year of jubilee would come to rejoice the hearts of the poor so that their patrimony could be returned to them. Paul seemed to have this passage in mind in I Corinthians 7:29-31. This passage in Ezekiel, moreover, does not contradict Jeremiah 32:15, 37, 43. Ezekiel had in mind his contemporaries and the conditions of his day; Jeremiah was looking on toward the future and the circumstances of the restoration. Finally, Ezekiel indicated the foolishness of the man who thought he could strengthen himself in the very iniquity which called down the wrath of God. Hardening oneself in sin would not accomplish immunity from punishment. On the contrary, it would assure it all the more.

Sin had so eaten away the vitality of the nation that their military power would fail them in the hour of danger and need. It is true that preparations for war had been carried out, but there would be neither power nor courage to withstand the enemy. Safety would be found nowhere, for the sword would cut down those without the city, while pestilence and famine would do their stealthy and deadly work within (cf. Deut. 32:25; Lam. 1:20). If any of the unhappy nation managed to escape and flee to the mountains, theirs would still be a mournful plight as they contemplated the havoc wrought by their iniquity (see Isa. 38:14; 59:11).

MOURNING OF THE SURVIVORS (7:17-22)

After describing the helplessness of the people in the city under attack, the prophet elaborated on the distress within the doomed city. Terror would so grip them all that they would be powerless to withstand the enemy. Strong expressions were employed for complete loss of strength. Shame and horror would cover them like a garment, and marks of mourning would be in evidence on every hand (see Isa. 3:24; Micah 1:16). In that hour of extreme distress they would recognize the uselessness of the things in which they trusted. Their wealth would not provide safety, nor would it furnish the needed sustenance for their hungry bodies. They had misused their silver and gold to make idols; now they would see how utterly worthless these abominations were (cf. Prov. 11:4). The "unclean thing" (v. 19, ASV) has reference to sexual impurity (Lev. 20:21). The stumbling block is unquestionably their idols as in 14:3; 18:30; and 44:12.

Verse 20 has been variously interpreted. One position takes the ornament to mean the silver and gold of the people of which they made their idols, as just noted. The other and better view understands Ezekiel to be speaking of the temple of the Lord. The very place God meant to be beautified, they had polluted with multiplied abominations which are described in 8:3-17. Since Israel had already profaned the temple of God, He saw no further purpose in keeping it from the desecration of the enemy. Thus the temple with all its sacred appointments was given over to the invading army. But this act could never have transpired unless the Lord had deliberately removed His protection from His sanctuary. When the Lord turned His face away from Israel, the enemy was able to carry out its wicked devices. That which was profaned was not the temple treasure or the wealth of the land in general, but the holy of holies, the central and focal point of all Israel's worship. God has no desire to keep mere outward worship in operation as long as such worship is accompanied with and encrusted over by idolatries that profane the very essence of that worship. Therefore, we read repeatedly that all would be profaned.

CHAIN OF CAPTIVITY (7:23-27)

Ezekiel was commanded to perform a symbolic act by making a chain which was emblematic of the captivity awaiting them (see Jer. 27:2; Nahum 3:10). To be sure, the chain was actually of their own forging. All sin carries with it the seed of its punishment. In Numbers 32:23 the matter is confirmed beyond a doubt. Jerusalem which was meant to stand for righteousness and godliness had become full of violence and crimes of the deepest dye. The worst of the nations who would chastise Israel would be the Babylonians. Both home and sanctuary would be violated by their depredations. In such an hour peace would be welcome but would not be found. An attempt to sue for terms of peace would possibly be made with the Chaldeans but would not be successful. Calamity would follow calamity and rumor would succeed rumor. All classes of people would be involved in the distress. Neither prophet nor priest nor elder would be able to help then. The prophet was mentioned for the immediate revelation from the Lord, the priest for instruction in the law (Mal. 2:7), and the elder for counsel in civil matters (cf. II Kings 23:1; Jer. 26:17). Since the people had not heeded the words of prophet, priest or elder for so long, there was no good to be gained by giving further truth or advice. The ruin would be a national one involving king, prince and people. And all that they would be called upon to endure would be in direct proportion to their way and their deserts, literally *judgments* and *deeds*. Abraham was right: the Judge of all the earth always does right (Gen. 18:25). Thus concludes the first series of prophecies (chaps. 4-7) given within a little over a year's time.

"THE END IS COME"

There is a note of finality in these words that grips the heart. How solemn they are and how much agony they foretell. But this pronouncement had reference to the physical destruction of the land of promise. Can anyone compute their seriousness when they are thought of in relation to eternal issues? Yet the day of grace is not endless; it will close. What then? Judgment will await those who have rejected the Saviour. Before that end comes, we need to be about the Lord's business as never before.

8

IDOLATROUS ABOMINATIONS IN
JERUSALEM

THIS CHAPTER introduces a new section of the book (chaps. 8-11) comprising a series of visions. The visions in chapters 3-7 were directed against Judah and Israel; those of chapters 8-11 refer to Jerusalem and the remnant of Judah under Zedekiah. The purpose of the visions of chapter 8 was twofold: to show the Jews in Babylon the righteous judgment of God upon His people for their sins and to forewarn that continuance in these outrages would result in a final and complete exile of Israel from the promised land. The present chapter amplifies the reason for the threatenings found in 7:20-22. Since Ezekiel's coreligionists had been captive almost six years, the people and their leaders may have looked for an early end to their exile. Instead, they were told that the inhabitants of the homeland had grievously persisted in their sins.

IMAGE OF JEALOUSY (8:1-6)

Ezekiel carefully dated the visions of this chapter as in the sixth year, the sixth month, and the fifth of the month. This was August-September, 592 B.C., a year and two months after the first vision (1:1). Seated in his own home in Tel-abib, the prophet was visited by the elders of Judah—leaders of the community in exile. They had probably come to consult him on the state of affairs in the nation, and especially in the homeland.

Suddenly the hand of God was upon Ezekiel and he saw the glory of the Lord as in the first vision (1:26-27). The element that dominated the scene was fire (Heb. 12:29). Then the Lord took the man of God by a lock of his head (an act recorded nowhere else in Scripture), and brought him to Jerusalem. How was this accomplished? Was it a physical transporting, or was it in ecstasy or trance? The first position has been advocated by some, pointing to such passages as I Kings 18:12; II Kings 2:16 and Acts 8:39. No one will deny that such activity was well within the power of God to carry out. However, the words "in the visions of God" (v. 3) prove that all that follows was clearly a vision from the Lord.

Ezekiel was transported in spirit, not in body, to Jerusalem. That he did not actually leave Babylon is clear from 11:24. He was carried back in spirit to Babylon after the visions were completed (11:22-25). What follows in the chapter is not a description of deeds done sometime in Israel's past but a retrospective survey of Israel's spiritual condition. Ezekiel saw conditions as they existed in his day at that very hour (11:13).

Once set down at the door of the gate of the inner court of the temple, facing northward, the prophet saw the image of jealousy. The image (in Hebrew an unusual word, *semel*) was an idol (see Deut. 4:16; II Chron. 33:7, 15). It may have been the Asherah set up by Manasseh (II Kings 21:3, 7, ASV) and destroyed by Josiah (II Kings 23:6), but we cannot be certain. It was called the image of jealousy because it provoked the Lord to jealousy (5:13; 16:38, 42; 36:6; 38:19; Exodus 20:5). A sweeping contrast is indicated between the image of jealousy and the glory of the God of Israel, the God who had chosen them in love, who should have been worshiped instead of the idol then in the temple. Northward of the gate of the altar Ezekiel saw the abominable idol in the entry. The worshipers may have been prostrating themselves before the idol. As grievous as their actions were, the prophet was told that they were performing even worse abominations, such as ultimately would drive the visible presence of the Lord from their midst. Previous sins had expelled Israel from their land; now the Lord warned them He also would no longer grace His sanctuary. Even though they had so shamefully defiled and polluted it, God still referred to it as "my sanctuary." God in grace was still hovering over the abode of His deliberate choice.

SECRET CULT (8:7-13)

The second form of idolatrous worship to be described was introduced in an atmosphere of secrecy and of the clandestine. At the door of the court Ezekiel was shown a hole in the wall. When he had dug in the wall, he was confronted with a door. Upon entering it he saw portrayals on the wall of all sorts of reptiles, abominable beasts and all the idols of the people. And before these base pictures seventy elders of Israel were worshiping with censers in their hands. There is no question that such practices were carried on by more than one nation of antiquity, but the consensus of interpreters is that these were the animal cults of Egypt (see Rom. 1:23). In Egypt such worship had perhaps its highest and most extensive development in ancient times. Jaazaniah (some detect an emphasis on the meaning of his name—"the Lord hears"), the son of Shaphan, was in the place of leadership and prominence. If he was the son of the Shaphan who read the book of the law to Josiah (II Kings 22:8-11; Jer. 39:14), we have some concept of the level to which the leaders in

Israel had fallen in their degraded and senseless worship of idols. The seventy men were obviously not the Sanhedrin which was not organized until the restoration from Babylon. The reference is probably to the pattern given in Exodus 24:9-10 and Numbers 11:16. These seventy in the time of Ezekiel represented the laity, as the twenty-five mentioned later stood for the priesthood. The Lord had appointed seventy leaders in years past, and their chief duties were to guard against idolatry. What a perversion this was of their high calling! As heinous as was their outrage against the holiness of the God of Israel, Ezekiel was told that what these perform in the dark, they each do individually in his chambers of imagery. The last phrase has been variously interpreted. Some understand it to refer to other chambers in the temple. It is doubtful that there were seventy such places available as individual cells or compartments for such use. Others interpret the words to mean the imaginations of those concerned. This would be strange, for throughout the prophecy we have depicted that which was carried out openly by the offenders. There remains the possibility that Ezekiel was speaking of acts taking place in the homes of the people. They had carried the idolatry of the temple into their private homes. Public and private worship was permeated with the God-dishonoring idolatry. And they were smugly complacent in it all. They were certain that the Lord did not take note of them, for He had forsaken the land. If God had not left the land, surely He would have saved them from the Babylonian invaders, they reasoned. Thus, they were denying the omniscience and omnipresence of their God. As though the depths of their degradation had not yet been plumbed, Ezekiel was assured that he would see other great abominations they were practicing. Strange is the fascination of that which brings down the judgment of God upon the unhappy perpetrators.

TAMMUZ WORSHIP (8:14-15)

Whereas the idolatries of the mysterious cult were of the Egyptian type, the worship of Tammuz came from Babylon through the Phoenicians (Canaanites) and then the Greeks. Tammuz, mentioned nowhere else in the Scriptures, was the Babylonian Dumuzi, beloved of Ishtar, and is to be identified with the Greek Adonis. He was the god of spring vegetation, who died and was revived after the scorching summer heat. Women joined Ishtar in mourning a dead lover in the intense drought during our months of June and July, so that vegetation might be assured. The fourth month of the Hebrew calendar still bears the name Tammuz. With the worship of this god in ancient times were connected the basest immoralities. With the greatest of abandon women gave themselves up to most

shameful practices. Idolatry and immorality are inseparable twins throughout the history of the world. How much baser could the people of God
become? But Ezekiel was immediately informed that he would witness
yet greater abominations than these. The expression "yet greater abominations" (v. 15, ASV) has not been employed before in the chapter, so
we are alerted for the climax of their idolatrous ways. There is continual
degression in sin, just as there are advance and growth upward under the
Spirit of God in the things of grace and sanctification of the redeemed
spirit.

SUN WORSHIP (8:16)

In the inner court of the Lord's house between the porch and the altar,
a most sacred place where only the priests had access (Joel 2:17), Ezekiel
saw the crowning insult to the Lord of heaven and earth. Twenty-five
men in that hallowed place were worshiping the sun, the object of Persian
idolatry. Moses had warned them against this ever present danger (Deut.
4:19); Josiah the king had sought to extirpate it from the land (II Kings
23:5, 11); Job disavowed any such senseless devotion (Job 31:26) and
Jeremiah seems to have had this worship flaunted in his face (Jer. 44:17).
The twenty-five men represent the twenty-four Levitical priestly courses
with the high priest at their head. The apostasy of the laity and of the
women has already been noted; now it is revealed in the ranks of the
priesthood. Like priest, like people. Think of it! That which was intended
best to manifest the glory of God in creation (Ps. 19), is perverted to de-
tract from the glory of God and the worship of Him exclusively. While
they faced toward the sun in adoration, they turned their backs toward
the temple of God. It was an attitude of defiance toward God and rejection of His worship. This was as complete a repudiation of the Lord
as possible (see II Chron. 29:6). The cup of their iniquity had been filled
to the brim. Such heartrending passages as these call for humility and
heart-searching on our part, lest we also be ensnared with the things of
the world and be drawn in idolatrous worship (I John 5:21) to the passing things of this world.

ANNOUNCEMENT OF JUDGMENT (8:17-18)

No matter in what light others may view these heinous deeds against
the thrice holy God, He considered them as a provocation of His anger
and as filling the land with violence. When God is not given His rightful
place, man fares ill through the violence of man against his fellowman.
The phrase "put the branch to their nose" is obscure. Jewish commentators understood it to refer to some revolting and wicked rite. If it was

a ritual act in an idolatrous cult, then it is grave indeed. But no such ritual act is known among Semitic peoples. Some take it to be a gesture of contempt toward God. Apparently this was the understanding of the translators of the Greek Old Testament who rendered it, "They are as mockers." One suggestion sees here a reference to sacred trees which served as symbols in idol worship. It has even been thought to refer to phallic worship. Yet another proposal is that what is meant is the holding up of a bundle of tamarisk branches (known as barsom) to the nose at daybreak, as they sang hymns to the rising sun. Suffice it to say, there is no room here for dogmatism since there is no certainty in the matter; it has not been satisfactorily explained as yet. However, the general sense is clear; an insulting practice is indicated. God's decision, on the basis of the evidence presented, was to deal with them in wrath. He would neither spare nor pity. It would be useless to supplicate Him, for He would not hear in spite of their loud cries for help (Isa. 1:15). How this unsparing judgment was to be carried out, is dwelt upon by Ezekiel in the following chapters.

"MINE EYE SHALL NOT SPARE"

In these days of grace how strangely do such words of incisive condemnation fall upon our ears. We are so accustomed to hearing the sweet strains of heavenly harmony that woo us to trust Christ as Saviour, that the words of Ezekiel have a foreign sound to us. But they are as true as the words of John 3:16. If the lost are not told the truth of John 3:16, they must be left to the judgment of God. Shall we help to avert the judgment of that coming day?

9

GOD'S THOROUGH DESTRUCTION

S<small>UCH</small> <small>ABOMINATIONS</small> in Jerusalem as described by Ezekiel in chapter 8 called loudly for the visitation of God. The judgment, now set forth, was to be thorough, although it was intended to be selective as well. Execution of this judgment awaited them at the hands of the Chaldeans in the last invasion and deportation under Nebuchadnezzar.

T<small>HE</small> M<small>AN</small> <small>WITH</small> <small>THE</small> I<small>NKHORN</small> (9:1-2)

As in all His works God carries out His judgments in order and with precision. Thus the chapter begins with the preparation for judgment on those who have committed the abominations of chapter 8. The threat of 8:18 is being initially carried out in this chapter. The Crier of verse 1 is the Lord Himself; the same is true in verse 4. The charge is issued with a loud voice to show the greatness of God's displeasure. In 8:18 they cried to the Lord with a loud voice; now it was His hour to cry out His signal for the judgment. Those who had charge over the city were those whom God set to watch over the welfare of the city. They were not earthly agents, but heavenly. Angels are frequently called men because of their outward appearance. The angelic executioners (see Dan. 4:13, 17, 23) came fully equipped with weapons of destruction ready in hand.

It is readily admitted that the six men and one man fit in with the prominence of this sacred number elsewhere. However, it is unnecessary and far afield to see here unconscious reminiscences of the seven gods of the planets which were venerated throughout the ancient world. Interpretation, to be seriously considered, must do more than dwell on superficial resemblances without any basic relationship in thought. The angelic executioners came from the way of the upper gate which was built by Jotham (II Kings 15:35), called the upper Benjamin gate (Jer. 20:2) or the new gate (Jer. 26:10; 36:10). The gate was toward the north of the city, the direction from which the Babylonian invaders came, as well as the area where the idolatries had taken place. These men were equipped with slaughter weapons, that is, maces or battle-axes. But the seventh man was attired differently. He was in the midst of them clothed in linen and with a writer's inkhorn at his side. Certain features are of interest here. This man's position is significant: he was clearly superior to the others. Linen indicates high rank and special service (cf. Dan. 10:5; 12:6). Some think Gabriel was the scribe, but there is nothing to connect him with such a specified ministry. While admittedly there is not much upon which to base such a conclusion, a comparison of this passage with other scriptures leads to the probability that the figure was the Angel of the Lord, the Guardian of Israel. From His clothing and the nature of the work He is seen to accomplish later, it is to be inferred that the Chief of the company was the Angel of the Lord, the preincarnate Christ.

The rest had weapons of destruction; He held an inkhorn. This was a small case for pens, ink and a knife—all the instruments of the Oriental scribe. The inkhorn may well remind us of the book of life (see Exodus 32:32; Ps. 69:28; 139:16; Isa. 4:3; Dan. 12:1; Phil. 4:3). Ezekiel saw the emissaries of the Lord go in and stand beside the brazen altar, which was the symbol of God's righteous requirement on earth. The altar had been especially desecrated and polluted by the nation's abominations. Now the servants of the Lord were in an attitude of those awaiting the Lord's command. All was in readiness for the judgment to follow.

UTTER DESTRUCTION OF THE UNGODLY (9:3-8)

Before the agents of the visitation performed any deed of judgment, an ominous act took place. The glory of God moved from the cherub (here used collectively for the two cherubim above the mercy seat) to the threshold of the temple. If the altar was rejected, then the blood on the mercy seat was also lacking. Thus God Himself had to depart from the people where there was no propitiation. The departure of the glory of the Lord from Israel is one of the basic disclosures of this prophetic book, so Ezekiel traces it very carefully in its different stages (cf. 9:3; 10:18-19; 43:2-5). From His position the Lord issued His charge to the Man in linen with the writer's inkhorn. His commission specified that the Man with the inkhorn was to pass through the midst of Jerusalem in order to mark on their foreheads all those who lamented over the abominations committed in the capital city.

It must be remembered that apostasy in Israel was never absolute. The principle of Jeremiah 31:29-30 and Ezekiel 18:4, 20 was operative. The lamentations of the marked ones were proof that they did not participate in the idolatrous abominations of the populace at large. Grief is always the portion of those who know the Lord in an evil day. The marked ones were penitent and faithful at a time of widespread departure from the will of the Lord. Their sealing was doubtless for the purpose of insuring safety. There is a remarkable similarity between what is stated here and in Revelation 7:1-3 (see also Exodus 12:32; Gal. 6:17; Rev. 13:16-18; 14:1 for the varied usage of the mark in Scripture). Jewish writers have explained the use of the last letter of the Hebrew alphabet (which is literally "mark" or "sign") as a signature in three ways: (1) since it is the last letter it denotes completeness; (2) it is the first letter of the word "torah" (law); or (3) it is the first letter in the Hebrew word for "thou shalt live." Incidentally, it is also the first letter in the Hebrew word for "thou shalt die." Christian interpreters have seen a somewhat prophetic allusion to the sign of the cross. In the earlier script the last letter of the Hebrew alphabet (*taw*) had the form of a cross. Ezekiel, of course, could not have thought of Christian symbolism nor is the passage a direct prediction of Christ's cross. It is a remarkable coincidence, however.

The first command to issue from the Lord was a word of grace and mercy to the godly remnant in the nation through the Man with the writer's inkhorn. Then the pronouncement of doom was uttered against the remainder, and there was to be no sparing or taking pity. They were to slay utterly (literally, to slay to destruction), implying that there was no possibility of escape. Where the visitation of God was concerned there was no consideration of age or sex that would change the situation: old men, young men, virgins, little children and women alike would bear the consequences of their transgressions. As the guilt was personal, the judgment discriminated between the godly and the wicked, thus the prohibition not to harm any with the mark on their foreheads. Perhaps the most striking feature of the punishment is that God designated specifically the place where the blow was to fall first, namely, at His sanctuary (see I Peter 4:17 for the divine principle). Judgment must always begin at the house of God. Privilege brings responsibility in every age of man's history. Where the greatest privilege and responsibility rest, there the judgment alights. In the sanctuary God should have been most honored, but there He was most dishonored and provoked, and there His holiness would most fully and certainly be vindicated. According to 8:11 the elders of the nation were foremost in the apostasy, thus divine retribution would begin with them (cf. Amos 3:2).

The final order to the destroyers was to defile the temple and to fill its courts with the dead. For such a command to come from the Lord Himself reveals the tragic degradation of the nation in that hour. The greatest possible defilement according to the Mosaic law came from a dead body (note Num. 19:11; I Kings 13:2; II Kings 23:16). The house of the Lord was to be defiled by their dead bodies, as they had already defiled it by their idolatry. The directives given, the agents of destruction proceeded to carry out their somber duty. Their work was executed with such diligence and thoroughness that Ezekiel, viewing the carnage around him, cried out in horror, asking the Lord whether He was purposing to destroy all the residue of Israel in His wrath. The prophet's intercession was surely directed against a complete annihilation of Israel. The slaughter seemed so universal that he felt that he alone remained. Elijah's feeling at Horeb was similar, as recounted in I Kings 19:10 and Jeremiah 5:1. The residue spoken of are those in Jerusalem who had survived the deportation in 597 B.C. in which Ezekiel himself had been exiled from his homeland. The compassion of the man of God for his fellow countrymen found beautiful expression in that hour. This passage reveals how wrong is that evaluation of Ezekiel which sees him as only a merciless religious zealot. The prophets of God had a heart for the people to whom they had to preach condemnation and judgment.

CAUSE OF THE AFFLICTION (9:9-11)

God answered the prayer of Ezekiel with the declaration that the guilt of Israel was so prevalent that punishment could no longer be averted. According to God's just requirements they could not be spared. The cup of their iniquity was indeed full; they had filled the land with the blood of innocent victims, and their city was full of the perversion of justice (see Exodus 23:2). As though these acts of violence were insufficient to incur the wrath of God, they had taken the attitude that God had forsaken the land and was no longer concerned with what went on in it. Vividly this reaction describes the hardness of their hearts. They spoke as though they owed God no more trust nor loyalty, since He had not spared them their troubles. Their attitude was an avowal that God did not take notice of their misdeeds. Whenever this position is taken, all restraint against God is cast off.

Israel's departure into sin was so deliberate and of such long standing that the Lord stated repeatedly that His eye (and they thought God did not see, v. 9) would not spare, neither would He have pity. God delights not in judgment but in extending mercy and providing salvation for trusting hearts (for the recurring thought see 5:11; 7:4; 8:18). Ezekiel, in keeping with the practice of all the prophets, was loath to conclude his message on the sole note of destruction. He had to strike the note of God's grace and pardon. Thus he gave the report of the finished work of the Man clothed in linen. All had been carried out according to the command of God. In the midst of widespread judgment, God had not forgotten the godly remnant nor His promised grace to them.

"I HAVE DONE AS THOU HAST COMMANDED ME"

These grand words are reminiscent of the declaration of the Lord Jesus Christ in John 17:4. How worthwhile and fruitful was that life! Has it ever gripped your redeemed heart that God has allowed you to remain on earth to this hour because of a work you are commanded to do? You may be sure that work includes glorifying Him in thought, word and deed, and involves getting the gospel to all men.

10

JUDGMENT BY FIRE

THIS CHAPTER CONTAINS the vision of the fiery coals and parallels the description of divine glory in chapter 1, with the living creatures of chapter 1 referred to here as cherubim. The reason for this new unveiling of divine glory was to show that the destruction of Jerusalem was the penalty for the nation's sin. The basic truth of the chapter is that God controls all the forces of judgment that He employs. Thus there is the appearance of the throne of the Lord. While this chapter is hard to outline, it falls into a twofold division: (1) In verses 1-8 Ezekiel foretold how Jerusalem was to be destroyed by fire and (2) in verses 9-22 he predicted how the Lord would abandon His sanctuary.

FIERY COALS OVER THE CITY (10:1-8)

In 9:3 the Lord had descended from His throne above the cherubim to the threshold of the temple; in 10:4 He returned there again. In the meantime He must have taken His seat again above the cherubim, as verse 1 states by implication. Although the throne was likened to a precious stone, there was no mention of any occupant upon the throne. The cherubim awaited God's departure from the city by means of the chariot-throne. The Lord on the throne spoke to the Man clothed in linen, the same Person who held the place of pre-eminence in 9:2-4. He was the Angel of the Lord into whose hands judgment was entrusted (cf. Rev. 8:3-5 for a parallel in the time of the great tribulation). Whereas His activity in chapter 9 was one of grace and mercy toward the godly, here it is a ministry of judgment upon the ungodly. He was commanded to go in between the whirling wheels, of which there were four, in order to ready Himself for the work of destruction. Like Sodom and Gomorrah of old, the city was to be destroyed by fire. Vastly different from the fire on the altar, which bespeaks God's proffered grace (Lev. 6:12-13), were the coals of fire in the hands of the Man clothed in linen (see Isa. 33:14). In Isaiah 6 the coals were for the purification of the prophet; here they were for the destruction of the wicked. Where evil is concerned, it is true that "our God is a consuming fire" as stated in Hebrews 12:29.

In this calm before the storm the cherubim were seen as stationed on

59

the southern side of the sanctuary. The reason for the right side may
have been because it was more directly toward the city than the north or
east side. In any case, judgment was impending; but the cloud, the sign
of the Lord's presence, was not lacking (cf. Exodus 19:9; 24:15-18; Num.
9:19; 12:10; I Kings 8:10-11). Now we witness the beginning of the
gradual withdrawal and departure of the glory of the Lord from the city.
But God was not leaving this dwelling place forever; some day He will
return to make it His permanent abode. At this point it should be noted
that the presence of the Lord was as glorious in His departure as it was in
His entrance (Exodus 40:34-35; I Kings 8:10-11). Even the fluttering of
the wings of the cherubim was indicative of important issues to follow;
the sound presaged coming revolutionary events. For the very name God
Almighty (*El Shaddai*) views Him as sovereign over nature. Psalm 29
reveals that the voice of the Lord has reference to the sound of thunder
(see especially v. 3). The Man in linen obeyed the charge of the Lord
immediately and went in, not into the temple, but between the cherubim.
Fire was taken to be scattered over the city, but that fact is not stated
because it was the obvious purpose of the action. The cherub seen is the
one approached by the Man in linen. Emphasis on fire in this chapter is
noteworthy, because it looked forward to the fire which destroyed Jerusalem in 586 B.C. (II Kings 25:9). Mention of a man's hands demonstrates
that this is a theophany, one with many similarities to that of chapter 1.
The prophet did not describe the burning of the city, because his attention was drawn rather to the cherubim. There is to be a further description of the living creatures and God's chariot.

VISION OF THE DIVINE GLORY (10:9-17)

The similarity of this portion to the vision of chapter 1 is clear enough.
The mention of the four wheels indicates that more details were added
as Ezekiel got a closer view (see 1:15-16). The wheelwork described in
verse 10 is almost an exact repetition of the account given at the beginning of Ezekiel's important prophetic ministry. The wheels followed not
some outside force but were guided by an inner impulse from the Lord
transmitted to the cherubim. They moved in the direction that the front
of the chariot pointed with unity of purpose and oneness of goal (cf.
1:12, 17). Characteristic of all the cherubim and the wheels was the fullness of eyes, speaking of the omniscience of God (Gen. 16:13; Zech. 4:10;
Rev. 4:6). The mention of body, backs and hands reveals that these
angelic beings appeared in human flesh.

Verse 14 has presented unnecessary difficulty to some interpreters.
Four faces are mentioned as in 1:10, but in place of the face of an ox,

10:14 designates the face of the cherub. The rabbis questioned why the face of an ox is omitted here. One claimed that Ezekiel prayed to the Lord regarding the ox, and that it was transformed into a cherub. Such claims cannot form a solid basis for the serious interpretation of the text. Others hold that the substitution of cherub for ox is a mistake. Reverent Bible students will do well to treat difficulties in the text as problems rather than errors and to continue the search for meaningful solutions. Yet others suggest that, because of the use of the article, *the* cherub was a special one with a place more important than the rest (v. 7). Another explanation seems more probable. It is clear that each cherub had four faces (1:10); Ezekiel is evidently speaking only of the face that was turned toward him at the time.

Now the cherubim have mounted up in preparation for the tragic departure, and the identification with the theophany of chapter 1 is stated conclusively. Cherubim and wheels worked in unison; all moved in view of the anticipated departure of the Shekinah glory (see v. 18). Unity of action and performance is emphasized by the response to the directing spirit of the living creature. It is, as it were, the ominous calm before the rending storm.

DEPARTING GLORY OVER THE CHERUBIM (10:18-22)

In this last section of the chapter Ezekiel set forth the fulfillment of the warning uttered by Moses (Deut. 31:17), and later by Hosea (Hosea 9:12). God had determined to forsake His sanctuary. There are several steps in His action, showing the Lord's great reluctance to abandon the abode of His own choosing. First He removed the cherub to the threshold of the temple (9:3); next, He lifted His throne over the temple's threshold (10:1); with the cherubim remaining on the right side of the house (10:3), He mounted up and sat on the throne (10:4); finally, He and the cherubim, after lingering at the door of the east gate (10:18-19), left the house (11:22-23) and did not return until the time of 43:2. There was a lingering of the glory at the east gate, but it was ultimately to depart. The gate was the main entrance to the outer court. God was about to desert the temple, and soon there would be written over the entire structure, as well as their entire religious life, "Ichabod" ("the glory has departed").

The affirmation in verse 20 belongs earlier as to time, but it adds emphasis to what has preceded. As a priest Ezekiel could have learned about the cherubim from the high priest or from the Mosaic instructions for the tabernacle. The prophet's people were to live a long time without benefit of the temple and its service, so he repeated the different features of the faces and wings, that they might know and recollect the glory and majesty that once dwelt among them. Again the identification is made which links this vision with chapter 1. The final word is that every cherub went straight forward, thus proclaiming the impossibility of thwarting or frustrating the plans of God. They kept their object and mission undeviatingly before them at all times (see Luke 9:51, 62).

How To Abide the Eternal Burnings

The Prophet Isaiah asked a searching question "Who among us shall dwell with the devouring fire? Who among us shall dwell with everlasting burnings?" (33:14). And Ezekiel knew full well that no sinner could pass unscathed through the judgment of the burning coals of fire. Does not eternal doom await those out of Christ? What does this mean to our redeemed hearts? This is the hour of rescue, the hour of glad tidings.

11

"I WILL JUDGE YOU"

CHAPTER 11 of Ezekiel's prophecy closes the series of messages begun in chapter 8. The complete departure of the Lord's glory is stated here and emphasis is now put on punishment of the corrupt princes. Many have commented on the order of this chapter, as though it were misplaced, but it is entirely in keeping with Hebrew style to resume the same theme from a different angle.

THE CALDRON AND THE FLESH (11:1-13)

Ezekiel was carried to the temple court in spirit; the east gate was the place which the glory of God had left in 10:19; this was the porch of Solomon. Here twenty-five men were gathered. Are these the same as the group mentioned in 8:16? The number alone cannot be decisive as to the identity of the men; their activity and function must be taken into account. Jaazaniah is mentioned in both passages, but the Jaazaniahs are not the same, as the names of their fathers evidence (8:11). The princes are not to be equated with the priestly group of 8:16. They do not stand where the priests did (between the porch and the altar), and they are expressly designated as secular princes, "princes of the people." They may represent the lay authority in the nation. To them God has a special message of solemn import through the prophet.

The Lord seated between the cherubim (10:2) denounces the godless leaders in specific charges. Some have suggested that the wicked counsel was the plan to rebel against the king of Babylon, which took place three years later. It is of little weight to hold that they were advocating such revolutionary action, when their advice is stated in verse 3. The words of verse 3 are difficult and have been the subject of differing interpretations, but the probable sense is that Jeremiah (29:5) in his concern for the exiles had written to the elders in captivity, foretelling the duration of the exile and counseling them to build and settle down in the land of their exile. They scorned Jeremiah's word, building instead in Jerusalem. The passage underscores the false security and pride of the leaders. They felt they did not need to heed the words and warnings of the prophets. Those afar off in exile might build if they wished, but as far as these residents of Jerusalem were concerned, it was too remote a factor for them to trouble themselves about. In the figure of the caldron and the flesh the thought is that, just as the caldron protects the flesh from the fire, so Jerusalem would be their refuge and protection from doom. To see a reference here to Jeremiah 1:13 is far-fetched.

Unbelief, then, marked all their counsel. In scorning Jeremiah's words they were declaring that building of homes in exile was a long way off. Jerusalem would not fall into the hands of the enemy. Rather, the city would be a shield about them as the caldron is to seething flesh. Thus they were scorning the message of God's prophet, and relying on a false confidence in Jerusalem and its power to withstand siege and ultimate exile. With repetition to convey great earnestness Ezekiel was exhorted to prophesy to the wicked princes of the people. He was clearly under divine compulsion to proclaim the message of judgment (cf. 3:21).

First of all, Ezekiel's contemporaries needed to be told that the contempt they had manifested toward God's warnings had not escaped His notice. God never takes lightly the scorning of His gracious warnings and entreaties. Because of refusal to hearken and obey God's timely word and because of their deceptions and unbelief, they were actually responsible for the multiplication of the dead in the streets of Jerusalem. Ezekiel reverses their interpretation of the figure of the caldron. The flesh represented the slain in the streets of the city, whereas the city was a caldron surrounded by the fires of judgment. They had boasted of the protection of Jerusalem, but Ezekiel showed that the city would be a secure place only for those who had fallen in it. It would provide no refuge for the living; they who had trusted in the city would be brought out of it by force. What a reversal this was of their haughty vauntings!

In the remaining verses of this section (8-13) the judgment is stated as certain. The sword which they so feared would be brought upon them, and that by divine appointment. They would be powerless to avert the calamity. By compulsion at the hands of strangers, the Babylonians, they would be evicted from their homeland. Again their vain hopes found a direct and unwavering denial. To those brazenly defying God's word the city would not be a caldron nor any form of protection, for God would remove them to the border of Israel to their doom. They would be driven from the city's area to the frontier. This prophecy was literally fulfilled at Riblah as is attested by II Kings 25:18-21 and Jeremiah 52:24-27. The root of their trouble was that they had followed the infectious and bad example of the nations around them, forsaking God's righteous statutes and ordinances and accepting the idolatrous ordinances of their heathen neighbors.

As Ezekiel prophesied he saw in his vision what actually happened in Jerusalem at this time or immediately afterward. Pelatiah the son of Benaiah died, a striking confirmation of the truth of Ezekiel's message. Pelatiah may have been the leader of those who scoffed at God's word (vv. 1-3). His death was a foretaste of what awaited the rest whom Ezekiel had warned. The prophet asked whether God was going to visit destruction on all, even the remnant (9:8), perhaps fearing that the slaughter would be extended to all. At the moment he wondered if deliverance would be granted anyone. The answer to his petition follows in the next division of the chapter.

A SANCTUARY FOR A LITTLE WHILE (11:14-21)

These verses are the Lord's answer to Ezekiel's intercession, giving the first promise of restoration in the book. The subjects of the message are emphasized by a threefold mention: they were the fellow exiles of Ezekiel from Judah. The prophet's concern was to be not with those in Jerusalem but with those in exile with him. These brethren were the men of his kindred, literally, of his redemption, the nearest relative whose duty it was to vindicate and redeem a threatened inheritance (see Lev. 25:25). The thought is that Ezekiel was to exercise the duty of kinsman-redeemer to the exiled of the nation. The prophecy is then broadened to include all the house of Israel, doubtless those from the northern kingdom deported in 722/721 B.C. The attitude of those still left in Jerusalem toward the exiles was one of pride and disdain. For them exile from the land was tantamount to departure from the Lord and His protecting care (cf. I Sam. 26:19; Jer. 16:13; Hosea 9:3). According to their reckoning, since they inhabited the land it belonged permanently to them. To offset this arrogant claim the Lord made a glorious promise to the scattered of the nation. The language employed by Ezekiel indicates more than the Babylonian exile of his day; the Lord conveyed to the prophet the disclosure that He would be a sanctuary for a little while to His cherished remnant in Israel. It is not a "little sanctuary" (v. 16, AV, which could never be true of God), but "for a little while" (ASV). God would watch over the remnant. No place would again be called God's sanctuary where He had set His name, but He would be accessible to any willing and obedient heart. The Aramaic Targum on Ezekiel paraphrases: "And I gave them synagogues which rank second to my temple." Thus the Jewish name in the Middle Ages for a synagogue was "little sanctuary." The suggestion of the Targum is interesting and may have been heartwarming to many, but the Lord is not speaking of an outward structure or edifice, but of Himself.

Now Ezekiel predicts the future return from exile. Verses 17-21 speak of repentance and conversion, and refer to the millennial period. Both Jeremiah and Ezekiel link the promises of the future with those in exile, not with those left in the land. The gathering is to be by divine direction and from all lands and countries of their dispersion. And the promise is unequivocal: "I will give you the land of Israel" (v. 17). Is it not pointless then to speak now as though the land of promise may belong to the Arabs or Israel? When did God reverse His land grant? It will not do to claim that the Jews now in the land are unbelieving; their neighbors are equally unbelieving. No, God's promise must stand and it will be literally fulfilled in God's good time and hour. The promise clearly awaits a future fulfillment, even with reference to the removal of the detestable things and abominations, which are their idols. Although every trace of idolatry was removed by their exile in Babylon, this practice would again fasten itself upon the unbelieving mass of the nation (read Matt. 12:43-45; Rev. 13:11-18).

When the Lord Jesus Christ was interviewed by Nicodemus (John 3), He stated that His inquirer should have known the truth of the new birth. But where is this truth stated? It is here in verse 19. The new heart, the heart of flesh, and the new spirit can be realized only through the new birth, a birth from above. Thus are new creatures created unto God (II Cor. 5:17). The stony heart is that of the unregenerate, which refuses to heed and submit to the will of God (see Zech. 7:12). On the other hand, the heart of flesh can be responsive to God's voice and message if it seeks God wholeheartedly. Nothing here suggests removal of sectional jealousies between north and south, as is stated in 37:22. No more important theme is treated in the Old or New Testament than that of the new heart (cf. Deut. 30:6; Jer. 31:33; 32:38-39; Ezek. 36:26-27). It is the opposite of the willful and divided heart mentioned in Isaiah 53:6.

As soon as the new life is imparted the new nature manifests itself in a new walk and fruit for God. The statutes and ordinances of God, formerly rejected and broken, will now be fulfilled in the new life. In whatever sense this may have been realized in Zerubbabel's or Ezra's day, or even in the Maccabean era, the promises look for more complete fulfillment in the future. More than eradication of idolatry, accomplished during the Babylonian exile, is meant here. The repetition of "heart" in verse 21 shows the emphasis on the positive condition of complete renewal mentioned in the preceding passage. The figurative expression denotes those who were so wedded to idolatry and its abominable practices.

Departure of the Glory (11:22-25)

There is an interesting Midrash (commentary) which reads: "Rabbi Jonathan said, Three years and a half the Shekinah stayed upon the Mount of Olives, in the hope that Israel would do penance; but they did none." All readers of the New Testament know this was the length of the earthly ministry of our Lord to the lost sheep of the house of Israel. Sadly enough, they did not repent and He did depart from them (cf. Hosea 5:15 with Matt. 23:37-39). The rabbis have enumerated ten stages whereby the Shekinah withdrew. These stages unmistakably reveal the loving and longing reluctance of God to leave His sanctuary where He dwelt in the midst of His beloved and erring people. Before He departed, however, He set forth the consoling promise of restoration for the remnant which we have been considering. From the midst of the city the glory of God ascended and remained temporarily on the Mount of Olives which is on the east side of Jerusalem. From this very place the Lord Jesus Christ left the earth (Acts 1) and to it He will return (Zech. 14; cf. also Luke 21:20 with Matt. 24:3; Luke 24:50-51; Acts 1:11-12). The Mount of Olives is higher than Jerusalem and affords a view of the entire city. Thus God forsook the temple altogether.

Verses 24-25 state the purpose of the revelations: that Ezekiel might communicate them to the captives for their instruction and consolation. The words "in a vision" contain the key to the transactions; they were in ecstatic vision. When Ezekiel returned to his normal state, he related to his fellow exiles the things revealed to him by God in vision.

Ichabod over Israel

It would be difficult for anyone today to state how downcast the godly in Israel must have been when they viewed the departure of the glory of the Lord from His sanctuary in Ezekiel's day. It is no wonder that the disciples were disheartened when the glory of God in Christ left them. But the presence of the risen Saviour meant all the difference in the world. There is only one way to reverse the Ichabod in the heart of any man. Acceptance of Christ brings the Spirit of glory to rest in the heart of the formerly desolate soul.

12

CERTAINTY OF DESTRUCTION

Chapters 12-19 may be classified as a distinct division of the prophecy. They are not dated as to time given or recorded, but the theme is still one of judgment for the nation's continued disobedience. Chapters 4-11 have repeatedly shown the certainty of Jerusalem's destruction; chapters 12-19 present the necessity for it. The emphasis in these chapters is the moral cause of the exile. Whereas the messages of chapters 8-11 centered about the temple, chapter 12 deals with the throne. Ezekiel's main purpose was to reveal how baseless was the people's confidence that the kingdom and its capital would be spared, and to arouse the remnant to repentance. The action here was not in the vision, but actually performed, because the people asked its meaning in the morning (v. 8).

Captivity Symbolized (12:1-7)

The message of Ezekiel was addressed to his fellow exiles who were as hardened as those who remained in Jerusalem. They were still intent on a return to Jerusalem, so they would not accept his message of destruction. The symbolical action was performed because of their hardness of heart which prevented them from seeing with proper perspective the significance of events around them. It is not difficult to identify the people of the nonseeing eyes and the nonhearing ears. These designations are repeatedly used of Israel throughout the Scriptures (see Deut. 29:1-4; Isa. 6:9-10; Jer. 5:21; Matt. 13:13-15; Mark 8:18; John 12:39-40; Acts 28:26-27). They were indeed a rebellious house (see 2:8), but the God of grace was eager to give the heedless ones multiplied opportunities to obey His word. Thus Ezekiel was commanded to prepare stuff for moving (literally, baggage for exile), just those scant supplies that could be taken by a captive from his country: staff, wallet, provisions and vessels needed for the way. This was to be done as publicly as possible, as explained in verse 11. Ezekiel was to play the part of an exile, reenacting a scene all the exiles had painfully experienced when led from their land. He dramatized the fate of the inhabitants of Jerusalem in order to convince them, despite all appearances to the contrary, that God was determined to carry through His moral aims in deporting the nation from their country. This was to be proof that the land would come under God's judgment in spite of the fact that the majority felt deliverance and restoration would soon be realized. In spite of their rebelliousness the people were to view the symbolical action, so that perchance some might yet heed; the possibility of repentance was still held out to them.

The material was to be prepared during the day and deposited in an accessible place for ease when he escaped. After removing it earlier, he was himself to seek an exit at night. And that was to be done in a singular way: he was to dig through the wall. It has been suggested that this was the city wall, but city walls would hardly be susceptible to such treatment. Babylonian houses were constructed of sun-dried bricks. Digging through the wall pictured the desperation with which they would seek to escape. In the dark Ezekiel was to carry forth his belongings with covered face so that he might not see the land. The covering of the face was also in order to avoid recognition, a mark of humiliation for a person of noble birth. The historical account of the siege and destruction of Jerusalem in the time of Zedekiah reveals that he did not see the land; he was taken to Riblah and blinded. Then he was carried captive to Babylon (see II Kings 25:4-7; Jer. 39:2-7; 52:7-11). Such blinding was a common custom of the Babylonians for the dethroned. Ezekiel carried out the command of the Lord in detail.

ACTIONS EXPLAINED (12:8-16)

Apparently Ezekiel's contemporaries in exile had asked the meaning of his actions on the previous evening. The reply was given the next morning. For a similar situation see 24:19-21. The language of verse 9 is a strong indication that the actions were actually performed and not merely narrated from a vision. The form of the question in the original implies a positive answer; they had asked the prophet. The answer was to the point. The burden (v. 10) was a threatening prophecy concerning the prince—literally, "the prince is this burden." The subject of the message was King Zedekiah, who was always spoken of by Ezekiel as prince, never king. Jehoiachin was regarded as the true king (17:13), the Babylonians having never formally deposed him. In ration tablets found by archaeologists in Babylon, Jehoiachin was still referred to as the king of Judah. (Note the dating of the prophecy in 1:2; cf. II Kings 25:27-30.) Although the prophecy centered in Zedekiah, it was for all the house of Israel; they would share the calamity that would befall him. In all this Ezekiel was a sign to the exiles. Whatever happened in Jerusalem to the king had significance for them too; for one thing it would effectively dash any hopes they might have cherished as to an early return to the land of Israel. Every word of prediction would come to pass upon Zedekiah and the inhabitants of Jerusalem. Ezekiel stated emphatically by repetition (with two different Hebrew words) that exile would be their lot.

How literally these words were fulfilled may be seen immediately from the vivid historical account in II Kings 25:1-7 (ASV):

> And it came to pass in the ninth year of his reign, in the tenth month, in the tenth day of the month, that Nebuchadnezzar king of Babylon came, he and all his army, against Jerusalem, and encamped against it; and they built forts against it round about. So the city was besieged unto the eleventh year of king Zedekiah. On the ninth day of the fourth month the famine was sore in the city, so that there was no bread for the people of the land. Then a breach was made in the city, and all the men of war fled by night by the way of the gate between the two walls, which was by the king's garden (now the Chaldeans were against the city round about); and the king went by the way of the Arabah. But the army of the Chaldeans pursued after the king, and overtook him in the plains of Jericho; and all his army was scattered from him. Then they took the king, and carried him up unto the king of Babylon to Riblah; and they gave judgment upon him. And they slew the sons of Zedekiah before his eyes, and put out the eyes of Zedekiah, and bound him in fetters, and carried him to Babylon.

The blinding was meant not only for punishment, but it rendered Zedekiah unfit to rule because of his violation of his oath to the king of Babylon.

The net and snare the Lord would spread for Zedekiah were the Babylonian army. Verse 13 repeats the statement of the previous verse that Zedekiah would not see the land of Babylon, though he would die there. Josephus the historian had a strange account:

> Ezekiel also foretold in Babylon what calamities were coming upon the people, which when he heard, he sent accounts of them unto Jerusalem. But Zedekiah did not believe their prophecies, for the reason following: It happened that the two prophets agreed with one another in what they said as in all other things, that the city should be taken, and Zedekiah himself should be taken captive; but Ezekiel disagreed with him, and said that Zedekiah should not see Babylon; while Jeremiah said to him, that the king of Babylon should carry him away thither in bonds. And because they did not both say the same thing as to this circumstance, he disbelieved what they both appeared to agree in, and condemned them as not speaking truth therein, although all the things foretold him did come to pass according to their prophecies. . . .[1]

Whether Josephus was correct or not, no one can verify, but the prophecies of both Jeremiah and Ezekiel were fulfilled to the letter: Zedekiah

[1]Josephus, *Antiquities*, X. 7. 2.

was taken to the land of Babylon, but he never saw the country because his eyes had been previously blinded at Riblah.

In the hour of most desperate need Zedekiah's army would be powerless to rescue him. God's hand would be with the forces of the enemy; they would be His rod of correction. Then the people of Jerusalem would know by experience that God is the Lord, when these trials prophesied of them came to pass. But all would not be wiped out; a few would be left to show the nations that the calamity of Israel was not due to God's lack of power to help them, but because He brought it upon them to vindicate His holiness. The nations among whom they would be scattered (a word that seems to look on to a far distant future time as well), would also be convinced by the manifestation of the power of God.

DISTRESS IN THE SIEGE (12:17-20)

It is not stated that this sign was carried out by Ezekiel, but it is surely implied. Ezekiel was to act with every indication of alarm. Some think that the mention of bread and water is not necessarily an indication of scarcity of food, since the words are the usual way of stating the elements of a meal. But times of siege are hours of distress in many ways. Here are underscored the privations of the invasion of Nebuchadnezzar. The people would sadly learn that the punishment for violence was to be violence. Desolation was decreed upon the whole land; there would be no turning back the stroke.

EVERY VISION FULFILLED (12:21-28)

In the two messages of verses 21-28 appear the reasons why the people had disbelieved the prophecies of Ezekiel. The first is in verse 22: delay gave the impression that the stroke would never come. The second is in verse 27: delay led those who apparently believed the prophecies to feel that the hour of calamity was far off. The answer of God in both cases was: every vision would be fulfilled, and the time would not be deferred any longer. A saying (v. 22) had become current among them because God's long-suffering, which should have led to repentance, was made an argument against His word (cf. Eccles. 8:11; Amos 6:3). There were always false prophets in the land to give events an interpretation that suited the people's fancy. The nation thought they were secure because Ezekiel's predictions had not yet been fulfilled. The same condition obtains in our day as reflected in Matthew 24:48; 25:5 and even more pointedly in II Peter 3:3-4. Time passed then and no prediction was realized. After the exile of King Jehoiachin many may have believed that conditions would get no worse. And all the while the mercy and patience of God were waiting for their faith in Him and His promises. But to the carnal eye and mind prophecy had failed; it was ineffective and failed of fulfillment. Ezekiel began to prophesy (1:1-2) in the fifth year of his captivity, but it was not until the twelfth year (33:21) that word reached him by messenger that Jerusalem had actually fallen. It was in the intervening years that skepticism had a good opportunity to fasten itself upon the hearts of the people.

God's delay was now over. They could well discard their convenient proverbs. The execution of the prophecies of judgment was certain; there would be no room now to consider the predictions a failure. That which added to the confusion in the minds of the nation was the presence of false prophets, for the people found it hard to differentiate (then as now) between true and false prophets (read Jer. 28 for the contest between Jeremiah and Hananiah). False prophets used the means employed by the Canaanites to ascertain the minds of their gods (see Deut. 18:10; I Sam. 6:2; Ezek. 21:21). Their divination was flattering (literally, smooth), and thus they instilled doubts in the minds of Israel. God was going to bring to an end all false prophecy in the land. The complacence of Israel in the hour of her testing and danger finds a striking parallel in the attitude of professing Christendom today. Ezekiel was quite explicit about the time of fulfillment: "in your days" (v. 25), that is, in your generation. Another method of circumventing the force of the prophetic word was to claim that the fulfillment was a long way off. Thus they needed not to be concerned about it at the moment. The ones using the proverb of verse 22 were out-and-out unbelievers; those of verse 27 were the carnally secure. With great solemnity and finality God assured the nation that there would be deferment no longer. The great truth here set forth is that prophecy has its validity and worth, not by virtue of a certain time element alone, but because of the unchangeable demands and requirements of God's righteousness and justice.

EVERY WORD FULFILLED WITHOUT DELAY

The obedient believer today realizes that God stands behind every word He has uttered, and also knows that God will shortly wind up His purposes on earth. Thus time is a most precious commodity; it is short.

13

LYING PROPHETS AND FALSE
PROPHETESSES

THE PROPHET EZEKIEL has already pronounced the judgment of God on the city of Jerusalem, the princes and the king. Now he rebukes the false prophets. The test of a prophet is found in Deuteronomy 13:1-5 and 18:21-22. Jeremiah carried on a long struggle against the false prophets (see Jer. 5:30-31; 14:13-18; 23:9-40; 29:8-10, 21-23), and this chapter may profitably be compared with Jeremiah 23. Ezekiel in exile watched with sorrow and righteous indignation the spiritual condition of his people at home in Judah. False prophecy, which had long flourished in Judah, had in some measure been transplanted to Babylon as well. This chapter, one of the most important in the Old Testament on the abuses of the phenomenon of prophecy, may be considered an elaboration of the truth in 12:24.

WORKS OF THE FOOLISH PROPHETS (13:1-7)

When the Lord instructed Ezekiel to prophesy against the prophets of Israel, He used the term "prophet" in an ironical sense, as the entire chapter reveals. In no sense were they prophets of God, for the source of their message was their own heart, as it is with the false teachers of our day (cf. II Peter 2:1-2). They were misled by their own desires, which is the scriptural method of asserting they were not inspired of God. The wish was father to the thought, and they spoke accordingly.

When the false prophets were termed foolish, moral rather than intellectual folly was meant. There is a play on words in the original, and the strongest of the several Hebrew words for "fool" is employed (see Ps. 14:1). Their sin was that they followed their own human, fallible spirit instead of the divine, infallible Holy Spirit; but this availed them nothing, because they saw nothing. These prophets of falsehood were likened to foxes in waste places, preying on the desolation around them and undermining foundations and causing havoc everywhere. As foxes they were crafty, mischievous and destructive (cf. Matt. 7:15; Acts 20:29).

In outlining the failure of the false prophets Ezekiel used two figures: one of a repairer of a breach in a wall (Isa. 58:12), and the other a warrior in a battle. The wall represents the moral and spiritual defense of the people which was needed for the coming catastrophe. The breaches in the walls were those made by the enemy. Those who encouraged the people to repent and turn to the Lord were called restorers of the breach (22:30). The breaches looked ahead to the fall of the theocracy in Israel. The day of the Lord came when the Babylonians attacked Jerusalem and destroyed it in 586 B.C.

The godless prophets, in using the phrase "The Lord saith," were falsely employing the authenticating formula of the true messenger of God. They were self-appointed and self-commissioned. Satan was behind their falsehoods and lying divinations (see I Kings 22:6-28; I Tim. 4:1). The detrimental effects of their preaching are clear enough. Some believe that this passage should be translated "have hoped"; it would then indicate they were self-deceived instead of deliberately falsifying a message. They had deceived themselves into expecting a fulfillment of their baseless pronouncements. Others suggest that the prophets had no basis to expect their predictions to come true because they had no authority to utter them in the first place. That deception has a reflexive effect on the deceiver is clearly witnessed in Scripture (II Tim. 3:13). The tragedy of deception is that liars are often duped into believing their own falsehoods. First they set out to deceive the nation Israel and then were caught up in the meshes of their fabrications. Ezekiel challenged them directly to acknowledge that they had never received their pronouncements or messages from the Lord. This was the necessary and first step in extricating themselves from their sad predicament.

GOD'S JUDGMENT ON THE WICKED PROPHETS (13:8-16)

The judgment of God upon the prophets was to be threefold (v. 9): (1) They would not come into the council of God's people; (2) They would have their names omitted from the register of Israel (Ezra 2:62); (3) They would never return to the land. When it was affirmed that they would not come into the council of God's people, the sense is that they would lose the place of authority and respect they held among the people by virtue of their alleged calling. Not to be written in the writing of Israel has been taken by some to mean that they would not be found on the list of the godly in the coming kingdom of blessing. Others believe the meaning is excommunication from the commonwealth of Israel, whereas still others consider that their names would be erased from the family and tribal registers (Jer. 17:13). The idea originated from the register that was kept of a city's citizens (see Exodus 32:32; Ezra 2:62; Isa. 4:3; Dan. 12:1). The Ezra passage shows to what use such registers were put, a literal fulfillment of this threat. However, Ezekiel was speaking of a public dealing on earth with eternal implications (cf. Luke 10:20; Rev. 3:5; 20:15). The final warning was that the peddlers of falsehoods would not return from captivity (20:38; Jer. 29:32). The expression "my people" is found seven times in the chapter, a constant reminder to the culprits of those whom they have misled.

Verses 10-16 show that their work would come to nothing, like building a wall with untempered mortar. Such a wall could never stand a storm. Verse 10 begins with a solemn and formal statement in the style of judgment. The characteristic of the false prophet was to promise prosperity and quiet. The detrimental effect of his words lay in that he lulled the people into a false and unwarranted security by encouraging unfounded hopes among the people. Ezekiel's statement reveals that the final siege of Jerusalem had not yet taken place. The false prophets were compared to those who build an unsafe wall and cover up its defects. The untempered mortar was actually whitewash, which is useless for strengthening insecure walls. Smooth words of false messengers hid from the people the actual seriousness of their spiritual condition. To daub with untempered mortar, in the metaphorical sense, is to flatter, to use hypocrisy. When the false prophets confirmed the people in their evil ways, by their approval they were whitewashing the flimsy spiritual structure of Israel. Such a wall was bound to fall, especially when an overflowing shower and hailstones were sent from God Himself. The hailstones were addressed directly. They were unusual in Palestine, but they could be very destructive (see Matt. 7:27). Stones measuring an inch in diameter have been known to fall. The Babylonians are figuratively in the hailstorm. When the disaster would come, for which the Hebrews were unprepared, they would inquire in derision of the builders, of what good their work had been. For the New Testament use of this figure see Matthew 23:27 and Acts 23:3.

When God signified in verse 13 the threefold judgment that awaited them, namely, the stormy wind, the overflowing shower and great hailstones, He specified that each would be accompanied by His wrath and anger. When the wall would be utterly flattened and its foundation uncovered, the wicked prophets would be buried in the ruins. By divine justice they would be undone by their own godless doings, and there would be a complete annihilation of the false spiritual structure they had erected. Finally, Ezekiel laid aside the use of figures and pointed out the false prophets as those who had been doing the disastrous plastering he had mentioned.

WAYS OF THE FALSE PROPHETESSES (13:17-19)

Sadly enough, there were not only false prophets preying upon the unhappy people but false prophetesses as well. With boldness Ezekiel
turned to denounce them. Although women were rebuked by Isaiah (Isa.
3:16–4:1; 32:9-12) and Amos (Amos 4:1-3), this is the only place in the
Old Testament where false prophetesses are mentioned. Women held a
higher place in Israel than among most other nations. While there were
no priestesses in Israel, the nation knew the prophetic ministry of women
such as Miriam, Deborah, Huldah and Noadiah, although it was rare (cf.
Exodus 15:20; Judges 4:4; II Kings 22:14; Neh. 6:14; Acts 21:9; I Cor.
11:5). Jezebel is pointed out as a false prophetess in Revelation 2:20.
Sorcery was practiced mainly by women (Exodus 22:18). It has been
suggested that, whereas the false prophets carried on their work publicly
and in the political realm, sorceresses plied their trade on the susceptible
in private.

The false prophetesses, who today would be called sorceresses and for-
tune-tellers, employed pillows and kerchiefs in their trade according to
the Authorized Version. The pillows and kerchiefs have been variously
explained. Some words in the passage are difficult because they occur
nowhere else in the Old Testament. Some take the expressions figuratively
to mean smooth and soft things upon which the hearers would rest their
confidence and faith. Others suggest the pillows were cushions upon
which the sorceresses leaned to show the peace and calm which would
be the portion of those who consulted them and followed their advice. Yet
others, on the basis of a better translation of pillows as bands on the
wrists, claim they were a means of sympathetic magic. The bands were
supposed to transmit into the consulting one the magic power of the sor-
ceress to bind and loose. This was a common practice among the Babylonians, but it is difficult to say whether the practice was carried over into
Israel. The kerchiefs were probably veils which were made to fit every
inquirer. Veils were worn by Roman augurs. With aroused indignation
the prophet asked whether they would continue to hunt souls for their
own advantage. One suggestion is that they adorned themselves as harlots do to attract unwary inquirers. But the entire passage emphasizes an
altogether different concept, namely, their seducing fortune-telling.

The handfuls of barley may indicate that they carried on their nefarious
activity for meager fees as their rewards, although it is possible that the
barley was not their pay but the means of their divination. Centuries later
in Syria divination was carried out with barley bread. It is less likely that
Ezekiel was referring to the baking of cakes to the queen of heaven (Jer.

44:17). What is unmistakable is that they degraded the name of the Lord by linking it with superstitions and magical practices. They claimed the prerogative of God alone over life and death, falsely asserting that the godly would perish and the ungodly would survive. They led on to destruction souls that were meant for life, and saved their own which were worthy of destruction (see II Cor. 2:15-16 for the principle involved). Their sin was all the worse since it was perpetrated on God's people, His peculiar nation and treasure.

Visitation of God on the Ungodly Sorceresses (13:20-23)

Verses 20-21 correspond to the warning in verse 18, just as verses 22-23 answer to verse 19. The thought in this portion is not that the sorceresses made their victims fly as birds, but rather to fly into their nets to ensnare them as fowlers catch birds. God would deliver the people from the misrepresentation of their deceivers. This He had to do, for the Lord must be the Lord and ever prove Himself to be such. The godly, who were opposed and threatened with evil because they followed the true prophets, would have their cause championed by the Lord of hosts. The sorceresses saddened those against whom the Lord had not spoken condemnation, with prophecies of evil, while they held out false hopes to the ungodly. It has been suggested that the complete loss of influence by the false prophetesses indicated their sin as less heinous in God's sight than that of the false prophets. This does not necessarily follow and is not a strong argument. God will bring false prophecy and sorcery to an end (Amos 8:11; Micah 3:6-7; Zech. 13:1-6). The sad feature of all the condemnation is that when the people heeded the messages of the false prophets and prophetesses they were in no position to follow the true message of the prophets of God.

"I Will Deliver My People"

All God's promises are sure. When He says He will deliver His people, He means just that. When He promised repeatedly to send deliverance in Messiah the Lord, He kept His promise to the letter. But of what avail is it if Jew or Gentile has not been told this good news?

14

IDOLATROUS ELDERS DENOUNCED

THIS CHAPTER IS A REBUKE to the elders of Israel who had evidently come to inquire of the Lord (v. 3; 20:1). The false prophets preyed upon Israel and made merchandise of them (chap. 13), but they were able to do so because the nation was ready for such false predictions because of the misleading of their elders. Though Ezekiel addresses the exiles in the first instance, his message is designed for the entire nation.

REBUKE OF THE HYPOCRITICAL INQUIRERS (14:1-5)

The elders were supposed to be the spiritual leaders of the nation while it was in exile in Babylon. They sat before Ezekiel to await a message from the Lord. There may be an indication of a measure of anxiety and apprehension because they were probably concerned about the future of Jerusalem and the homeland, and hoped Ezekiel could enlighten them on these themes. Perhaps now they realized that the smooth messages of the false prophets were worthless, and that the Babylonians were not to be turned back from their attack on Jerusalem. As the elders sat before the prophet, who could have had no way of knowing the condition of their hearts, the Lord spoke to him to reveal the inner springs of their souls. God disclosed that the elders had taken their idols into their heart. The figurative language does not mean they had actually set up the stumbling block of their idols in their presence, for the wording excludes the open practice of idolatry. Instead, they were longing after the old worship they had once carried on, which was the cause of the judgment of God on the nation. Their thoughts were occupied with idol worship; they were enamored of idolatry, and their affections were centered on worthless vanities. Since they were so hypocritical, God asked whether He should allow Himself to be inquired of them at all. A strong negation is implied. Their very asking was an affront and insult to God as long as they were determined to go on in their idolatry if given the opportunity. The divided heart, part for God and part for anything or anyone else, was condemned by Elijah on Mount Carmel (I Kings 18:21) and later by the Apostle James (James 1:8).

Since inquiring of the Lord was merely pretense while idolatry was firmly rooted in their heart, the elders could expect no oral answer from the Lord whom they did not reverence in truth. Rather, the Lord would answer them by deeds, not in words merely, but by acts of judgment. The reply would come not through any intermediary, but personally. Furthermore, the answer of God would take into consideration the degree to which the inquirer had become wedded to the practice of idolatry. One is reminded of the sad words of Hosea 4:17 concerning the northern kingdom: "Ephraim is joined to idols; let him alone."

The Lord expected to call them to account for their sinful desires toward idols. They would be taken in the snare of their own making, and the Lord would unveil the ungodliness and deceit of their hearts which had become estranged from obedience to Him. The thought is that their hearts would be subjected by judgment, not for the purpose of remedying their wicked condition.

Certain Judgment of the Offenders (14:6-11)

Though it was only the elders who sat before Ezekiel, the message of God was directed to all the house of Israel. It was a clear and unmistakable call to repent and turn from their idolatry. The situation called for a clean break with all idolatrous practices. Ezekiel's message was one of repentance, while the Lord answered the inquirers Himself (v. 7). God can be satisfied with nothing less than thoroughgoing repentance, for halfway measures neither deceive nor please Him.

The proselyte had equal rights and responsibilities with the rest of the nation, for the one who lived in the community of Israel was bound to observe the law of the land, a situation which is paralleled everywhere today. Since Israel was a theocracy, its laws against idol worship were binding on the stranger as well as the citizen of the land (cf. Lev. 17:10; 20:1-2). He who separated himself from the Lord (literally, apostatized from Him) dedicated himself away from following God (see Hosea 9:10). To be sure, this was not done for the glory of God but for himself, for his own pleasure and satisfaction.

The punishment outlined echoes the wording of Deuteronomy 28:37 and the earlier warning in Leviticus 20:3, 5-6. God would set Himself against that man until he was destroyed from the midst of Israel. Verse 9 sets forth an important principle of divine dealing. When the false prophet, sensing the desires of his idolatrous inquirers, gave them a prediction, a prophetic word in keeping with their wishes, thus aiding their apostasy and delusion, the prophet himself had been deceived by his wicked heart; and ultimately it was the Lord who had enticed him. There is an elimination of secondary causes as in Isaiah 45:7 and Amos 3:6.

Because of their continuance in disobedience God had permitted false prophets to deceive them and prepare them for their doom (see I Kings 22:13-23). When men obdurately refuse the truth, the Lord gives them over to falsehood. This passage is cited as an instance where the Old Testament bypasses secondary causes and relates all actions ultimately to God and His law (cf. I Kings 22:20-23; II Thess. 2:11; and the case of the hardening of Pharaoh's heart). The deception, of course, is not direct (James 1:13) but through the flesh, the ungodly and Satan. This happens only to those who willingly take deceit into their hearts. It is a righteous judgment on their willful blindness. William Cowper put it well:

> Hear the just law, the judgment of the skies:
> He that hates truth must be the dupe of lies:
> And he who *will* be cheated to the last,
> Delusions strong as hell must bind him fast.

Just as God is impartial in His offers of grace, mercy and love, so is He no respecter of persons in judgment. Inquirer and false prophet would suffer the same punishment, for they were alike guilty. The responsibility was mutual. They would bear the punishment of their iniquity, that is, the Lord would allow them to be duped by the prophets from whom they sought pleasant and smooth messages.

The intent of the rebuke was a gracious one, for there was still hope held out if they would turn to God; they would again be recognized as the people of God. Such is the hope set before them in the midst of darkness. The fiery judgment consumes the sinner but cleanses the nation at the same time (Isa. 4:4). The dealings of God were actuated by love throughout. In the last days of the Judean kingdom false prophecy was allowed to flourish so that the righteous could be distinguished from the wicked in order to purge and purify the nation.

No Hope in the Godliness of Others (14:12-20)

The wording of verse 12 implies an interval of silence of undetermined length. Questions may have arisen in many minds after the previous oracle. Was there to be no sparing of the ungodly because of the righteous? Had Ezekiel overdrawn the gravity of their condition? Would God deal with Israel now in a manner different from His dealing with Sodom in Abraham's day? Jeremiah 7:16 and 15:1-4 afford a close parallel to this section. According to Jeremiah even Moses and Samuel, well known for their power in intercessory prayer, would not avail to deliver the doomed city of Jerusalem and her people (see Exodus 32:11-14; Num. 14:13-20; I Sam. 7:8-12).

Ezekiel spoke of a land, purposely leaving it indefinite so that they would seek the application for themselves. Fourfold judgment was threatened: (1) famine, (2) evil beasts, (3) sword and (4) pestilence. Physical life is dependent in the first instance upon food, so God would break the staff of bread by sending famine. Man's life is sustained by bread as on a staff, hence the expression. They had arrived at the place where God would not hear intercession on their behalf. Noah, Daniel and Job, saints whose intercession came at strategic points in history, could deliver only their own souls from the impending calamity.

There seems to have been a view current among the nation that Jerusalem would be spared if there were righteous men among her inhabitants. But when a land had sinned as willfully and long as Judah had, even the presence of godly men could not avert the coming judgment. Moral responsibility is not transferable. Instances like Genesis 18:22-32 and Jeremiah 5:1-4 are exceptions and not to be counted upon in every case. In short, Israel was beyond the help of any human mediation, even of the most righteous. With Abraham (Gen. 18) God was willing to spare even wicked Sodom if ten righteous men were found in the city, but in Israel there was no hope that the merit of the godly would avail for the ungodly majority. Noah was the means of sparing his family (Gen. 6:18); Daniel, his friends (Dan. 1:6-20; 2:17-18); Job, his friends (Job 42:7-10). Questions have been raised about the inclusion of the name of Daniel, but he was a well-known contemporary of Ezekiel at the court of Babylon. It is not a reference to an older Daniel of whom nothing is stated in the Old Testament. Daniel's fame for wisdom and piety was already widespread in Ezekiel's day. Possibly the names are arranged not chronologically but to form a climax: Noah delivered his family with himself; Daniel, his friends; but Job, not even his children. Whether or not this be Ezekiel's intent, the order is the same in each mention. The righteousness referred to is not that of works but of grace, as throughout the Scripture.

The second visitation was that of evil beasts. It has been suggested that these may have been the Gentiles (Dan. 7), but there is no reason these cannot be literal, just as the other punishments were. The beasts would ravage (literally, bereave) by robbing them of their children. Though Noah, Daniel and Job could each individually accomplish much in his day, all three together would be powerless in Ezekiel's day. Even members of the same family, sons and daughters, would not be spared. If a third calamity, invasion of their land by the enemy, were to befall them, both man and beast would be overwhelmed by it. And again, the notable righteous ones could not help one whit by any intercession. Finally, pestilence would also be an irresistible judgment: God's wrath in blood, that is, in death. With repeated blows Ezekiel masterfully brought home to his people bent on departure from God, the utter hopelessness and helplessness of their estate. If they would only heed!

GOD's JUSTICE VINDICATED (14:21-23)

For the four judgments mentioned here, observe carefully Leviticus 26:22, 25-26. The number four conveys the idea of completeness with an allusion to the four quarters of the earth. The logic is this: If there would be no sparing in one judgment, how much more certain would the universal judgment be in the case of four devastating judgments? Verses 22-23 speak of a remnant, but it is a remnant of the wicked and not of the righteous. They also would go into exile to Babylon, where the contemporaries of Ezekiel were at the moment. The reason a remnant would be spared at all would be to show the earlier exiles the enormity of the sin of the more recent exiles. This would be proof positive that the judgment of God was called for. They would see that God's judgments were neither excessive nor arbitrary. They would be comforted (mentioned twice) in the sense of acquiescing in the rightness of the judgment of God. No matter how much Ezekiel loved his countrymen, no matter how much he was pained at their judgment, yet he had to acknowledge that the dealings of God with His people were in justice. The question of Abraham comes ringing down the centuries: "Shall not the Judge of all the earth do right?" (Gen. 18:25). Ezekiel vindicated the divine justice, and so must we.

GOD's OBJECTIVE

Repeatedly in times of declaration of coming judgment God intersperses the word that His ultimate longing for Israel is that they may no more go astray, but may be His people and He their God. The pleasure of God can never rest upon any man until he has found salvation through Christ's work on Calvary. When hearts are engaged with Calvary love, there will be no occasion to seek after the idols of this world.

15

THE PARABLE OF THE VINE

IN CHAPTERS 15-17 appear three parables which show there is no hope of deliverance for Israel. Chapter 15 takes place during the last days of the reign of King Zedekiah. The people were hoping for aid from Edom, Ammon, Tyre, Sidon and finally from Egypt (17:15). In a certain sense this portion briefly introduces what is set forth in greater detail in chapter 16. It also carries on the truth of chapter 14. Some may have questioned whether the Lord would carry out such a thoroughgoing purge of His people, for they were after all the vine of His own choice and planting.

THE FIGURE OF THE UNFRUITFUL VINE (15:1-15)

The vine is an old figure for the nation (read Deut. 32:32; Ps. 80:8-12; Isa. 5:1-7; Jer. 2:21; Hosea 10:1; Matt. 21:33 ff.). The vine tree here is the wild vine. Josephus indicates that the temple of Herod had the characteristic vine and clusters.[1] Ezekiel asked wherein lay the preeminence of the vine tree. Actually it is of no value in comparison with other wood. The only use of a vine is for fruit-bearing, he declared. Apart from this it is worthless. Other trees, fruit-bearing or not, are employed for art or construction or other purposes, but not so the vine. Because the vine is crooked, it cannot be used for building. Because it burns so rapidly, it is of little value for fuel. Because it is soft, it cannot be employed where anything needs to hang on it. The pin referred to is the large wooden peg utilized in Near Eastern homes, upon which household utensils are hung (see Isa. 22:23-25 for a symbolic use). God desired the fruits of righteousness and piety. Apart from God's choice of the Hebrews for bearing the fruits of godliness, they were inferior to their neighbors in age, land, army, resources and other respects. The people of God in every age are like the vine—most valuable when bearing fruit for God, but worthless when barren and sterile.

Casting the vine into the fire for fuel spoke of judgment to be carried out by Nebuchadnezzar and his invading forces (cf. II Kings 25:9; see John 15:6 for a similar picture). The ends of the vine that suffered burning were probably the kingdoms of Ephraim and Judah. The havoc of

[1]Josephus, *Wars of the Jews*, XV. 11. 3.

previous invasions and deportations had left the nation without value or worth.

If the vine be of limited usefulness when it is intact, of how much less value would it be after it had suffered burning in the fire (see Amos 4:11; Zech. 3:2)? Obviously its life of fruit-bearing was over.

THE APPLICATION TO ISRAEL (15:6-8)

Then Ezekiel made his application to the nation Israel in such a way that there would be no mistaking his meaning. As the vine is given over for burning, so the inhabitants of Jerusalem would see their city burned with fire. Israel had lost her value in the eyes of the Lord.

Ezekiel's warning at the beginning and at the end of the verse was that God would set His face against His people. They would be given over to fire—a figure for any kind of calamity (Ps. 66:12). Whether they were in the fire or going forth from the fire, fire would overtake them on every hand; there would be no escaping it. In the great tribulation it will be so again (cf. Rev. 14:18). Here the meaning of the burning by fire is stated literally as a desolation of the land. This visitation would occur because of the trespass they have committed. Rather than a specific reference to the rebellion of Zedekiah, the statement may be taken to refer to the corporate guilt of the nation.

GOD DESIRES FRUIT

It is clear from Matthew 21:33-41 and other passages that God desires fruit. This is spiritual fruit, fruit of the spiritual life. Instead, God finds sour grapes or none at all. Unless men come into vital relationship with the true vine, there can be no fruit. The vital link must be formed by faith.

16

ISRAEL THE UNFAITHFUL WIFE

IN CHAPTER 15 the emphasis was on Jerusalem's worthlessness and use-lessness as a fruitless vine; here it is on her base iniquity. There were few peoples of ancient times who were more patriotic and more proud of their national heritage than Israel. In fact, again and again in the Old Testament Scriptures the people of God were reminded of the privileges bestowed on them by their gracious God. Such knowledge on their part was to be accompanied by gratitude and obedience to the Lord. When this was lacking in Israel, as it largely was, the prophets pointed out the worthlessness of the nation in God's sight.

No passage in Ezekiel is more forceful or vivid than this chapter which is a remarkable and unparalleled setting forth of God's dealings with Israel from the beginning and their response to His ways with them. It also is a beautiful illustration of what God does in grace for any believing sinner. The chapter is reminiscent of truths found in the prophecies of Isaiah (1:21) and Hosea (1:2). Ezekiel, too, saw Israel's sin as one of unfaithfulness to the boundless love of God.

The prophet saw that repentance was produced not by the thunderings and terrors of Mount Sinai with its law, but by the tenderness of the gracious God with His love. In his treatment of Sodom and her restoration he manifested that the love of God would reach down even to the lowest depths of moral corruption. A parallel is chapter 23, which is also an allegory. Here, in the longest chapter in Ezekiel, the story is told in detail in all its sordid, loathsome character, so that God's infinite abhorrence of Israel's sin may be clearly seen. According to Rabbi Eliezer ben Hyrcanus in the Mishna, the chapter was not to be read nor translated in public. A sad parallel to this narrative is the course of Christendom in its departure from the purity of God's Word and the life of godliness.

THE ABANDONED CHILD (16:1-5)

Ezekiel was charged by God to declare his message to Jerusalem as representative of all Judah, and even the entire nation. The burden of his prophetic communication was the abominations of the people of God, namely, their many idolatries. Sin ever makes insensate, so there had to be impressed on Israel the necessity for God's judgment on her. A number of commentators feel that Ezekiel laid hold of a current tale and applied it for his purpose to Israel, but surely he was not so impoverished as to literary form nor style.

Amorite and Hittite were general names for the people of Canaan who occupied the land before Abraham. It has been suggested that the names refer not to the nation itself which came from Abraham and Sarah but to the Canaanitish origin of the city. This position is not tenable because the entire passage has in view the people of Israel and not the capital city for its own sake (see Gen. 15:16; 23:3, 10; 27:46). The names Amorite and Hittite are to be understood as a taunt, as though they were not descended from Abraham, Isaac and Jacob, in the same sense as the words of our Lord Jesus Christ in John 8:44. It is a moral rather than a historical notation (cf. Isa. 1:10; Gen. 15:16; 27:46). Being the most powerful of the nations in Canaan, they represented them all. Jerusalem was the Amorite and Hittite personified; she had their moral characteristics. Her spiritual origin was thus being set forth. In character and outlook she was thoroughly Canaanitish.

When the child was born, nothing necessary for its separate existence was performed for it. It was wholly neglected. Salting and swaddling of infants are customs which are still practiced (among Arabs of the Near East). In salting the child the skin is rubbed with salt to make it firm and clean. There seems to be no allusion here to any magical operation. The time indicated in this verse is the period in Canaan, then in the land of Egypt, when the nation was weak, defenseless and liable to perish. It received no tender care from any human source; no eye was turned in pity to the unfortunate child. Such exposure of infants to die prevailed as a cruel custom in the ancient world, where children were cast out into the open field; even worse, female children among the Arabs were buried alive.[1] As for Israel, in the day of its birth it was an unwanted and uncared for infant.

THE GRACE OF GOD TO HER (16:6-14)

When the Lord passed by the foundling, it was kicking convulsively in its blood. With an omnipotent word of grace God spoke life to the child. Twice the Lord proclaimed, "Live!" The time intended here is generally taken to be the patriarchal period. Ezekiel passed from the allegory to the reality when he affirmed the great growth of the nation Israel. Their extraordinary increase is confirmed in Exodus 12:37-38 and Acts 7:14. It was a growth in the field, without care, wild but flourishing. Physical

[1]Koran 81:8.

growth is stated in normal terms for maturing into adolescence and young adulthood. The foundling became a beautiful young woman, yet it is stated that she was naked and bare. The implication may be that she was without wealth and without the benefits of culture and civilization, as the world sees them.

Again the Lord passed by (visited) her, which is usually understood to mean the events of the exodus and Mount Sinai with its covenant. The Lord found that Israel had arrived at the time of love or the marriageable age. Thus He spread His skirt over her, a custom which meant espousal (see Ruth 3:9). Then God entered into covenant with the young nation. Making a covenant signifies marriage, which is a figure for the relationship the Lord sustains to Israel (read Jer. 2:2; 3:1 ff.; Hosea 2:2-23; Mal. 2:14). In this way she became the Lord's (Exodus 19:5). The washing with water may be compared with Exodus 19:14. Washing and anointing were ceremonies preparatory to marriage. These practices are often mentioned in connection with the tabernacle and its services through the ministration of the Levites. After washing and cleansing, clothing was next in order. "Sealskin" (v. 10, ASV)[2] is still used by the Bedouin for sandals. The word for "silk" in verse 10 is a Hebrew word which does not occur elsewhere. The clothing was costly. It is interesting that three of the four articles of apparel are prominent in the materials of the tabernacle.

The gifts next mentioned were marriage gifts customarily presented to a queen. The bridal jewels were carefully enumerated in the text, as a loving heart would go over them in reminiscence of that joyous occasion (see Gen. 24:22, 30, 47). The crowning may refer to the time of the reigns of David and Solomon, especially when the city of Jerusalem became the royal or capital city of the realm. Not only was the best of raiment granted her, but the bride was provided with the finest of food. Because of the unstinted favor of God lavished upon her, she attained and prospered to royal estate. Though Israel was actually a small kingdom with limited natural resources and limited area, yet the renown of this land became great among the nations. The Queen of Sheba (I Kings 10) came to verify the reports for herself, while the friendship of Hiram of Tyre for both David and Solomon is told in unmistakable terms in the books of Samuel and Kings. The majesty Israel wore was granted her and placed upon her by the Lord Himself. It was not intrinsically hers. How long a way the foundling has come from verse 4 to verse 14—from abandonment in the field to exaltation to the position of queen in a highly

[2]Sources seem to feel the skin was probably that of the dugong (like the dolphin) which is common in the Red Sea and Indian Ocean, and its skin is used for leather.

honored and respected realm! Such is an illustration of what the grace of God can do in the life of any sinner who will trust the redeeming grace of the Lord Jesus Christ, God's provision for a lost and perishing world. The Prophet Ezekiel takes the reader in a few verses (4-14) through the history of Israel from the time of her inception to the time of her highest glory and majesty in the era of the Solomonic kingdom. The natural and proper response to the many benefactions of the Lord to His people would be unswerving faithfulness to Him and a life of devotion and love. But the record reads in an altogether different manner.

THE MULTIPLIED FAITHLESS DEEDS OF THE FAVORED WIFE (16:15-34)

Rebukes of Israel's sin by the prophets of Israel are many and well known, but none is so vivid, vehement, sordid and piercing as these words. God had bestowed beauty, majesty and renown upon His bride Israel, but soon her pride led her astray (see Deut. 32:15; Jer. 7:4; Micah 3:11). Her beauty and renown were the material and spiritual blessings vouchsafed to Jerusalem. She played the harlot, that is, committed the sin of idolatry (cf. James 4:4). In verses 15-22 Ezekiel showed that she gave herself to the worship and religious practices of the Canaanites, her neighbors (Isa. 47:7, 10). In all these actions she was most indiscriminate.

Israel was not long in making high places decorated with richly colored fabrics—an indication of the idolatry of the Phoenicians and Canaanites with the richly colored carpets of the high places (see II Kings 23:7). The images of men referred to may signify obscene worship. However, Ezekiel may have had in mind the teraphim or household gods of ancient times (cf. Gen. 31:19; Judges 18:14; I Sam. 19:13). Nothing more may be intended than many kinds of Baal worship.

With shameless abandon every gracious gift of the faithful Husband was taken and devoted to the insanity of idolatry. The broidered garments were taken to cover the worthless idols (the practice of clothing idols is seen in Jer. 10:9). As though the idols could partake of them, oil and incense ("mine" stated twice in v. 18 shows to whom they belonged and whence they came) were presented as offerings to the idols. Every thought and consideration were expended for the worthless images, and there was no denying it, said the Lord with a note of finality.

As though these enormities were not sufficient, the favored and faithless wife offered her own children to vain deities. Human sacrifice was a part of this wicked worship, called Molech worship (cf. II Kings 16:3; 21:6). The children were borne unto the Lord because Israel was in covenant relation with God, so He claims as "my children" (v. 21) those who had been sacrificed to the idols and were devoured by fire. The children were first slain in this heathen practice, then burned (see Micah 6:7; II Kings 16:3—Ahaz; 21:6, 16; 24:4—Manasseh; II Kings 23:10—Josiah's abolition of it; Jer. 7:31; 19:5; 32:35—revived before Jerusalem's fall). The question of verses 20-21 shows that their sins were gradually getting worse, building up to a climax. The seat of the trouble was their ingratitude and thoughtlessness. The Lord in grace had remembered the early love (Jer. 2:2), but Jerusalem was so occupied with her infidelities that she had no time nor inclination to think of her early history.

The repeated woe (v. 23) is partly threat and partly lament. The second form of idolatry was the introduction of the gods and practices of Egypt, Assyria and Babylon. Israel allied herself (vv. 23-34) with foreign powers and adopted their religions. In the last days of the Judean kingdom there was an influx of foreign idolatry which brought the nation to an even lower spiritual level. The vaulted and lofty places which they built in every street and way were small shrines to foreign gods (cf. Jer. 2:20). She went on to prostitute her every God-given endowment. She made an alliance with Egypt (Isa. 30:1 ff.; 31:1 ff.), who always seemed a willing ally against Assyria or Babylonia. Alliances with foreign nations included recognition in some measure of their cults and idols. The phrase "great of flesh" may have an obscene connotation, as Egyptian idolatry was particularly base and debasing.

In order to bring her to her senses the Lord in love laid His hand heavily on her food (Hosea 2:9). Even the Philistines became ashamed of her lewd practices. They at least were content with their own idols and did not add those of other countries (cf. Jer. 2:11). "The daughters of the Philistines" is a phrase comparable to "the daughter of Zion" and refers to the Philistine cities. When the child of God wanders from the Lord, he even amazes the unbeliever and excites his contempt. There is no substitute for the path of faith and obedience.

Favoring Egypt was only a part of Israelite policy. In time and when it suited her pleasure, she turned to the Assyrians. The historical books recount the pro-Assyrian policy of both Ahaz and Manasseh (see II Kings 16:7 ff.; Hosea 5:13; 8:9; Amos 5:26).

Finally the faithless wife, unsatisfied with her past performances and misdeeds, pressed her conquests to the land of traffic (literally, Canaan, because the Phoenicians were noted merchants), which is here employed of the Babylonians who similarly excelled in trade. For reliance on Babylonia compare II Kings 20:12-19. And still she was not satisfied.

Ezekiel here exclaimed over the heart of Jerusalem which was sick with desire and passion. She herself was called an impudent harlot, one unbridled and without control. Even more strange, she had departed from the custom of all other harlots in that she scorned hire. The statements of verse 32 are exclamations of extreme disdain and disgust meant to quicken the culprit into some realization of her unheard of position. Her giving of bribes to her paramours refers to the heavy tribute and exactions Israel had to pay as the price of her godless consorting with forbidden powers and practices (see II Kings 16:8-9). She had nothing to gain from those with whom she committed iniquity, so her action was likened to giving of bribes. In all this she was different from both ordinary harlots and adulterous wives.

JUDGMENT DESCRIBED (16:35-43)

In this portion is a figurative representation of the shame and suffering brought about by the Babylonian invasion and destruction of the Judean kingdom. In the severest terms she was addressed, "O harlot." The picture of the harlot is bad enough, but she was seen as a murderess of her children as well. The reference is, of course, to Molech worship. The first step in her retributive judgment at the hands of the Lord would be public exposure before both her lovers and her enemies. Public exposure of profligate women and stoning of them were well-known customs in ancient Israel. Those she "hated" (v. 37) may well have included the Philistines with whom Israel had never formed an alliance, as far as is now known. The gathering of a large company points to the invasion and destruction of 586 B.C.

For infidelity and the shedding of blood in the murder of her children (vv. 20, 36), God's wrath and jealousy for His honor would mete out a bloody death. After the divine sentence had been carried out against her, she would be left naked and bare, and would sink back to her original lowly position (v. 7). Again public exposure of the adulteress was predicted. The penalty in the law of Moses for an adulteress was stoning (cf. Lev. 20:10; John 8:5). For a city, idolatry was punished by the sword (Deut. 13:15). Both are mentioned here, a double judgment for double wickedness, as it were. All this judgment would take place before her neighboring countries; she would be a spectacle and warning for all nations. By exacting the full penalty on the sins which evoked it, the Lord would cause His wrath and jealousy toward Jerusalem to be placated. In verse 43 there is a summary of the indictment thus far. Notice that the emphasis is similar to that in verse 22. If she had remembered, Israel would have had to be thankful; she did neither.

JERUSALEM COMPARED TO SAMARIA AND SODOM (16:44-59)

Jerusalem had actually fallen so low as to be the subject of a proverbial byword. The East is fond of condensing life expressions into maxims and proverbial sayings. "As is the mother, so is her daughter" is similar to our "Like father, like son." Judah had shown herself to be of like nature with Sodom and Gomorrah who were in the land before Abraham entered it. They had all departed from an original revelation of God (Rom. 1:21). Jerusalem had a real family likeness to them. Samaria may have been called the elder sister of Judah because of greater political influence and wider territory or perhaps because she went into idolatry first. Since directions are always given as though facing east, the left hand signifies north, as the right hand stands for the south, thus indicating the location of Samaria and Sodom relative to Jerusalem. Sodom was called the younger sister because she was smaller in territory as well as political power. The daughters of these cities were the minor towns that surrounded them. In wickedness and flagrant disregard of the will of the Lord, Jerusalem had far outstripped both Samaria and Sodom. Her abominations exceeded any of theirs.

Notice how pride was singled out as the root of Sodom's sin when her abominations were traced to their source. God had blessed her abundantly with fullness of bread (Gen. 13:10), but she monopolized these blessings for her own pleasures and basked in prosperous ease. Provision for her own needs made her insensible to the needs of others; she had no social conscience. Then she committed the abominations and enormities which are linked inseparably with her name. God took her away with a final blow when He saw it (Gen. 18:21). When the sins of Samaria are evaluated, they were not half so many as those of Judah. Judah was more guilty because she had more privileges from the Lord. She was said to justify her two sisters because her wickedness was so much worse than theirs that their spiritual condition seemed pardonable when compared with hers (for similar concepts see Matthew 10:15; 11:24). Judah refused to learn from the fate of Samaria and Sodom, and her much worse conduct set Samaria and Sodom in a comparatively favorable light.

Ezekiel then turned to words of comfort and promise, the first in this long chapter. When he spoke of turning the captivity, the thought is the reversing of the fortunes of anyone. The passage does not refer to those sinners who will endure eternal fire (Jude 7); it is not treating the restitution of the wicked dead. Ezekiel was speaking of national restoration and the rebuilding of these cities in the millennium. It has been suggested that since there was no population of Sodom to be restored, the reference was to the small heathen cities surrounding Israel. Others point out the sparing of Zoar. But the restoration of Sodom will pose no difficulty for the omnipotence of God; her restoration was mentioned first to do away with all boasting. The daughters of Sodom were the cities in her neighborhood which suffered divine punishment along with her. Samaria and Sodom, who suffered God's judgment first, will be first to be restored. The basic passage on the restoration of Israel is Deuteronomy 30:3.

When Judah surpassed Samaria and Sodom in wickedness, she made them feel less guilty concerning their defections from God. Thus she was a comfort to them. Now all were on the same level of God's dealing, although when Jerusalem was in her proud position before her own wickedness had been revealed to her, she would not condescend even to mention the name of her disgraced sister Sodom. When once her perfidy and unfaithfulness were brought to the light, the Syrian and Philistine cities made the most of the situation, reproaching and disdaining her. When Ezekiel stated that Jerusalem has borne her lewdness and abominations, the presupposition is that the destruction of Jerusalem in 586 B.C. had taken place. The final threat of this section is that Jerusalem would suffer her punishment according to her deeds, and would fall. Her grievous sin stemmed from the fact that she had despised the oath she made to the Lord at Sinai that she would obey in all things, and she had broken the covenant.

RESTORATION OF ISRAEL BY COVENANT (16:60-63)

God can no more help being gracious than He can cease being God. He is the God of all grace, and He always finds a covenant basis on which He can exercise His grace. Judah may forget her origin, the many benefactions received at the hand of the Lord, even the heinousness of her sins, but the Lord will remember the Abrahamic covenant made with Israel in the days of her youth. Restoration will be because of grace and not merit. The everlasting covenant, which is so closely related to the Abrahamic covenant, is the new covenant spoken of in Jeremiah 31:31-34; Isaiah 59:21; 61:8; and Ezekiel 37:26. Again, Jerusalem was reminded that all God's work of restoration will rest not on her demerit, nor on that of Samaria or Sodom, but on His work in grace. The basis will not be the covenant at Sinai (notice the contrast between "my covenant" in v. 60, and "thy covenant" in v. 61) into which they entered and assumed responsibilities, which they never carried out, nor indeed could they in the weakness of the flesh.

When God establishes His everlasting covenant, then Judah will know that God is the Lord, not—as so often in this book—because of the judgments of God upon her, but because of His entirely gracious dealings toward her. God in grace will overrule and blot out the past, but Jerusalem will remember it and, in doing so, be impelled to faithfulness to her gracious and forgiving God. Because of the remembrance of her former guilt and the grace of God in pardoning her, she will not open her mouth again; evidently in the sense of boasting. She will surely open her mouth to magnify and extol His grace and love to her (see Luke 7:47).

God's Everlasting Covenant

The ramifications of the Abrahamic covenant run throughout the Word of God and defy human imagination in their comprehensive sweep. The features of the new covenant are actually the outworking of the basic elements of the promises to Abraham. In his seed all the families of the earth are to be blessed. But God meant, first of all, for the Seed of Abraham to be a blessing to His own people Israel. They do not now enjoy these blessings and provisions. Christ does not yet see of the travail of His soul for them so that He may be satisfied. We can be used of God to make it possible by giving the gospel to Jews throughout the world. The hour is late and the opportunity is fleeting with the day calling for immediate obedience. May it be gladly and fully given.

17

THE PUNISHMENT OF TREACHERY

THIS CHAPTER IS DATED about 588 B.C. (approximately two years before the destruction of Jerusalem), although some place it a little earlier. Emphasis is on Zedekiah's judgment for breaking the oath he had made to Nebuchadnezzar in the name of the Lord. The meaning of the chapter is not in doubt because the interpretation is appended. For the history of the period the following passages must be studied: II Kings 24:8-20; II Chronicles 36:9-13; Jeremiah 37; 52:1-7. This chapter has points of relationship with Isaiah 11; 53; Daniel 2:34-35, 44-45; and Micah 4.

PARABLE OF THE EAGLES (17:1-10)

The message of the Lord to Ezekiel is called both a riddle and a parable. It is a riddle in that its meaning needs to be explained; there is a deeper meaning which underlies the figurative form, for something in its presentation is obscure. It is a parable in that it is an allegory. This account narrates the international affairs of Judah, Babylon and Egypt between 597 and 588 B.C. The first date marks the exile of Jehoiachin and Zedekiah's accession to the throne of Judah as a vassal king paying tribute. The second date was the year Zedekiah revolted against Babylon while relying on the promised help of Egypt.

The eagle, the king of birds, is supposed to have been the symbol of the Assyrian god Nisroch, but there is no proof of this. Here it undoubtedly refers to the king of Babylon, Nebuchadnezzar, who invaded the Judean kingdom. The same symbolism is found in Daniel's prophecy (7:4; cf. Jer. 48:40; 49:22). The great wings and long pinions speak of great power and vast dominion, while the feathers of the eagle suggest the many nations subject to Babylon under the world monarch Nebuchadnezzar. Different nationalities are represented in the empire by the diverse colors, rather than the colored portrayals of the eagle as an emblem of royalty on Babylonian monuments. Lebanon, to which the eagle came, stands for the land of promise, especially Jerusalem because the palace and temple were made of the cedars of Lebanon (see I Kings 7:2; Jer. 22:23 for this usage). The top of the cedar removed by the king of Babylon was Jehoiachin who was taken into exile in 597 B.C. (II Kings 24:8-16). The topmost of the young twigs that was cropped off was not Zedekiah but rather Jehoiachin, as noted earlier. The twig was carried away to a land of traffic, literally, the land of Canaan, a name applied to a trader. Here it was employed of Babylon (16:29), the great center of commerce in all Asia. In previous pronouncements of judgment in Ezekiel the denunciations had been against the entire nation. Then it was against the faithless ruler of the land.

In an act of leniency Nebuchadnezzar replaced Jehoiachin with a native Judean prince, Zedekiah, instead of with a foreign ruler. The new king was the youngest son of Josiah. Formerly called Mattaniah, he was renamed Zedekiah by the Babylonian king (II Kings 24:17; Jer. 37:1). Zedekiah was surrounded by favorable conditions for his reign, represented in the parable by the fruitful soil, the many waters and the planting as a willow tree (Isa. 44:4). The benevolent attitude of Nebuchadnezzar helped Zedekiah to prosper in his rule. If he had remained faithful to his oath of fealty to Nebuchadnezzar, the kingdom of Judah could have continued to prosper as a tributary kingdom. The hope of the king of Babylon was that Judea would remain dependent on him. The security of Judah depended on Babylon, and Zedekiah at first was an obedient vassal to the dominant power of the day.

But this state of affairs did not continue, for another eagle was introduced. This was Egypt, specifically Pharaoh Hophra who came to the throne of Egypt in 588 B.C. To him Zedekiah foolishly looked for help to throw off the Babylonian yoke after he had been befriended by Nebuchadnezzar. (For the details of the events see II Chron. 36:13; Jer. 37:5-7; 44:30; 52:11.) It was Jeremiah's purpose to keep Zedekiah from an alliance with Egypt, but he failed in his objective. For a time Egypt did cause Nebuchadnezzar to lift the siege of Jerusalem, but Jeremiah warned the nation that relief would be temporary.

Ezekiel continued to portray the favored condition of the kingdom under Zedekiah, if he had been satisfied with subordination to Nebuchadnezzar. The seed of the land had good soil, many waters and every opportunity to sprout branches, bear fruit and be a luxuriant vine. There was no valid reason for Zedekiah's revolt; he was neither oppressed nor deprived. Perfidy, ambition and ingratitude led to insubordination. But his treacherous scheme would not prosper, as the rest of the chapter predicts. The question of verse 9 implies a strong negative answer. Summary judgment on Zedekiah through the instrumentality of Nebuchadnezzar was announced. Isaiah had opposed an alliance with Egypt (Isa. 30:1-7) as had Jeremiah (Jer. 37:7). It has been suggested that only a small part of Nebuchadnezzar's army would be required to accomplish the ruin because God was behind the visitation in wrath (Jer. 37:10). The probable meaning is that Judah would not recover from its fall by the help of Egypt or any other nation's forces. Carrying through the same figure and the same question, Ezekiel indicated that the doom of Zedekiah would be effected in the way vegetation is turned to dust under the blasts of the east wind or the sirocco, here a figure of Nebuchadnezzar's invasion from the east (cf. 19:12; Job 27:21; Isa. 27:8; Hosea 13:15). It is an interesting commentary on the words "where it grew" (v. 10) that Zedekiah was captured at Jericho (Jer. 52:8).

INTERPRETATION OF THE PARABLE (17:11-21)

It is not clear whether the parable was explained when given or after a lapse of some time. If the latter, the content of the allegory could more deeply impress the minds of the nation. The rebellious house was Israel in the homeland and in Babylon. The king taken to Babylon was Jehoiachin in the year 597 B.C. (see II Kings 24:10-16; Jer. 24:1; 29:1). The indication is that a large number went into captivity with the king. Nebuchadnezzar, acting on political principles to his advantage, took Mattaniah, a son of Josiah, made him king, and named him Zedekiah (II Kings 24:17). Zedekiah swore by the Lord (II Chron. 36:13) in the making of the covenant. The language seems to imply the ancient ritual set forth in Genesis 15:9-18 and Jeremiah 34:18-19. The mighty of the land were taken away as hostages, a precautionary measure against a possible revolt. Nebuchadnezzar wanted to be certain that there would be no further revolts, and undoubtedly imposed humiliating terms, insuring that the kingdom would be base. The Babylonian monarch's previous experience with the Judean kingdom made him desirous of insuring loyalty to his rule. He did purpose that the state might continue, for he would be drawing tribute from it all the while.

Zedekiah became weary of his covenant and sent for help to Egypt, although it was always useless to look to Egypt for help (cf. Isa. 36:6; Ezek. 29:6-7). But Egypt was famous for her chariots and horses, which had been her main strength for the millennium after 1600 B.C. (see Exodus 14:7; I Kings 10:28-29; II Chron. 12:3; Isa. 31:1; 36:9). Zedekiah sent for reinforcements of men for his army also. But would the plan work? Could such treachery, which had called upon the name of the Lord in the beginning of the transaction between Nebuchadnezzar and the vassal king, avoid punishment at the hands of the God who had been so insulted? The question is repeated with a wrathful denial understood. Zedekiah's treachery against the Babylonian king was similar to Israel's against the Lord. The sanctity of an oath was ingrained in Israel. Even an oath made by fraud was to be honored; for example, that with the Gibeonites (cf. Joshua 9 with II Sam. 21:1-2). Jeremiah had warned Zedekiah against treachery and duplicity.

Now the details of the disloyal king's fate are mentioned. In the very land where the king reigned whose power had made Zedekiah king, and whose authority and covenant he had despised, would the culprit die. The punishment was to be commensurate with the crime. The Pharaoh with the mighty army and great company is the Apries of the Greeks, successor to Necho (cf. Jer. 37:5-11). The casting up of mounds (v. 17, ASV) was not the tactic of the Egyptians against the Babylonians, but of the latter against Jerusalem when they recovered themselves from their first setback. The Egyptians would not be able to counteract the second siege. Their baseless and disappointed hopes are stated in Lamentations 4:17. As plainly as he could declare it, Ezekiel showed that Judah's political disaster was traceable to moral weakness and deceit. When once the hand was given in token of agreement, that word should have been all the bond needed. Zedekiah had called on God in his oath-taking. Probably a sacrifice was offered in ratifying the covenant, so God called it His oath and His covenant. Thus the Judean king's actions were a patent insult to God. International contracts carry with them high responsibilities. Though Nebuchadnezzar carried out the will of God in judgment, the Lord was seen as the moving One who took Zedekiah in His net and snare (12:13). In Babylon the wicked king would know the issues involved and why he was bearing the severe penalty for his unprovoked treachery. Once punishment overtook the king his followers would fare no better, for without a leader they would be scattered and decimated. The Targum and Syriac by transposing two letters render "fugitives" (v. 21) as "chosen men," but the verse is clear without this assumption. Besides, the Greek and Vulgate versions confirm our translation "fugitives." Thus God's anger was eminently justified in His dealings with the final stages of the Davidic monarchy in the sixth century B.C. (see II Kings 24:20).

PROMISE OF BLESSING IN MESSIAH (17:22-24)

These concluding verses without question introduce a Messianic prophecy (cf. Isa. 2:2-4; Micah 4:1-4). Though this portion is couched in the same figurative language as the rest of the chapter, it strikes a new note and presents a promise of future blessing in the Messiah. In grace God would raise up a branch in David's house which would be fruitful (in contrast to Zedekiah, v. 4). Psalm 89 demonstrates unequivocally that God had provided so that His covenant with David would never be void nor annulled. This reassurance at this time was most heartening since the people of Israel would see no Davidic king on the scene of their national horizon until the Messiah Himself appeared in His first advent.

After all human instrumentality has accomplished the purpose of God, He intervenes directly and takes the lofty top of the cedar, in contrast to that of Nebuchadnezzar (vv. 3-4). The top of the cedar refers to a descendant of the house of David. The "tender one" is the Messiah, the Son of David (see Isa. 11:1; 53:2; Jer. 23:5-6; 33:15; Zech. 6:12; Rev. 22:16). The suggestion that Zerubbabel is the subject of the prophecy falls short of the requirements of the passage. The Messiah's human and lowly origin is in view. Ezekiel's later prophecies enlarge on this King from the Davidic house (34:23-24; 37:24-25). The high mountain is Mount Zion. In the mountain of Israel, God will establish His chosen One (Ps. 2:6); He shall prosper and all nations under His worldwide rule will be blessed. For the same figure of dwelling in security under the great of earth see Daniel 4:12, 21; Matthew 13:32; Mark 4:32. What a contrast between the vine of low stature and the goodly cedar. It is the Lord who will bring down Gentile world rule and restore the kingdom of Israel. Then all the nations of earth will know that the One who makes the promise is able to fulfill it.

The chapter began with judgment and punishment; it ends with mercy and grace. The dethroned and blind Zedekiah is overshadowed by God's King who is full of power and glory. Kingdoms are but the lengthened shadows of kings.

THE CHANNEL OF BLESSING

The Bible has one unified message whether before the cross, now after the cross, or in the future ages: there is blessing in the Lord Jesus Christ alone. His kingdom will fill all the earth with righteousness and equity for all the world. But personal participation in these assured glories comes only through personal faith in the Redeemer. How can men enter into these joys if they believe not? We must face our responsibility to transmit the message to them.

18

INDIVIDUAL RESPONSIBILITY BEFORE GOD

ONE OF THE GREAT PRINCIPLES of Scripture is enunciated in this chapter: judgment is according to individual conduct. The judgments Ezekiel introduces here are temporal judgments, and the death dealt with is physical death. Ezekiel was not at this time dealing with the problem of the suffering of the innocent, vicarious suffering or corporate suffering. He had foretold national punishment, but he had to bring home to them an individual sense of sin. The subject of justification by faith should not be pressed into this chapter; it is not under discussion. As for reconciling the truth of this passage with such portions as Exodus 20:5; 34:7; and Deuteronomy 5:9, some do so on the basis of the entail of physical consequences that issue from the misdeeds of ungodly parents. This subject is discussed later. Ezekiel deals with individual responsibility apart from this chapter in these portions: 3:16-21; 14:12-20; 33:1-20. It was not a new idea (see Deut. 24:16; II Kings 14:6).

THE SCORNFUL PROVERB IN ISRAEL (18:1-4)

Evidently with some spirit and force in the matter Ezekiel asked the nation what they meant by using the proverb then current among them. They were apparently charging God with injustice in His dealings by claiming that they were suffering for the sins of their fathers. The emphasis is on the "ye." But how could they use this proverb when they were being punished for their own sins, not for those of their fathers? Their use of the proverb shows they had been overtaken by a spirit of pessimism (for the same attitude, cf. Jer. 31:29-30; Lam. 5:7). They were actually dulling their sense of individual responsibility for their sins and the just judgment due them. The eating of sour grapes by the fathers is said to have set on edge or blunted the teeth of their children, but this proverb was singularly inapplicable because they were far from innocent of complicity with the evil for which the Lord was judging the nation. With a strong oath the Lord declared that the practice of using the proverb must stop at once because its use implied God was unjust.

Then Ezekiel enunciated the great principle of the chapter: all souls belong equally to God. God as Creator loves all the creatures He has made, so what possible objective could He have besides absolute equity in every case? Individual responsibility is the only explanation of the dealings of God. If they complained of suffering for their fathers' sins, they should have been ready to suffer for their own. The soul (the person) who sins must die. This does not contradict the principle in Exodus 20:5 because it is well known that children have a tendency to repeat the sins of their fathers (see Matt. 23:32, 34-36). This death is physical death, and its punishment is a figure of exclusion from the Messianic kingdom. Ezekiel was doubtless speaking of suffering punishment, which is an experiencing of the wrath of God by being deprived of physical life. Life is used to mean continuance in this world, and death means removal from it. These solemn words leave no doubt as to where God lays the obligation for individual conduct.

THE CASE OF A JUST GRANDFATHER (18:5-9)

Ezekiel now gives a concrete example of the truth he set forth in verse 4. Three generations are presented in verses 5-18: a just grandfather, an ungodly son and a godly grandson. Three kings of Judah fit these descriptions—Hezekiah, Manasseh and Josiah.

The just man is not to be understood as the righteous one of the New Testament who has all the light of added revelation after the coming of Christ. Nor is the emphasis on sinless perfection. In view here is one who is living up to the Old Testament standard. He does that which is lawful and right, just as Paul declared was the manner of his life (Phil. 3:6). His conduct revealed his heart attitude toward God.

Typical virtues are pointed out. Eating on the mountains was connected with immoral worship and Israel's idolatrous feasts. According to Deuteronomy 12:13-14 there was one place only to sacrifice to God. The just man had not lifted up his eyes in adoration to the idols of the house of Israel. Along with those of the heathen, Israel had her own idols. The upright man was careful to observe the rights of others; he gave man his due as well as God. He respected the marriage rights of his fellowman (cf. Exodus 20:14; Lev. 20:10; Deut. 22:22). Even more, he was careful and chaste in his relationships with his own wife. There were definite regulations in the Mosaic law regarding women in their impurity (see Lev. 15:24; 18:19; 20:18).

The just man under consideration wronged no one; he had a godly concern for all. Ezekiel's ethical standards are thus as high as those of any prophet, although he has been labeled time and again as formalistic, legalistic and ritualistic. According to the law's commands the debtor's pledge had been duly restored to him, an expression of genuine consideration for others (cf. Exodus 22:25-27; Deut. 24:6, 10-13; Amos 2:8). No gain by robbery had found its way into the home of the just man. It is an error to conclude that the prophet was concerned only about external acts, and unconcerned as to the condition of heart from which these deeds proceeded. Furthermore, the godly man observed and carried out acts of benevolence, distributing his bread to the hungry and providing the naked with clothing (see Isa. 58:7).

The portrayal of the just man continues with the observation that he had not allowed himself to take interest of any kind on money he had loaned. Such interest was allowed by the law of Moses in dealing with foreigners (Deut. 23:20), but was strictly forbidden in loans to Israelites (Exodus 22:25; Deut. 23:19; Isa. 24:2). They were to be motivated by the bond of brotherhood toward their fellow countrymen. The just man kept himself from whatever he might wrongly turn to his own profit. Moreover, he was quick to see that justice and equity were meted out in the relationships between man and man. In short, his outward actions revealed a heart obedient to the Lord and willing to fulfill God's moral law. God's pronouncement on him was that he had dealt in truth, kept God's commands and was surely just. This statement, we must caution again, does not have eternal life in view, but life on earth. Eternal life is not obtained on the grounds mentioned in this portion of the chapter.

The Case of an Ungodly Son (18:10-13)

This is the case of the unjust son of a just father. He was far from considering the welfare of others, for he was a robber (literally, a violent one), and a shedder of blood, a murderer. He was best characterized as one who did all the things from which his godly father abstained. Moreover, he gave himself to none of the duties which occupied the attention and life of his parent. Idolatry, adultery, oppression, indifference to the needs of the unfortunate, and unlawful gain were the order of the day for him. His life was completely profane. He cared nothing for positive, good deeds and was diametrically opposite to his father on every moral and humane issue. The great question was: Could this man possibly claim the merits of his father's godly life? Should he live? In the strongest language Ezekiel showed he could not claim the worth of another. Natural relationship would profit him nothing, for his character would have revealed him as no true son of his just father. So it was futile and worse for Israel to claim natural relationship with Abraham in an endeavor to enter into his merit. Character and conduct showed there was no true sonship to faithful Abraham. Compare the pertinent words of our Lord in John 8:37, 39. God is surely impartial: He will not lay to the charge of children the misdeeds of parents; but conversely He will not lay to their credit the godly conduct of parents when they themselves scorn every righteous precept of the Lord.

THE CASE OF A GODLY GRANDSON (18:14-18)

Another case in contrast is presented—this time it is the just son of an ungodly father. It is universally known how easy it is to follow a bad example, but here is an exception. The son of an unjust father took to heart the unbecoming life of his father. He weighed the issues and concluded that the manner of life that had been before him was one to be avoided. The fear of God was his guiding principle, and he could not complacently live such a life of callous ungodliness. He conformed in particular after particular to his godly grandfather and not to his ungodly father. Would God visit the sins of the ungodly father upon the just son? The Judge of all the earth would do right (Gen. 18:25). Just as He could not and would not credit the merit of a just father to an ungodly son, so He would not charge the misdeeds of a nonobservant father to a godly son. The ultimate status and condition of all three men went back to the individual manner of life of each one. How could God be more impartial? And how could the proverb current in Israel be seen to be more unfounded and false?

GOD'S PERFECT RIGHTEOUSNESS (18:19-29)

It seems from verse 19 that the nation was arguing on the other side of the question, but they evidently had in mind the second commandment of the Decalogue (see Exodus 20:4-6). They had failed, as many do today, to see the force of the words "hate me" and "love me." Thus, if they individually loved God, they could not be suffering the penalty of their fathers' sins. God's answer was clear that He would never condemn the son for the wrongs of his father. Now follows what may be taken as a summary of the teaching of the entire chapter. Whether father or son, each would reap what he had himself sown. The righteousness referred to is not in the absolute sense, for then it would contradict the rest of the Scriptures which declare that no man is truly righteous. It relates to one's seeking the godly life as far as revealed in the Old Testament.

Ezekiel introduced another factor in verses 21-24. He took the hypothetical case of a wicked man who radically changes, and forsakes his wicked ways in order to do God's righteous will. The implication is clear that man has the ability to determine his final condition. Such a man will not die but surely live. Thus, not only is a man free from his father's misdeeds; he can also break with his own ungodly past if his heart desires. This man will live in (not "for" or "on account of") his righteousness. His past will be no deterrent to the blessing of God. The standing of the individual is determined by his final choice of good or evil. It is a man's moral condition at the time of judgment that is determining.

What is God's ultimate objective in human life? He does not delight in the death of the wicked. His pleasure is that the wicked turn from his evil way and live (cf. John 5:40; I Tim. 2:4; II Peter 3:9). But when one who was formerly outwardly conforming to the statutes of the Lord, commits apostasy, not merely backsliding or occasional offenses, he must die in his sinful condition. Of course, the ways of God do not please the natural man, so Israel charged that the principle of God's dealing was inequitable and unfair. Again, the standard of God's reckoning is declared with reference both to the righteous man and the wicked. God is vindicated in all His actions and must ever be, otherwise there can be no moral universe. Let this ever be the anchor for every soul.

EXHORTATION TO RETURN (18:30-32)

In the closing verses of this great chapter God declared that He treats every man according to the individual's attitude toward Him. It was still the hour of opportunity for Israel, and Ezekiel longed that they might avail themselves of it. The road to blessing was clearly marked. God required the casting away of their transgressions and a new heart and a new spirit (see Ps. 51:10; Ezek. 36:25-27). God's answer to the question of verse 23 was that He delights in the salvation of men, not their destruction. Judgment is God's "strange act" (Isa. 28:21), and the possibility of condemnation is designed to spur men on to the acceptance of His grace. Ultimately God's help must be sought for life and salvation. Ezekiel was a preacher of repentance and of God's proffered mercy to the penitent.

THE SINNING SOUL AND DEATH

Though Ezekiel was speaking of physical death and punishment for sin, it is clear from the rest of the Bible that sin is attended by spiritual and final (second) death. God has gone to great lengths to provide a way of escape for the sinning soul. Is it too much that God asks us to be the messengers of this good news?

19

LAMENTATION OVER ISRAEL'S KINGS

THE LONG SECTION of the prophecy on warnings and judgments (chaps. 12-19) closes with this passage. The chapter is an elegy in two parts (vv. 1-9, 10-14). While it is generally couched in figurative speech, at times its expressions are literal. The portion reveals something of Ezekiel's literary skill and deep emotion. The chapter is cast into the regular lamentation (kinah) meter, usually three beats followed by two beats. The passage treats of the captivity of kings Jehoahaz and Jehoiachin (also called Jeconiah and Coniah), and the collapse of the Davidic dynasty under Zedekiah. The last four kings of Judah were of the same spirit and outlook in their reigns, but the main emphasis of this section is a lament over Jehoahaz who languished in an Egyptian prison, and Jehoiachin in Babylonian captivity. The "princes," a general designation for "king" in the prophecy of Ezekiel, relate only to those of Judah because no other dynasty than David's was recognized by God and His messengers.

THE LIONS OF JUDAH (19:1-9)

The persons to whom the lamentation is addressed are clearly pointed out at the beginning as the princes of Israel. It has been suggested that the mother lioness was the wife of Josiah (Hamutal), mother of Jehoahaz or Shallum. She was a woman of great influence (II Kings 24:12; Jer. 13:18). The lioness must have been a personification of Judah, just as in verse 10 (cf. Gen. 49:9; Num. 23:24; 24:9; Rev. 5:5; and Isa. 29:1—used of Jerusalem). Lions were quite common in the land in ancient times, and the Hebrew language has five different words for them (Job 4:10-11). They were to be found in the thickets of the Jordan (Jer. 49:19; 50:44; Zech. 11:3), at Mount Hermon (Song of Sol. 4:8) and in the Judean desert (Isa. 30:6). Judah took her place majestically and securely among her neighbors. The whelps were the descendants of the house of David who were exposed to the corrupting influences of the surrounding heathen kings by whom they were nurtured. In Samuel's day the clamor had been for a king who would parallel those of the nations about them; this was accomplished through the years of the monarchy in Israel. The first whelp singled out was King Jehoahaz or Shallum. He was made king by the people of the land after the death of his father, Josiah, at Megiddo (II Kings 23:30). He reigned three months on the Judean throne, and did evil in the sight of God (II Kings 23:32). Jehoahaz was taken captive to Egypt in 608 B.C. and died there (II Kings 23:31-34). His wicked ways are indicated as the devouring of men. His actions excited the attention of his neighbor nations which determined to curb him. Just as it was customary for a community to gather together to catch a lion or wild beast, so Jehoahaz was taken by force by Pharaoh Necho to the land of Egypt.

King Jehoiakim, who succeeded Jehoahaz, was passed over, and Jehoiachin is presented next. Jehoiakim was probably omitted because his judgment was not so conspicuous as that of the others (II Kings 24:6). His life ended peacefully. Jeremiah reveals that the people of Israel had entertained hopes that Jehoahaz might return from Egypt, a false expectation whch Jeremiah tried to dispel (Jer. 22:10-12). When the restoration of Jehoahaz did not materialize, Jehoiachin succeeded Jehoiakim. Upon the death of his father he came to the throne at eighteen years of age. He reigned but three months, used the same methods as his predecessors, devouring men by oppression and injustice, and was taken captive to Babylon (II Kings 24:8-15). The particulars of verse 7 show how far the king went in his wicked self-will. Instead of "palaces" another reading is "widows," which would indicate to what lengths the cruel king went. However, Ezekiel was probably speaking of widowed palaces or places. The king wrought havoc everywhere he went, just as a rapacious lion would.

Again the nations about Israel were aroused into action against the perpetrator of these deeds, not because of their superior righteousness, but because of the judgment of God on the king. A statement of how these nations confederated against Jehoiachin's father, Jehoiakim, appears in II Kings 24:2. They were the Babylonians, Moabites, Ammonites and Syrians. History has a strange way of repeating such incidents. This time the place of imprisonment was eastward in Babylon (II Kings 24:15). The Babylonians and Assyrians were extremely cruel in their treatment of their captive prisoners. The figure states that King Jehoiachin was taken in a cage with hooks. Such a practice was not uncommon. The hook or ring was inserted in the nose of a captive (Isa. 37:29). The cage was that used for a dog or a lion. Ashurbanipal of Assyria said of a king of Arabia, "I put him into a kennel. With jackals and dogs I tied him up and made him guard the gate, in Nineveh."[1] As already stated, the Judean king had ruled only three months; then Nebuchadnezzar took Jerusalem and deported the king. He was in prison for thirty-seven years. Released at the

---

[1]Luckenbill, ARAB. II. 314.

age of fifty-five (II Kings 25:27-30; Jer. 52:31-32), he no longer had a chance of restoration to his lost throne, and no hope of successors among his children (Jer. 22:29-30). The concluding reigns of the kings of the house of David were indeed covered with shame, and the nations of that day were no longer impressed with the splendor of the kingdom which had been David and Solomon's.

THE END OF THE KINGDOM (19:10-14)

The allegory which occupies the rest of this chapter parallels that in 17:5-8. Although there is not unanimity of views as to who is meant by this allegory—whether Jehoiachin or Zedekiah—it seems best to hold with the majority of interpreters that Zedekiah is the king under consideration. The mother is, as above, Judah or the people of Israel. The vine is a usual figure for the land of Judah (cf. Ezek. 15:1-5; 17:6-10; Ps. 80:8-11; Isa. 5:1-7). The Hebrew word translated "in thy blood" is variously interpreted. Some translate "in thy repose," that is, in the time of your secure prosperity, but it is not a convincing rendering. The verse seems to mean she lived in (through) the life of her children. The passage may contain an allusion to Genesis 49:11 (see also Deut. 32:14). Surrounded with every advantage for growth, the vine did splendidly. There was no lack of water to produce fruitfulness (Deut. 8:7-9).

In time the vine shot forth strong rods, which indicate the scepters of those who ruled in Judah. There is no need to specify who the rods are; they include all the powerful native kings who reigned in the land of promise. Of course, the time of greatest exaltation of the monarchy was in the days of David and Solomon, but there is no need to limit the reference to them. This period would parallel the time in the earlier part of the chapter when the young lions devoured men. But when God was ignored and forgotten in the counsels of the kings, the vine, that is, the nation, was plucked up in fury. While the kingdom declined gradually, its end came by a sudden stroke of God's wrath. From great exaltation the Judean dynasty was abased to the ground. The Babylonian invaders from the east are represented by the east wind; they shriveled up the fruit of the land. The fire of judgment did its work of retribution. The result was that the vine was planted in a dry and thirsty wilderness. Such is the description of her condition in exile after 586 B.C. Transplantation of this kind meant complete loss of productiveness.

The concluding verse (32) assesses the blame for the catastrophe that overtook the Judean kingdom. The fire from the rods of the branches of the vine refers undoubtedly to King Zedekiah whom Ezekiel never calls king. The judgment was directly due to the wickedness of the ungodly kings, especially Zedekiah who was responsible for the destruction of Jerusalem through his treachery (cf. Jer. 38:20-23, especially v. 23). The visitation is seen as having already occurred in words reminiscent of Judges 9:15. Thus the people of Israel were left with no rightful king to reign over them. This condition continues to the present. So stirred was Ezekiel to think that the royal house was responsible for the ruin of the nation, that he closed the passage with a repetition of the thought of lamentation. His message was a lamentation for the destruction already carried out; it would be a lamentation for the desolation yet to be accomplished. Though the prophets preached and taught from God's viewpoint, they were not unfeeling channels of messages of rebuke and destruction. The disclosures they uttered deeply touched their own hearts.

No Scepter to Rule

For almost two and a half millennia the people of Israel have had no king of David's line to rule over them. God intended the greatest era of the kingdom to occur when the Messiah, the Son of David, appeared to His people. However, they would not have Him rule over them; they preferred the rule of Caesar. Now again they have "no strong rod to be a sceptre to rule" (v. 14). But Messiah became the Saviour through His glorious work on Calvary and has made available redemption for Jew and Gentile alike. When He returns in power and glory, He will indeed establish the kingdom for which men in all ages have yearned.

20

A HISTORY OF REBELLION

WITH THIS CHAPTER Ezekiel begins a series of oracles which comprises chapters 20-23, the last prophecies before the fall of Jerusalem in 586 B.C. The chapter reviews the past and indicts the nation for its present sins. Ezekiel gives a historical survey of Israel, a literal presentation of what had been described figuratively in chapter 16. The chapter is remarkable in that it shows a uniform moral plane sustained by the nation throughout its history. Numerous repetitions are used to carry home Ezekiel's message to the hearts of the people.

ISRAEL'S SIN IN EGYPT (20:1-9)

The time of the prophecy is stated quite explicitly to be about July or August, 591 B.C. By comparison with 8:1 it is clear that this communication from God came less than a year after that in chapter 8, about midway in the first portion of Ezekiel's ministry. A group of elders of Israel came to Ezekiel (cf. 14:3) to inquire of the Lord. Sitting expectantly before the prophet, they doubtless represented the orthodox contingent of their day, but the Lord had no word of reply for them. The nature or subject of their inquiry is not stated, although they probably had in mind some question about their present status. God's answer to the nation was one of emphatic rebuke; He categorically refused to be inquired of by them. Since they were not sincere nor repentant in their asking, God was not interested in their hollow trifling and would brook it no longer.

Instead of merely answering their questions, Ezekiel was commanded of God to judge them, that is, to set forth God's case judicially before them. The repeated question is tantamount to an imperative, perhaps with an element of emotion. The theme of the prophet's address was the abominations committed by their fathers. The Old Testament generally uses the word for abominations with reference to idolatry. All of God's dealings with Israel were founded on His sovereign choice of them for His own people, so Ezekiel emphasizes this primary relationship and transaction (see Exodus 6:2-4 for a restatement of this choice). It is found not only here in Ezekiel, but also in Jeremiah 33:24, frequently in Isaiah 40-66, in Deuteronomy 7:6 and elsewhere. The covenant relationship was

108

confirmed by an oath, as in Genesis 15:17-21; Exodus 6:8; and Deuteronomy 32:40. God made Himself known to them in a higher and fuller way through His redemptive work in Egypt (cf. Exodus 3:6-7; 6:3). In infinite grace and compassion God promised them He would deliver them from Egyptian bondage. Moreover, He had already searched them out (speaking after the manner of man) a land of unusual fertility and productivity, described as flowing with milk and honey, an expression proverbial for the land since its first usage in Exodus 3:8. The land was further described as the glory of all lands. When the people of Israel entered the land of promise under Joshua, there was every indication that the land satisfied the high hopes of the people (see Joshua 23:14; Jer. 3:19; Dan. 8:9; 11:16, 41, 45).

The command mentioned in verse 7 is noteworthy. From no other source do we learn of Israel's idolatry in Egypt as explicitly as here. However, intimations to this effect are not lacking (see 23:3; Lev. 17:7; 18:3; Joshua 24:14; Amos 5:25-27). The incident of the golden calf (Exodus 32:4) was not without background gained in Egypt. Their eyes, following the bent of their hearts, were directed toward the idols (by way of contrast see Num. 15:39). The defiling character of the worthless images and their detestable nature in the sight of God were made plain to the ancestors of the prophet's contemporaries. At that early time in their national history did they desire to obey God? The record shows they rebelled against God's leading and would not heed His word (cf. Ps. 106:7). Even then God considered destroying them, for sin always deserves punishment in God's moral government. The account in Exodus centers on Israel's conflict with Egypt and Moses' ministry among his own people, but these portions in Ezekiel supplement and in no wise contradict the record there.

God did not carry through His rightful judgment, however, for mercy triumphed over judgment. When God could find no basis in them for extending to them His mercy and grace, He did it solely for His name's sake, that is, for His own glory. This is a very common concept in Ezekiel, as it is in the latter portion of the book of Isaiah. God's name stands for all He is, has revealed of Himself, and expects to accomplish in the affairs of men. God acted for His glory (cf. vv. 14, 22). The Lord did not want His glory and power to be disregarded or lightly esteemed by the nations of the earth. To profane the name of the Lord is the opposite of sanctifying it. If God had poured out His wrath on His people, though they warranted such action by their multiplied transgressions against Him, the heathen could well have concluded according to their reasonings that God was unable to deliver His nation from their enemies. Moses used this valid argument effectively in His intercession for Israel in the wilderness (Exodus 32:12; Num. 14:16). Why this rehearsal of the nation's sins of the past to the prophet's countrymen in exile? The reason is clear: their father's sins were mirrored in their own lives, as is demonstrated in the course of the message.

THOSE DELIVERED FROM EGYPT (20:10-17)

According to His infinitely wise counsels and the abundance of His grace the Lord determined to bring His people from the bondage of Egyptian servitude. In one pointed verse Ezekiel summarized the numerous transactions whereby the Lord delivered Israel. Notice the moving Personality throughout is God, all secondary agents being passed over. In the wilderness at Sinai the Lord gave them His law with statutes and ordinances (Deut. 30:15-20). The promise of life which accompanied the law ("if a man do, he shall live in them," v. 13b) was genuine, but there was no enablement provided to keep the law (Rom. 8:3), nor was there life for those dead in trespasses and sins (Gal. 3:21). It is clear that more was required than some external conforming to God's precepts. Obedience would have brought life physically and spiritually, temporally and eternally (see Deut. 4:40; 5:16). It insured life and prosperity, whereas disobedience brought with it disaster and death (Hosea 8:3; Amos 5:14). From among all His laws given to Israel the Lord specifies His Sabbaths. Six references to this day are found in this chapter and in each case God designates them as His. The Sabbath was the central sign of the old covenant (cf. Isa. 56:2, 4). Repeatedly it is shown that the law of the Sabbath was not legislation by which they could gain life but rather the sign of the covenant between God and Israel. It was a sign that they were Israelites and were being set apart unto the worship and service of the Lord alone. From this chapter and Nehemiah 9:14 it is certain that the Sabbath was given at Sinai and did not date from Eden, all the fallacious arguments of the Sabbatarians to the contrary notwithstanding (see Exodus 31:12-17). There is not a word here of a previous committal of the Sabbath to Israel as an institution antedating the exodus. The plural is for the regular recurrence of the day and does not include the other feast days of the sacred calendar.

But the tragic account of rebellion continues. In the wilderness they opposed every provision of God for their blessing and good. They were no better out of the land of Egypt than they had been in it. Only two profanations of the Sabbath are recorded in Exodus 16:27 and Numbers 15:32, but the people failed to keep the day in the widest sense (cf. Neh. 10:31-33; 13:15-22; Isa. 56:2-4; 58:13; Jer. 17:21-27; Amos 8:5). The entail of disobedience was the righteous wrath of God which would have consumed them. But the grace of God found a way to spare them, and God wrought for His own glory so that the nations might not receive an erroneous impression of His power. It is vital to realize that the Lord was concerned as to how the nations would view His acts as well as the response among His people Israel. However, the sins of the wilderness issued in judgment on the transgressors who were refused entrance into the land of promise. The rebellion of the ungodly at Kadesh-barnea could not be viewed lightly (Num. 14:11-19, 22-23, 29; Deut. 1:35; Ps. 95:11). God was impartial in His judgments, for even Moses was similarly refused entrance into the land on the ground of his disobedience to an express command of God. Moreover, in the wilderness as in Egypt the heart of the wicked went after idolatry. This tendency, always latent, came out into the open from time to time. Numbers 25:3-9 reveals how easily they were enticed from the way which pleased the Lord. However, God was not minded to wipe out the nation completely, for He allowed His pity for them to overrule their wickedness (cf. Ps. 78:38).

The Wilderness Generation (20:18-26)

The children of verse 18 are the second generation in the wilderness. They were solemnly warned of God not to follow the wicked ways of their fathers who had shown themselves to be incorrigible. The entire message of Deuteronomy was one constant reminder and warning in this regard. Repeatedly the Lord insisted upon the relationship He sustained to them in order to evoke their obedience and observance of His statutes. Had they heeded these admonitions, great would have been their blessedness, and they would have come to know the Lord in a way inconceivable in any other manner. But transgression for transgression the children were but carbon copies of their fathers. They too deserved the wrath of God, but He determined to manifest grace that the nations might know Him as both omnipotent and gracious. God withdrew His hand from meting out to them the punishment their deeds deserved. But even as early as the wilderness era God had predicted Israel's worldwide scattering among the nations (Deut. 28:64-68). The Babylonian captivity was only a partial realization of this prophecy by Moses. Insofar as the nation's moral conduct was the same as that generation in the wilderness, it could expect just such universal dispersion as has overtaken it to this hour. And the basis of all the misery was the inveterate bent of their hearts and eyes after their fathers' idols, a fatal and senseless attraction.

Ezekiel's statement that the Lord gave His people statutes which were not good, has been difficult for Bible students for a long time. Possibly no solution will please all where there is such divergence of opinion, but certain features should be pointed out. First, the position that the statements in verses 25-26 are the blasphemous words of the people, is indefensible. Clearly the Lord is speaking. Second, for the same reason the words cannot be characterized as casuistry, which would not be worthy of the Lord. Third, the passage is not a reference to verse 11 (as many have thought it to be in ancient and modern times) or to any aspect of the Mosaic law. Those who have so argued have based their view on Romans 3:20; Galatians 4:9; and Hebrews 7:19; 10:1. But Romans 7:12 is explicit as to the intrinsic nature of the law and its commandments. Account must be taken of the argument of Romans 7:13 where Paul denies that what was inherently good, was made evil to them because of their disobedience. Furthermore, the immediate context in Ezekiel (vv. 13, 21) shows that the statutes were such that they were expected to "live in them."

Finally, a step toward the solution is made when it is realized that the statutes which were not good were the Molech worship of verse 26. Undeniably, this heathenish worship was never promoted by God, but rather strongly condemned by Him many times in the Old Testament prophetic messages. Ezekiel was declaring that in retribution the Lord allowed them to go after their own ways in order to punish them according to their deeds. The passage is speaking in the sense of a judicial sentence. The problem is susceptible of solution if we see that God identifies Himself with the instruments of His wrath and His providential chastisements which He brings upon Israel in answer to their sin. The Lord gave them these worthless and unprofitable statutes in the same sense as Isaiah 63:17. Disobedience leads to greater sin. Sin becomes its own punishment (Ps. 81:12; Ezek. 14:9; Acts 7:42; Rom. 1:24-25; II Thess. 2:11). The statutes were not good in the sense that they did not lead to life and welfare ("whereby they should not live," v. 25b). Of course, the matter of justification by the law is not in view here. An example of the outworking of the principle in verse 25 is to be found in Numbers 25. The Lord punished Israel by allowing the worshipers of Baal to tempt them to idolatry, and then by judging them for their departure into idolatry.

Verse 26 is the divine commentary on verse 25. In the polluting worship of Molech, children were cast into the fire as a sacrifice to the idol. Judicial blindness from God resulted in this degradation, not a misinterpretation of Exodus 22:29, as though it demanded the sacrifice of the firstborn. The gifts referred to were all God had given them, the produce of the ground and their children. The firstborn of man and animals (Exodus 13:12) belonged to God, and were not to be offered to Molech

(Deut. 18:10). The unbelieving were deluded continually and increasingly until they ended in death.

They Rebelled Against God

The history of all created beings has been one long and wearisome story of rebellion. Rebellion against the moral government of God is an ancient and always disastrous occupation. But is there not rebellion in our hearts when confronted with the command of God to take the gospel to a lost world through godly life and faithful witness?

Approximately half of Ezekiel 20 is devoted to a recital of Israel's defections in the past, whether in Egypt or in the wilderness. The purpose of this portrayal is to lead up to the generation contemporary with Ezekiel.

The Nation's Sins in the Land (20:27-32)

In spite of the grace of God repeatedly shown to Israel in Egypt, in the exodus and in their wilderness wanderings, they had not determined to obey the Lord, for they blasphemed God through their acts and transgressions. Disregarding their failures and disobedience in the wilderness, the Lord brought them into the land of promise. In Canaan they were quick to assimilate the heinous practices of the people of the land. On high hills they entered into the abominable cult of Asherah or Ashtaroth (Isa. 57:5; Jer. 2:20; 3:6). As for the thick trees, the idolatrous Canaanites thought these were inhabited by divine beings. Archaeological findings in the Near East have shown how degraded and sensuous were the idolatrous religious rites of the Canaanites. Instead of exterminating these practices and those who followed them, Israel entered into these enormities themselves. The sacrifices, the offerings, the sweet savors and the drink offerings that rightly belonged to God were poured out upon the worthless idols of the land. Verse 29 has been taken as a play on words as if the Hebrew word (bamah) for high place came from the two words "go" (ba) and "whither" (mah); or "what [mah] . . . go [ba]," a contemptuous pun. Others take such an interpretation as fanciful, if not a trifling with the text. However, the latter part of the verse indicates that Ezekiel is eager to make something out of the name Bamah.

When Ezekiel's contemporaries were asked whether they had polluted themselves or played the harlot, the answer was a strong positive. As a matter of fact they were more guilty in following the idolatry of Canaan than their fathers had been in serving the idols of Egypt. They could read the disastrous consequences of such folly in the fate of their fathers. With this in mind Ezekiel asked whether the elders of his time had any right to think God would be inquired of by them. It is as though he expressed surprise that those who had continued in sin and emulated the disobedience of their forefathers should still expect to receive fresh revelations from God. They were told categorically that God has no intention of communicating further messages to them. God knew full well what was in their minds that very hour. They had decided deliberately to pattern their idolatry after that of the heathen about them. They did not care for their separated and distinct position in the plan of God. Just as their fathers had assimilated the idolatries of Canaan in their religious observances, they in exile had decided to imitate the idolatries of their neighbors. They did not want the odium of being different from other peoples with a special and distinctive God; they had decided to conform. It is the cry and enticement of the world to the people of God in every age and clime. But God determined to overrule their desire to be like all the nations; He had never chosen them for this.

FUTURE JUDGMENT FOR ISRAEL (20:33-39)

Ezekiel looked far ahead to the future of Israel in verses 33-44. To seek to apply them to the prophet's day or any age already past requires a strange handling of the plain statements of the passage. As with all the other prophets, Ezekiel saw in the historic events of Israel's past the very matrix and mold for events that still lie in the distant future. God manifested His irresistible power over the defiant Egyptians with His mighty hand and outstretched arm (cf. Deut. 4:34; 5:15; 7:19; 11:2). This same power He will exert to manifest His sovereign will over Israel after a long history of disobedience and rebellion. Beyond any return from Babylon to the land of promise Ezekiel is foretelling a divine regathering of His people from all the countries where they have been scattered. The prophetic Scriptures are replete with this theme (see Deut. 30:1-10; Isa. 11:11-16; 49:17-23; 60:1-22; 61:4-9; Jer. 23:1-8; Ezek. 36:22-31; Amos 9:11-15; Zech. 10:8-12). These passages, only representative of a large number, will repay closest scrutiny, for they treat one of the dominant themes of all prophecy. If one be confused here, God's prophetic program must remain obscure and out of focus.

Having regathered His people from the corners of the earth, God will bring them into the wilderness of the peoples for the purpose of judging them. The wilderness of the peoples has been taken as the barren plateau— the Syro-Arabian Desert—between the Jordan and the Euphrates Valley where the nations who influenced Israel lived. But since the text is speaking of all peoples and all countries, it would seem incongruous to restrict the wilderness of the peoples to a circumscribed locality like the Syro-

Arabian Desert. It is truer to the context to understand the words to refer to the wilderness condition of the people of Israel, their spiritual status while in worldwide dispersion. The judgment under consideration will be face to face without any intervening parties. So that Ezekiel's contemporaries would have a point of comparison, he likened the coming judgment to God's dealings with their rebellious ancestors in the wilderness of the land of Egypt. Even the method of procedure is outlined in broad sketches. As a shepherd's staff is employed to count the sheep (Jer. 33:13), so the Lord will bring the entire flock under the rod, this time with the purpose of separating the godly from the wicked. The godly will be brought more firmly into the bond of the covenant, whereas the rebels will be purged out; those who have transgressed against the Lord will be brought out of the land of their sojourn but denied admission to the land of promise. Just as in Matthew 25 in the judgment on the nations (an event which takes place in the same general prophetic period of the latter days for Israel) there is separation of sheep individuals from goat individuals, so in this purging judgment on Israel. This is an exclusive judgment on Israel which will take place during the time of Jacob's trouble, probably at the end of the period.

There is a difficult transition from verses 33-38 to verse 39. Some consider the words as irony or suggest that by transposition of the text it be made to read, "But as for you, O house of Israel, if ye will not hearken to Me, go serve every man his idols! Yet hereafter ye shall no more profane My holy name in you." Transpositions of the text are a desperate measure and should be avoided. The viewpoint that takes the verse as irony explains that God would have them open and out-and-out idolaters rather than the hypocritical patronizers of His worship which they have been thus far (see I Kings 18:21; II Kings 17:41; Amos 5:21-22, 25-26; Matt. 6:24; Rev. 3:15-16). Perhaps Ezekiel was stating that if they persisted in their stubborn opposition to God's will, He would allow them to follow their own inclinations to their doom.

Future Blessing in the Land (20:40-44)

Once Israel has known the purging and refining work of the Lord (Zech. 13:7-9), then all the hopes and promises of her full spiritual restoration will be realized. So blessed will it be then to live in the land, that Ezekiel refers to the land six times in verse 40. The goal of the work of restoration is that they will serve the Lord wholeheartedly in the land after idolatry has been done away with forever. All will be present too, because the breach in the nation will finally be healed. A united nation will participate in a united and purified worship (see Isa. 11:13; Ezek. 37:22-23).

They will render priestly service to God, for the word "serve" is the technical term for priestly ministry (cf. for this commission Exodus 19:6). The Lord will not only accept their offerings and holy things, but will seek them. Isaiah uses a bold figure for the same truth in Isaiah 60:7. Then the regathered and cleansed nation will no longer be a cause of profanation of the Lord's name among the heathen, but rather a sweet savor, a delight to the Lord and the means of His being exalted and sanctified before the nations. This is reason enough to justify the existence of any nation. Israel will have fulfilled her objective in world history.

In that hour Israel will review their long career and dwell on their past deeds and pollutions with sincere conviction of heart and loathing for their past transgressions (16:61). To look at God in His holiness and majesty is to abhor self with all its sinful ways (cf. Job in Job 42:5-6 and Isaiah in Isaiah 6:5). So loathsome will be their past history of defection that they will never return to idolatry. They will see it in all its stark reality for what it really is: suicide of the soul. They will realize too that the foundation of all God's dealings with them has been in grace and solely for His glory.

THE JUDGMENT OF FIRE (20:45-49)

In the Hebrew text of Ezekiel, verse 45 of this chapter is the beginning of chapter 21, where the connection is clear and the figure is explained in direct prophetic discourse. The time in view is no longer the far distant future for the nation, but the immediate future, the desolation soon to be carried out through the invasion of Nebuchadnezzar. The parable of the forest does not relate to Babylon, but to the land of Israel. The south referred to is Palestine, which was always invaded, as far as the Mesopotamian powers were concerned, from the north. Three different words are employed for south. The first designates it as the region on the right hand as one looks east (47:19); the second term signifies the shining land (Deut. 33:23); the third word is the most popular today and has come to be used as a proper noun, the Negev, the dry land (Joshua 15:21). To "drop a word" is used of the message of the prophets. The picture is of water from a tilted vessel (cf. 21:2; Deut. 32:2; Amos 7:16; Micah 2:6, 11). The land is called forest because the area was more densely covered in those days. "Field" is employed in the sense of country, as so often is done in the historical accounts of the Old Testament (see Ruth 1:1).

With such a detailed introduction Ezekiel must have had a matter of importance to convey. It was the devastation of the land of Judah under the figure of a fire. A striking parallel is the message in Zechariah 11:1-3. The green tree refers to the one who is generally or manifestly righteous, whereas the dry tree speaks of the life of the sinner which is spiritually withered (cf. Luke 23:31). The flaming flame, kindled by the Lord Himself, is a strong expression indicating a most vehement flame. And it will touch every life. What will be judgment for the godless will be refining for the godly. So it was when Nebuchadnezzar invaded the land for the third time, bringing about the dissolution of the kingdom in 586 B.C. No power on earth could hinder his visitation; it was inaugurated by God and carried out through him. Through the messages of godly Jeremiah and Ezekiel no one in the nation was in doubt as to who brought about the catastrophe. Ezekiel was alert to the reactions of his contemporaries, and knew what they were saying of his method of presentation of truth. They refused to comprehend his message. Men find difficulty in understanding a message which is distasteful to them. Some even take the question as a statement of the people's skepticism. It is well known that to the unwilling heart any message from God appears to be difficult of comprehension. The parable forms a transition to the next chapter where Ezekiel speaks in nonfigurative speech.

"King over You"

In a soon coming day God has indicated He will make known His sovereign rule and will in Israel with a mighty hand and an outstretched arm. But no one can enjoy that reign who is not prepared by faith in the Lord Jesus Christ. It is the glorious privilege of the hour for us to be co-workers with God to spread the message of redeeming grace among the lost sheep of the house of Israel. They have waited so long for an interest in our prayers, our efforts and our witnessings. Need they wait longer?

21

THE SWORD OF THE LORD

No CHAPTER IN THE BIBLE speaks more prominently and fully of the sword of the Lord than does this chapter which has been called the sword song or the prophecy of the sword. As previously stated, 20:45-49 is joined to this chapter in the Hebrew text; but the English text follows the Septuagint, Syriac and Vulgate versions. Chapter 21 has been characterized as a series of rhapsodies. The historical background of this prophecy is Nebuchadnezzar's 588 B.C. campaign to quell revolts in Tyre, Judah and Ammon.

THE SWORD IS COMING (21:1-7)

The Prophet Ezekiel was commanded of the Lord to address himself directly toward Jerusalem and to drop (as in 20:46) or utter his predictions primarily against the sanctuaries of the capital city, but ultimately against the entire land of Israel. The sanctuaries included the courts, the holy place, and the holiest of all, the holy buildings in Jerusalem (see 7:24 and the use of the plural in Matt. 24:1). The thrust of the message was that God was the antagonist of the nation and would draw forth His sword to destroy both the righteous and the wicked. The sword was actually King Nebuchadnezzar of Babylon. As a rule liberal interpreters find verse 3 in contradiction with Ezekiel's teaching on individual retribution in 14:13-20 and chapters 18 and 33. The translators of the Septuagint version were so disturbed by the problem that they translated "unrighteous" for "righteous." But such attempts misunderstand Ezekiel's natural meaning. Just as a forest fire consumes the green with the dry (20:47), the judgment would be indiscriminate to all outward appearances, which is always true when an invading army takes over a land. In national calamities, of necessity the godly suffer the same temporal woes as the ungodly. The passage does not contradict such portions as 9:4-8 and those already mentioned, the truth of which is assumed throughout. So important is the warning that Ezekiel repeated it in verses 4 and 5. The sword of the Lord would not return to its sheath until it had carried out the purpose of God.

In order for the nation to realize more clearly the reason for Ezekiel's anguish, he was exhorted twice to sigh with bitterness and with all his strength. He was not communicating a message toward which he had superficial feelings, but one which he felt deeply. God would have Ezekiel experience something of what was in His own heart toward the rebellious nation. The loins were considered the seat of strength (cf. Job 40:16; Ps. 66:11; Isa. 21:3; Nahum 2:10). This was a heartbroken sorrow, and doubtless Ezekiel's anguish would not go unnoticed. In reply to the question of his people, Ezekiel would truthfully inform them of the coming devastating judgment, a visitation so thorough and terrifying that it would paralyze the people and render them incapable of resisting the enemy. Of the certainty of coming judgment there was no possible doubt. What God had purposed would be accomplished without fail.

THE SWORD IS SHARPENED (21:8-17)

In this portion the prophet vividly portrayed the work of destruction to be carried out by the avenging sword of the Lord. The repetition of the instrument of punishment was for emphasis. The sword was not only sharpened but was rubbed and scoured to make it bright so that it would gleam brilliantly and cut with sharp strokes. Widespread slaughter was the objective of the sword of God. In view of the fearful prospect, Ezekiel asked whether this was the hour for mirth, an hour of enjoyment and complacency. The implication was that any imagined basis for confidence was false.

The last portion of verse 10 is admittedly difficult, and neither the Septuagint nor the Vulgate helps here. The clause is obscure because of its brevity; in such cases the context does not help sufficiently for a decisive conclusion as to the meaning. Because of the mention of "the rod" and "my son," the passage has been referred to Psalm 2. But the connection between the two scriptural portions is not too clear. To state that the rod is that of discipline (Prov. 10:13; 26:3) still does not illuminate its meaning in this context. It has been suggested that the rod or the sword of Babylon with which the Lord will chastise His son (the people of Israel and their king) will exceed in severity all other chastisement (the rod of every tree). This is rather farfetched and calls for conclusions upon insufficient evidence. It is probably best to relate the verse to Genesis 49:9-10, where Jacob called Judah "my son" and referred to "the sceptre" (literally, rod). The interpretation, then, would be that the people objected to Ezekiel's denunciations of them by pointing out that God's promise to Judah was secure, no matter how great the obstacles it was called upon to overcome. So they imagined themselves safe whatever their offenses were against the Lord. But they would not be able to argue the promise of Genesis 49 against Ezekiel's prediction, for the sword would certainly come. Even this view leaves something to be desired, for the Genesis promise is introduced all too abruptly. Verse 13 is equally difficult, as we shall see.

Ezekiel dwells upon the manner in which the sword has been readied for its solemn and death-dealing work. The indefinite reference to the slayer is related specifically in verse 19 to the king of Babylon. With gestures of anguish, extreme grief and even despair (Jer. 31:19), the man of God was called upon to express the depth of his grief, and God's sorrow above all, for the calamity to befall His people and all their princes. Verse 13 has received various treatments by interpreters, as has verse 10, and some leave the problem unsolved. But the sense of this passage must be in agreement with verse 10. Ezekiel was not declaring that God's sword would put all under trial and testing. The trial had been made, but the agent is not clearly identified. Perhaps the reference was to victories Nebuchadnezzar had already won in his campaigns. Thus the sense may be that Babylon's strength had been proved and Judah's scepter, which despised it, would be done away with. Judah's royal house was soon to pass away (vv. 25-27). Difficulty in interpretation arises from the conciseness and brevity of the statement, not because of Ezekiel's impassioned and ragingly wild mood, as some have claimed.

Again, the command to Ezekiel was that he smite his hands together in great indignation. The sharpened and furbished sword flashed so swiftly in its movements—with a double or triple intensity—that it appeared to be two or three swords in one. Its destructive force would be multiplied. The third time had no allusion to the three attacks of Nebuchadnezzar against Jerusalem. Judging from verse 25, the deadly wounded was King Zedekiah. The great one was specified as the deadly wounded one; Zedekiah would be judged and pierced by the same sword that fell upon his people. That sword would penetrate into their innermost chambers, leaving them no opportunity for escape. If they decided to escape the city altogether, the sword would threaten them at the gates. All courage would vanish, for the slaughter would be so great that the living would stumble over the carcasses of the dead. Then the sword itself was addressed and commanded to slay on every side in indiscriminate fashion. Finally, the Lord made the prophet's gesture His own. In a strong symbol of grief He smote His hands together (see v. 14), for His wrath had spent itself upon the ungodly.

THE SWORD OF NEBUCHADNEZZAR AGAINST JERUSALEM (21:18-23)

In this section of the prophecy the king of Babylon and his divination are described. Ezekiel was to draw a sketch of the road from Babylon to Jerusalem and Rabbath. He saw the army on the march, and was charged to enact a symbolic action. The sword emphasized throughout the chapter was that of the king of Babylon, Nebuchadnezzar. The roads to both Judah and Ammon came from the one land of Babylon; south of Riblah the road southwest led to Judah and Jerusalem, that southeast to Rabbath and Ammon. Twice Ezekiel was commanded to mark or carve out a place (literally, a hand), the signpost or pointer to the city. Ammon had conspired in 593 B.C. with Judah to rebel against Babylon. The question was whether the king would decide to go against Rabbath or against Jerusalem. In Greco-Roman times Rabbath was called Philadelphia; it is the modern Amman in Transjordan, the Old Testament Rabbath-Ammon. Religious pagan that Nebuchadnezzar was, he did not venture to decide for himself. That had to be left to the gods, with their will ascertained by means of magic and divination.

The king of Babylon took his stand at the crossroads, and Ezekiel faithfully portrayed Babylonian concepts and customs. Even Nebuchadnezzar's superstition was overruled by God in order to carry out His purpose on Judah (for Babylon's divinations see Isa. 47:8-15). The king thought he was deciding by the help of his gods, but God was determining the course of his action. The parting of the two ways is literally "the mother of the way," the branches being like two daughters. Three kinds of magic were specified. Each arrow was marked with a name, a form of casting lots. They were put in a quiver, whirled about, then the one falling out first was the decision of the god. According to rabbinic tradition the teraphim was a mummified child's head. It is generally accepted that the reference was to household images supposed to be connected with good fortune (see Gen. 31:19; I Sam. 15:23; 19:13, 16; II Kings 23:24). The liver was considered the seat of life because it is filled with blood. Sheep were sacrificed for this kind of divination (called hepatoscopy), then the judgment was made on the basis of the color or marks on the liver. This was the most common method of divination practiced in Babylon. In all this divination there was no tacit approval from God on these heathen practices; rather, all of it was overruled of God to execute His judgmental purposes on Judah.

Amazingly enough, the lot fell on Jerusalem. It was the signal to make ready all the paraphernalia of warfare: battering rams, mounds and forts.

However, the people of Jerusalem thought it was all a false divination and that Nebuchadnezzar would not succeed in his objective against the capital. They may have secretly realized that all magical and idolatrous practices were worthless. At any rate they felt they were safe in spite of their betrayal of their oath of fealty to Babylon. The sworn oaths do not have in view the broken oath of King Zedekiah (17:16-18) but the sworn oaths or covenants from God to them, the people of Judah. Therefore the Hebrews believed they had nothing to fear from Babylon. Surely they could not be relying on the oaths of fealty to Babylon, for their King Zedekiah had expressly broken these. The one who brought iniquity to remembrance has been taken to refer to the Lord or to Nebuchadnezzar; probably the latter is better. They would be found out, arrested in their wicked ways and proved wrong in their false hopes.

PRIESTHOOD AND ROYALTY REMOVED UNTIL MESSIAH'S COMING (21:24-27)

Judah's sins had been so flagrant that they were manifest for all to see and long remember. Indeed, it appeared that all their actions were colored by sin. Lack of loyalty to their oath was but one of many sins for which the hand of the king of Babylon would forcibly seize and arrest them. It has been suggested that verses 25-27 provide a contrast between Christ and Antichrist on the basis of the words "the time of the iniquity of the end" (v. 25b, ASV; cf. Dan. 11:35-39). But such a view takes insufficient notice of the immediate context. The deadly wounded wicked one was the prince of Israel, Zedekiah. His fall was so certain that he was addressed as though he had already undergone his punishment. The manner in which he was addressed is one of the most severe in the Scriptures. His day was the day of his judgment. The time of the iniquity of the end pointed to the measure of guilt as full (see Gen. 15:16; Ezek. 7:2-3).

Since the hour had come for visitation, what was the procedure? Both the miter and crown were to be removed. This marked the commencement of the times of the Gentiles. The miter was the headdress of the high priest (Exodus 28:37); the crown, of course, belonged to the king. Priesthood and royalty were related in Israel. Now they were both to be interrupted, set aside for a time. Neither office was fully restored after the captivity. There were no Urim and Thummim, no ark of the covenant with the glory over the mercy seat (Ezra 2:63), and no king of the Davidic line. Even the new order of things would not remain stable. It would be no more the same (v. 27, literally, "this not this"). There would be continued and repeated changes and shiftings. Social upheaval and revolution would be the order of the day with complete revolution where normal values and positions would be reversed; the low would take the place of the high, and the high the place of the low.

How long would this state of flux and revolution go on? God indicated that He would interpose and cause even greater upheavals. The threefold mention of overturning underlines the awesome certainty of the prediction and expresses the highest degree of unsettled conditions. Ezekiel was not speaking of Jehoiakim, Jehoiachin and Zedekiah, nor of the destruction of Babylon, Greece and Rome. The reference is far more general and comprehensive as to both time and place. This overturning activity explains the breakdown throughout the world. It is important to recognize that world chaos and catastrophe are not working against God's plan and program but are actually leading up to it in the overruling providence of God. Instability and flux will be the normal condition until Christ's appearing. The words "until he come" are reminiscent of Genesis 49:10, and undoubtedly refer to the same Person. The Targum referred these words to Ishmael, the murderer of Governor Gedaliah, but later Jewish interpreters more soberly assign them to the Messiah. The "right" is that remarkable combination of priestly and regal offices (read Ps. 110:2, 4; Zech. 6:12-13; Ps. 72; Isa. 9:6; 42:1; Jer. 23:5; 33:17). The promise is that to the Messiah, and to Him alone, will God give this double right of high priesthood and kingship (cf. Heb. 5-7).

The Sword Against Ammon (21:28-32)

Nebuchadnezzar only postponed his chastisement of Ammon; he did not decide to give it up altogether. The judgment was to overtake the people of Ammon as well as Israel. They seemed to have escaped, but it was only temporary. In chapter 25 Ezekiel reverts to the theme of judgment on Ammon. Ammon rejoiced at the fall of Jerusalem (25:3, 6), just as Edom did (Obadiah's prophecy). The Ammonites were conquered and their country devastated when Nebuchadnezzar invaded Ammon a few years after Jerusalem's fall. Their name finally disappeared from the family of the nations. Ammon also had false prophets in their midst who led them astray with baseless hopes. The dead of Ammon would fall on the bodies of those already slain in Judah, whose day of judgment had already come (v. 25).

Verse 30 is not to be interpreted as an indication that Ammon seized the opportunity to curry favor with Nebuchadnezzar, when he marched against Jerusalem, by attacking Judah; whereupon the Lord commanded them to desist. Simply stated, Ezekiel was forewarning Ammon that resistance against Babylon on their part would be useless. Their punishment would overtake them in their own country. The figure of fire then replaced that of the sword. The brutish men, who were expert at destruction, were the Babylonians already referred to throughout this chapter. Israel was to have a future (v. 27), but the fall of Ammon was to be absolute and without remedy. The memory of them would perish.

"UNTIL HE COME"

The coming of the Lord for His church in the rapture is recalled in every celebration of the Lord's Supper: "till He come." Israel also has an "until He come." The Messiah will restore access to God in high-priestly ministry and righteous rule in royal ministry. How bright is the future for Israel! But how dark for any soul, Jew or Gentile, who is out of Christ now! We cannot know when God will begin to fulfill His prophetic plan; therefore, let us be diligent in our efforts to proclaim the gospel to all men.

22

THE INDICTMENT AGAINST
JERUSALEM

ANOTHER DESIGNATION for this chapter could well be "Jerusalem, the City of Blood." The sins of the religious center of the nation are described again. Not one section of the land nor one class of society is exempt from condemnation; all are implicated in the evil. This chapter, like chapter 20, vindicates the divine judgment on Jerusalem. There the emphasis was on the sins of their ancestors; here, on their own abominations. In the earlier portion their iniquities were set forth in the historical framework of the past; here, as a present reality. The chapter is usually outlined in three oracles (words) or prophecies: (1) the abominations of Jerusalem (vv. 1-16); (2) the smelting furnace (vv. 17-22); and (3) the sins of prophets, priests, princes and people (vv. 23-31).

JUDGING THE BLOODY CITY (22:1-5)

The urgency of the matter at hand is indicated by the repetition of the question by the Lord to Ezekiel as to whether he will judge the nation. If the prophet is to perform the function of a judge, he must state the bill of particulars in the arraignment, and he does precisely this throughout the chapter. The city is characterized as a bloody one in verses 2, 3, 4, 6, 9, 12, 13. (Cf. the use of the words for Nineveh in Nahum 3:1.) Jerusalem is so named because of the many deeds of violence and oppression committed in her. The plural of the original for "blood" points to numerous acts of bloodshed. The enormity of her sins must be declared to Jerusalem. The violent acts perpetrated have brought about the time of her judgment (see 7:7; 21:25). The result is stated as though it were purpose, according to a well-known Hebrew idiom found also in the New Testament. The people made no effort to avert the calamity by repentance. Jerusalem made idols against (literally, upon) herself, that is, as though to cover the city with idolatry, thus defiling her spiritually and morally.

Bloodguiltiness, which hung so heavily over the city, was brought about because of the children offered to idols and on account of judicial murders (notice vv. 6, 9; 23:27; 24:6, 9). Such violations of the revealed will of God have hastened the day of her calamity. Some, following rabbinical comment, refer the days to the siege of Jerusalem, and the years to the captivity in Babylon which resulted therefrom. But this is an arbitrary distinction for the days and years speak of the same time. As a result of much profession and little or no performance the Lord had made them a reproach and mocking to all the nations. Paul has the same concept in view in speaking of Israel in Romans 2:24. Strangely, God has linked His honor and dignity among the nations of earth with the kind of actions His people display. The same is true of believers in this age. The privilege is great; the responsibility is correspondingly so. Neighboring peoples, far and near, would recognize Jerusalem for what she actually was, an infamous one, literally, defiled of name. She was no longer worthy of the name of holy city where the visible presence of God had dwelt, because she had given herself over to all manner of abomination against God and all kinds of crimes against man. Social and spiritual tumult filled the city (cf. Amos 3:9). Sin ever works violence, tumult and shame.

LEWD DEFILINGS (22:6-12)

This section presents an itemized list of the moral arrears of the nation. The words are first addressed to the princes of Israel, the very ones who were expected to uphold the dignity of the law, yet were the most to blame. Nor was this an occasional lapse, for according to their power (literally, arm) they carried out their wicked designs. With them might was right. Also, their actions were arbitrary in the extreme. The only restraint on their deeds of evil was the limit of their ability. They did all the evil they could, and the shedding of blood seemed to be their chief aim in life. Judicial murders were evidently intended (see II Kings 21:16; 24:4). Again and again, eleven times in verses 6-12, it is stated that all this took place "in thee," that is, in Jerusalem.

Detail by detail the sad and sordid tale unfolds. Parents were lightly esteemed and robbed of the honor due them, even though honor to father and mother was one of the most frequently stated commands of the law (cf. Exodus 21:17; Lev. 20:9; Deut. 27:16). This relationship ultimately underlies the proper submission of citizens to their rulers. If parents were slighted, the sojourner could not hope for consideration. Him they oppressed, forgetting that they were formerly sojourners in Egypt (Exodus 22:21; 23:9). Those without human protectors, the fatherless and the widow, were wronged, the wicked forgetting that God had made Himself their special and sufficient Defender (Exodus 22:22-24; Deut. 24:17; 27:19). In the spiritual realm they despised the sacred appointments instituted by the Lord, and profaned the Lord's Sabbaths. Neither God nor man could hope for proper respect, honor or consideration.

Furthermore, slanderous men, informers who are the plague of corrupt governments the world over, plied their nefarious trade, bringing about the death of innocent victims by their lies (for the prohibition, see Lev. 19:16; for the practice, cf. I Kings 21). Eating upon the mountains was connected with the abominable idolatrous feasts in the high places with which unspeakable indecencies were associated. What manner of lewdness was practiced in the capital city is outlined next. It would appear that they willfully set out to violate the Mosaic legislation item by item. They were guilty of incest of a most vile character (see Amos 2:7; I Cor. 5:1—probably a stepmother is intended; for the prohibition, cf. Lev. 18:7-8; 20:11; Deut. 22:30; 27:20). No type of impurity could stay their evil desires (Lev. 18:19; 20:18). In their excesses they acted more like beasts than creatures of reason. God has placed restraints in every realm of human life with infinite wisdom, and it is worse than folly to disregard these warnings.

No moral standards were kept inviolate, whether they involved a neighbor's wife, a daughter-in-law or a sister, for impurity of every kind reared its ugly head. When a holy people forsakes its place of separation and godliness, the depths to which it sinks are unmentionable. Adultery, incest and sins of the deepest dye were the order of the day (for prohibitions regulating each act, see Lev. 18:20; 20:10; 18:15; 20:12 [for the deed, Gen. 38:16]; Lev. 18:9; 20:17; Deut. 27:22 [for the deed, II Sam. 13:12-13]). Bribery, usury and oppression were an ungodly trio that constantly dogged their steps. The corruptions began with the leaders and permeated the so-called lower classes of society (cf. Exodus 23:8; Lev. 25:36). How could the actions of the nation be explained? What had come over them? The basic cause of their wickedness was diagnosed as forgetfulness of God. Since God is at the center of all moral relations, all social and moral rights and proprieties are secure only when God is recognized in His sovereign rule. The application to our own hearts and our own day is obvious.

THREAT OF DISPERSION (22:13-16)

By a gesture of scorn and indignation the Lord took recognition of the many defections of His people, now summarized under the heads of dishonest gain and blood. In all fairness the Lord asked the nation whether it felt itself equal to the stroke that He was about to deliver. Was there the remotest chance that they would endure, or that their hands would sustain them in the crisis? A strong negative answer was anticipated. In stating the outpouring of God's displeasure upon Israel, Ezekiel saw not only the punishment of the near future, but at the same time he viewed the worldwide dispersion and scattering of his countrymen. How literally this has been fulfilled to this very hour! But mark the purpose of this scattering: for purging the nation of its filthiness. God chose this method of accomplishing this high purpose, and His ways are as far above ours as the heavens are above the earth.

The grammatical construction in the original of verse 16 is difficult. One suggested reading is "I shall be profaned through you." The profanation had come about both by the evil lives they led and their unbelief in the power of God to preserve His temple and people. Some translate, "Thou shalt take thine inheritance in thyself." But this hardly makes good sense of the passage. The concept of God's profaning His people by casting them out of their land is thought to be seen in Isaiah 43:28; 47:6; Ezekiel 24:21; 28:16. However, others doubt that God's judgment on them in this way can be denoted a profaning of them before the nations; but the parallel passages would appear strongly in favor of this position. Israel, in the depths of her humiliation and despair, would come to know the Lord in truth.

JERUSALEM A SMELTING FURNACE (22:17-22)

In chapter 15 when Ezekiel wanted to reveal the worthlessness of the nation in its sin, he likened it to a useless vine. Here he conveys the same truth under the figure of a smelting furnace (cf. Isa. 1:22; Jer. 6:28-30). By her apostasy from the truth of God Israel had become as the dross which requires the heat of the fire and the labor of the refiner (cf. Zech. 13:9; Mal. 3:2-3). It would appear that they had become all dross with no benefit in refining them. They were silver dross, a symbol of that which is worthless. Because they had become so degraded, they were to be gathered for the melting process in the city of Jerusalem. God is a consuming fire (Heb. 12:29), so He would undertake the refining operation. And Jerusalem, instead of being a refuge in such an hour of testing, would be the furnace where the anger and wrath of God would be poured out. A fiery furnace was an apt figure indeed for the coming dread trials to be experienced in the distress and siege of Jerusalem by Nebuchadnezzar in his third invasion of the land in 588-586 B.C. Thrice God's gathering of them was stated, and four times His wrath was underscored. It is always a fearful thing to fall into the hands of the living God in the hour of His anger. He who minimizes the wrath of God against sin does despite to the truth of the holiness of God without which there can be no basis for a moral universe.

THE WHOLE NATION GUILTY (22:23-31)

As strongly as he knew how, Ezekiel leveled the charge of corruption against all segments of his people. The degeneration of all ranks of the nation was the immediate and procuring cause of the coming catastrophe upon Jerusalem. It made impossible the deliverance of the kingdom. Various have been the interpretations of verse 24, but the probable meaning is that the land had had neither human tending nor the blessing of God in rain. According to Old Testament promise rain was one of the blessings in the material realm which attended a walk of obedience. It was withheld to turn their hearts back to the Lord. What was the day of indignation? Was it the time of Josiah's death at Megiddo (about 609 B.C.) or the destruction of Jerusalem in 586 B.C.? Both the trend in this passage and parallel references would decide in favor of the latter.

In the indictment the prophets were mentioned first because their sins had the widest influence for evil. Throughout the books of the true prophets (especially that of Jeremiah) the work of the false prophets is seen as opposed to the true prophets (see I Kings 22). The rise of false prophets had been foretold (Deut. 18:20-22). Ezekiel gives as strong a denunciation of false prophets as is found anywhere in Scripture. The prophets were directly responsible for the multiplication of widows in the land because their husbands went out to battle against the will of the Lord after being deceived by the prophets of lies and flatteries. The priests of that day must have had great influence because they were enjoying a place next to the ruling house. Instead of teaching and upholding the law of God, they made it their business to blot out every God-given distinction between profane and holy. They belied their calling in particular after particular with the result that, instead of being magnified in His holy requirements, the Lord was profaned among them. They were timeservers of the basest sort. And the ruling house was not one whit better than the prophets and priests. Human life was amazingly cheap in their eyes; they went ravening, shedding blood and destroying souls. A sinful people was cursed with wicked and unfeeling rulers. All was done for personal advantage and profit. Material profit outweighed every other consideration. When such is the case, sad and precarious is the lot of the subject.

In hours of darkness and grief the true prophets held out hope and bright promise to the godly, but the opportunist prophets only manufactured their messages to suit the hour without caring that they had no substance in fact. They were meticulous about claiming the same divine authority as the true prophets, even using the same sacred formula "Thus saith the Lord," but the Lord had no relation to their claims or messages.

How were the common people of the land affected by such dishonest conduct in every rank of leadership? They followed the bad example of their leaders, employing oppression and robbery of the poor and needy. Moral standards were broken down on every hand.

One of the famous passages of Ezekiel's prophecy is verse 30, which reveals God as seeking for a man who would fortify (as a wall does) the people in their hour of need, so that they by repentance might not be defenseless before the onslaughts of their enemies. But God found none. How is this statement to be understood? Some suggest that a lack of a prophet or a king is suggested. It has been held that Ezekiel was not in the land of Israel, and Jeremiah had been thrown in prison. Another proposal is that there were those in the nation who were godly, but no one of them was of such strong character that his prayers could avert the threatening disaster. Still another view is that the ungodly could not avert disaster, and the godly would not because they had been warned of the futility of doing so (Jer. 11:14). Actually, the meaning is quite simple. Ezekiel and Jeremiah as authenticated messengers of God were naturally considered apart from the people in this matter. Ezekiel was declaring that of the rest of the people there was no one who could intervene by intercession and encouragement to repentance, to draw the nation back from the precipice over which they were plunging to their national ruin. Abraham had filled such a gap (Gen. 20:7) as had Moses long after him (Exodus 32:11).

With the entire nation so given over to every displeasing act, and no one to intervene for them, judgment alone remained for them. So sure was this visitation that Ezekiel thrice expressed it as having already occurred. The judgment had to overtake them, and it did in the calamitous fall of the kingdom and monarchy in 586 B.C. Since Israel's true King and Messiah, the Lord Jesus Christ, was rejected in His earthly ministry, the effects of this disaster go on to this hour.

"I Sought for a Man"

When Adam and Eve revolted against the clear command of God, sin became a reality in the human family, death an ever present specter, and redemption man's paramount need. For this infinite task God the Father sought a man. Thank God, He found Him in Christ Jesus. Now that the work of redemption is finished, God is still seeking for men to carry out the work of evangelization.

23

OHOLAH AND OHOLIBAH

THIS LENGTHY PORTION is a parabolic presentation like that of chapter 16. There the emphasis was on idolatries as breaking the marriage relation and the sacred covenant with God, here it is on the nation's worldly spirit and worldly alliances for safety and national security. Recitals such as found in this and similar chapters justify God's actions toward Israel. Throughout all these descriptions, distasteful as they may appear, it must be remembered that the symbol only faintly conveyed the gravity of the sin which Ezekiel was denouncing.

THE TWO GODLESS SISTERS (23:1-4)

For the purposes of the allegory the two divisions of the nation, the northern and southern kingdoms of Israel and Judah, were viewed as separate from the beginning. The single mother indicated the original unity of the nation. Some have understood the reference to be of Sarah, but this is not necessary. The daughters of this passage were designated as sisters in Jeremiah 3:7. There had been a division between Judah and Ephraim even from tribal days (see Judges 8:1; 12:1; II Sam. 19:43). Parts of the nation early strayed from God in self-satisfaction and ultimate self-destruction. Could Ezekiel have been referring to the period of friendly relations with Egypt? (Cf. Gen. 45:10; 46:2-5; 47:1-6; Exodus 1:8.) The passage is clear concerning their defection because Ezekiel spoke twice of their unfaithfulness. The golden calf episode reveals they were both touched by the idolatry practiced about them (16:26; 20:7-8), and the comment of Joshua was both interesting and determining in the matter (Joshua 24:14).

The names of the sisters are not identical in meaning, as some contend, though based on the same noun form. Oholah means "her tent," whereas Oholibah signifies "my tent is in her." The names would seem to imply that the Lord never recognized nor identified Himself with the worship which Jeroboam the son of Nebat had set up for the northern kingdom; however, He did own and claim that His sanctuary was in the midst of Jerusalem. There are expositors who strongly deny this inference, but their argument appears to have little foundation. The city of Samaria is called the elder because she preceded Judah both in defection and captivity. Another possibility is that Ezekiel had in mind that the northern kingdom was the more populous of the two. In spite of their failings God had compassion on them, and they became His by covenant relationship (16:8). Even the northern kingdom had prophets, such as Elijah and Elisha; it was not completely forsaken though its kings to a man wrought evil in the sight of the Lord. To press Leviticus 18:18 in this connection is to follow a crass literalism indeed, and to be unaware of the ultimate force of the entire allegory. Yet some liberal writers are guilty in this instance.

SAMARIA'S SIN AND JUDGMENT (23:5-10)

Ezekiel began his history of the two sisters with their political alliances which incurred the wrath of God. While Samaria was still the Lord's, that is, while under His authority (Num. 5:19-20, 29), she went astray with the Assyrians. This reference has been taken as an allusion to Jehu's payment of tribute to Shalmaneser III in 841 B.C., recorded on the Black Obelisk of Shalmaneser, now in the British Museum. It has also been suggested that the defection began when Samaria allied herself with Assyria in Menahem's time (II Kings 15:13-20), when the usurper needed foreign aid to stabilize his seizure of power (see Hosea 5:13; 7:11-13). The Assyrians were called the neighbors of the northern kingdom though they were seen in verse 40 as coming from afar; but the emphasis here was not geographic nearness, but spiritual affinity.

Oholah doted on the Assyrians because of their striking apparel, their high offices and their costly means of travel. The appeal, then as now, was to youth, strength, position, wealth and self-gratification; that is, the world in all its dazzle and attractiveness. The term "governors" (or "captains," II Kings 18:24) was used of officers in Assyria and Babylon, but more especially of the officials of the Persian monarchs (Neh. 2:7; 5:14). The title "rulers" was employed of Assyrian, Babylonian and Jewish officials (Isa. 41:25, ASV; Ezra 9:2; Neh. 2:16). Horses and horsemen were mentioned because the Assyrians, as the Egyptians, used cavalry prominently. Israel was deficient here throughout her history except during Solomon's day (Judges 5:10; Isa. 36:8; Zech. 9:9). It is clear from verse 7 that political alliances were only a wedge whereby idolatry was introduced into the nation (cf. chap. 16). When the prophets of Israel preached against confederacies with pagan powers, it was not from the basis of a senseless isolationism, but because one realm of national life always sheds its helpful or baneful influence on all other aspects, especially the spiritual.

Evil is always tolerant of other evil, so persistence in wickedness is to be expected of those whose heart has not been turned to the Lord. The days of Egypt referred to may have been the pattern for the days of the calf worship of Jeroboam. At Dan and Bethel the calves paralleled the worship of the bull idol Apis. The infidelity denounced must include more than the political alliances; spiritual apostasy must be indicated. Throughout the Scriptures it may be discerned that divine retribution operates in such a way that the source of sinful pleasure becomes the source of punishment. Samaria's lovers became her destroyers. They exposed her to shame, robbed her of her dearest possessions, her children, then wrought extensive slaughter upon her, so that she became notorious (literally, a name) among the nations. In general terms the fall of Samaria in 722 B.C. was thus stated (II Kings 17:3-6).

THE AGGRAVATED TRANSGRESSIONS OF JERUSALEM (23:11-21)

Hegel, though an unbelieving philosopher, was a close student of the meaning or philosophy of history. He said, "We ask men to study history. The only thing that man learns from the study of history is that men have learned nothing from the study of history." Did Judah learn from Israel's sins and punishment? She was actually more perverse and corrupt than her sister. One needs only to consider the long and abominable reign of Manasseh (II Kings 21:1-16; II Chron. 33:1-9). She had the example of the northern kingdom clearly before her, both as to the gravity of her transgressions and the severity of the punishment for them, but no impression was made upon the heart to turn to God. Just as Oholah doted upon the Assyrians, so did Oholibah. Ahaz placed the southern kingdom under the protection of Tiglath-pileser III (II Kings 16:7-10), a political maneuver denounced by Isaiah (Isa. 7:3-17). Both sisters followed the same manner of life in disobedience to the revealed will of God.

Judah's conduct became baser and more blameworthy with the passing years. There was much to help her on her wayward course. She saw portraits of the Chaldeans done in brilliant colors. There was enough communication between Assyrians, Babylonians and Israel for this to take place. The exiles with Ezekiel were certainly aware of these facts. The Assyrians (and probably the Babylonians as well) ornamented their stately rooms with marble panels which were colored and carved with reliefs. In view of the confirmed commercial communication between Palestine and Babylon, such representations could well have existed in the palaces of Judah. Compare the case of Berodach-baladan in the time of Hezekiah (II Kings 20:12-19; II Chron. 32:31; Isa. 39:6-8). The flowing turbans are confirmed by the monuments of ancient Assyria. The princes (literally, threes) were heads of the military forces who fought by threes in their chariots: one drove, one held the shield and one fought.

Enamored of the foreign nobility, Judah sent ambassadors to Chaldea to form alliances or establish good relations (for the time of Zedekiah see Jer. 29:3). Political alliances again led to religious defection. Verses 17-19 indicate Judah's vacillating policy in turning from one great political power to another in order to gain the greatest political benefit from her alliances. After she saw the emptiness of Babylon's promises, she returned for help to Egypt after Josiah's death. But the revulsion that results from sated passion overtook ungodly Oholibah. All ended in political antagonism and hostility. But her disgust was not complete enough, so she reverted to her previous ways. Her obscenities were done openly and without shame. Having forsaken God for self-interest and having abandoned reliance upon Him, Judah came to experience the bitterness of God's alienation from her.

Now her old sins from the days of Egypt were renewed; she reverted to her old paths. The grossness of her immoralities is brought out strikingly by verse 20. In Egyptian hieroglyphics the horse represents a lustful person. Asses and horses are proverbially lustful (Jer. 2:24; 5:8; 13:27). Thus was described the return to her first degradation. There is here a probable reference to Judah's calls to Egypt for help against Babylon (v. 27; Jer. 2:18; 37:7). This portion concludes with a summarizing of her past history.

THE VISITATION UPON JUDAH (23:22-29)

Four punishments were threatened in verses 22-35. The entire passage vividly sets forth how her companions in sin were the very ones who visited judgment on lewd Oholibah. The names Pekod, Shoa and Koa have been variously understood by interpreters. They have been taken as allegorical names for Babylon (Jer. 50:21) because it is contended that geographically it has been hard to locate these names in the confines of the land of Chaldea. Some have understood the names to represent titles of Chaldean leaders (so also the Latin Vulgate). Still others claim they are names of nations or tribes east of Babylon (or according to another opinion, east of the Tigris) which appear in the Assyrian inscriptions as Pukudu, Sutu and Kutu. The Assyrians referred to are those who fought in Nebuchadnezzar's armies. The same qualities (v. 6) that attracted her at first were those which accomplished her undoing and destruction.

Cutting off the nose and ears did not signify the treatment of prisoners by their captors; rather, it was the punishment of an adulteress, a horrible deformity. Such was the custom in Egypt, Chaldea and elsewhere. Beautiful women in the East wore ornaments in the nose and ears. The upshot of the entire sordid episode was that unholy love would be turned to deepest loathing (see II Sam. 13:15).

The Cup of God's Wrath (23:30-35)

The figure of the cup is employed in Scripture in two diametrically opposite senses. In certain cases it refers to the blessings of God poured out in abundant measure (Ps. 23:5). At other times it points to the wrath of God for sinners (Ps. 75:8; Isa. 51:17-22; Jer. 25:15-29; Hab. 2:16). In the highest sense it is used of the death of Christ for sinners when He drank the cup of God's wrath for us (see Matt. 20:22 and parallel passages). Judah would not only drink to the full the cup of God's wrath, but she would even gnaw the sherds of the cup. Ezekiel vividly portrayed the utter despair of the outcast who would drink herself to madness, tearing at her breasts. It cannot be repeated too often that the basic reason for all her distress was that she had forgotten God (22:12). Now she was to be left to her own devices and the endurance of all the woe her transgressions had brought upon her. Infinitely tragic is the fate of the individual or nation that has forgotten God. To cast God behind one's back is to commit suicide of the soul.

The Detailed Indictment (23:36-42)

No recital of apostasy is heart-satisfying, and least of all when it concerns those so highly favored of God as the kingdom of Judah had been. There is not in the realm of all the great literatures of the world so incisive and so scathing, yet so majestic and worthy in objective, an arraignment of the moral defection of a people from their loving and holy God. Ezekiel detailed a summary, beginning with verse 36, of the entire case against the nation (see 20:4; 22:2). It was a double accusation against adultery and murder. They dared to worship in the temple of God on the same day that they made their sacrifice of their children to Molech worship. They did for their senseless and worthless gods what the Lord would never have required of them. In profaning the sanctuary it was not that they worshiped Molech in the temple of the Lord (see II Kings 21:4, 5, 7); but by their actions they put the Lord and Molech on the same level. They saw no incongruity in their actions, first, offering their children in the valley of Hinnom, and then attending the temple and its services.

Then Ezekiel pictured the practice of lewd women awaiting their paramours (cf. II Kings 9:30; Jer. 4:30). The eyelids were painted with a black powder (stibium) to set off the luster of their eyes (for a vivid parallel see Prov. 7:10-21). And she senselessly abused the gifts of God, utilizing them for her wicked pleasures. Think of the outrage of it—using in this unspeakable fashion that which belonged rightfully to the worship of the blessed God whom she had so shamefully forsaken. She mingled sacred and polluted in an outrageous manner (cf. Hosea 2:8). The drunkards from the wilderness may have been her neighbors, Arabs, Edomites and Moabites. It is a sad portrait of merriment, debauchery and wickedness.

PUNISHMENT FOR ADULTERY AND MURDER (23:43-49)

It was, indeed, a sad commentary on the spiritual state of both divisions of the nation that the prophet of God was called upon to address Judah as "old in adulteries." The habit had become too ingrained to be thrown off. She was so steeped in her sin that she would not alter her ways. Whatever could be predicated of the immoral among the nations was tragically true of her. The righteous men were probably the spiritual leaders and remnant of the nation (Deut. 21:21). Some believe them to be the Assyrians and Babylonians who executed God's wrath on the godless nation. But it was not unusual for them to be so designated (see 7:21, 24). For punishment the Lord would hand over the people of His choice to be robbed and plundered by the enemy. Since adulterers and adulteresses were stoned (Deut. 21:21; 22:23-24), such would be part of the all-encompassing destruction to be meted out to them.

By punishment of the guilty ones the Lord intended to convey a spiritual warning to all men. Oholah and Oholibah were to be an object lesson to all nations. There was to be no escape for their sin of idolatry. God rightly will brook no rival. Through visitation upon their transgressions the ungodly will learn by bitter experience who the Lord truly is and what His righteous requirements for human conduct are.

POLLUTION AND PUNISHMENT

Just as it is heartbreaking for a parent to point out the failings of a beloved child, so much more was it distressing for God through His prophet to denounce the flagrant and blatant sins of His people. But as the moral Governor of the universe the Lord cannot look upon sin complacently; expiation must be made for the guilt of sin, and cleansing for its pollution. This has now been accomplished in Christ's work on Calvary, and it is our privilege to herald to the world the royal reprieve.

24

THE FALL OF JERUSALEM

THE PROPHECIES OF CHAPTERS 20-23 were given in the seventh year of King Jehoiachin's captivity (20:1). This prophecy was given two years later, the ninth year after the deportation in 597 B.C. Interpreters understand it to be January, 588 B.C. The chapter ends with the irreversible word that the judgment of God must fall on His city and people.

THE FIGURE OF THE CALDRON (24:1-5)

One is struck immediately with the minuteness of detail as to the day, month and year. Ezekiel, three hundred miles from the scene of the invasion of Jerusalem by the forces of Nebuchadnezzar, was nevertheless fully aware of what was transpiring in the doomed city (see II Kings 25:1; Jer. 39:1; 52:4). According to Zechariah 8:19 the day was observed as a fast day. But what was the purpose of the revelation to Ezekiel? It was meant to show that God was carrying out His will. He was commanded to write down the very day because of its importance, and because in writing the nation would have tangible proof of the accuracy of Ezekiel's prophecies. It was a red-letter day for the religious life of Israel.

In order to make clear that a figure was being employed, the prophet was commanded to utter a parable. The rebellious house addressed (as in 2:3) was, in the first place, Ezekiel's hearers, then the whole nation of whom they were representative. The charge to set on the caldron was repeated for urgency. The pot was a symbol of Jerusalem and was readily understood from the proverb current among them (11:3; for a similar figure cf. Isa. 1:25-26; Jer. 6:29-30). The figure had been used either in an attitude of false security or in despair. Ezekiel continued by an enumeration of portions of flesh that were to be placed in the caldron, with the good and choice pieces and bones evidently meaning the leaders of the nation. Not only were bones to be set inside the caldron, but under it as well, for bones of animals were frequently used for fuel. Here the city's inhabitants were intended. The fire involved was doubtless that of war. What ravages sin works in the individual life or that of a nation!

137

THE EXPLANATION OF THE PARABLE (24:6-14)

Jerusalem was addressed with woe as the bloody city, not the holy city. The word "rust" occurs five times in verses 6, 11 and 12 of the American Standard Version and nowhere else in the Old Testament. Some translate the word as "scum," but "rust" is correct. It was a symbol of the corrosion and corruption of the city and may have represented the blood of victims slain through intrigue and oppression. The emptying of the pot pictured in vivid fashion the exile of the inhabitants whom the captivity would touch individually and by a number of successive attacks. This time there would be no lot cast in order to spare any of the population. It has been suggested that on another occasion (597 B.C.) lots were cast to determine who would go into captivity. Now there was no choice nor alternative allowed (for this practice see II Sam. 8:2; Joel 3:3; Obad. 11; Nahum 3:10).

The reference to blood was meant to cover the nation's many sins, even when not directly connected with the shedding of blood. The setting of blood upon the bare rock indicated the openness of Israel's sins (see Isa. 3:9), for as her guilt was manifest, so would be her visitation before all the nations. According to Genesis 4:10, blood which was uncovered called for God's vindication of it (cf. Isa. 26:21). When blood was not covered with dust, there was a violation of the Mosaic law (Lev. 17:13). And the punishment was in kind: her own blood would not be covered.

The principle was enunciated by Christ in Matthew 7:2. Again, Jerusalem was denounced as the bloody city; Nahum (3:1) used the same designation for Nineveh. The term has in mind both the judicial murders and the sacrifice of children prevalent at the time.

Ezekiel then returned in verse 10 to the figure of the caldron, explicitly going through the steps of preparing a meal, all representative of the siege and distress of Israel's capital city. But the judgment was to be unusually thorough. The caldron itself was to remain on the fire until it also melted, thus doing away with the rust. That it had been emptied signified that a full captivity would depopulate the land. Moreover, it was not sufficient that the people only be destroyed; the city itself had to be demolished (see the injunctions for the treatment of leprosy in a house in Lev. 14:34-45). There was no mistaking the intention of God; in order to purge the city He would have to destroy it completely. Some feel the figure intends to declare that purifying judgments would be prolonged long after the destruction of the city, but the context does not compel such a conclusion.

In concluding this theme Ezekiel passed from the figure into the realm of fact. The nation has proved itself incorrigible and all pleas had been

unavailing, with even preliminary and token punishments having failed
to achieve anything of lasting value in the people's spiritual life. The Lord
had sought to purge them through the ministry of prophets, providential
dealings and calamities, but nothing procured the desired result. They
were now left to the dire consequences of their evil deeds. Thrice positively and thrice negatively God declared His unchangeable purpose to
visit His wrath upon them. He did not intend to reverse His purpose nor
relax it.

THE SIGN OF THE DEATH OF EZEKIEL'S WIFE (24:15-18)

This is a strange charge, not duplicated in the Scriptures, although the
general truth may be found in Jeremiah 16:5, where it is shown that all
personal sorrow will be eclipsed in the hour of universal calamity.
When God reached down into the very homelife of the Prophet Ezekiel,
as with Hosea before him, it became evident that the prophet was in the
truest sense God's representative to His people. God forewarned Ezekiel
that He intended to bereave him of his wife. When the wife of Ezekiel
was referred to as the desire of his eyes, it becomes clear that the ac-
cusations of harshness and inflexibility leveled against the prophet were
quite wide of the mark. Here is sufficient evidence of a tender and warm
heart. The separation would be with a stroke, sudden death. The word
in the original usually refers to a plague (see Exodus 9:14). Since it was
so sudden, it would all the more naturally call forth expressions of deep
grief. But Ezekiel was distinctly charged not to mourn; he was to restrain
his natural feelings. His suffering was not meant to atone for the sin of
the nation (as the Talmud erroneously assumes), but was intended to be
symbolic.

He was not forbidden to sorrow, for even our Lord wept at the grave of
Lazarus. He was only prohibited from a loud manifestation of it, which
was in contrast to the usual loud wailing on such occasions. The bereaved
even hired mourners, a fact which the writer has witnessed in traveling in
the Near East. So universal a calamity would normally call forth the most
general mourning, but every indication of sorrow was denied the grief-
stricken one in this instance. The covered head (II Sam. 15:30); the bare
feet (Isa. 20:2); and the covered lip (Lev. 13:45; Micah 3:7) were prohibited Ezekiel. Priests could mourn their near kin (Lev. 21:1-3), but
Ezekiel was an exception for a special purpose. It was customary in ancient times to have a funeral feast; the friends of the bereaved sent the
food as a token of sympathy (for the custom cf. Deut. 26:14; Jer. 16:7;
Hosea 9:4). Faced with this directive Ezekiel exhibited complete subordination of his own will and feelings to his prophetic office in the will of

God. In spite of the fact that he knew his wife's hours were numbered, he went about the ministry committed to him. What an example of obedience!

Ezekiel's Actions Interpreted (24:19-24)

Ezekiel's contemporaries realized there was some deeper and symbolical meaning to his actions. He had carried out God's injunctions for the purpose of arousing their interest, self-examination and obedience, and they knew that his conduct was meant in some way to convey a significant message to them. What they had already profaned by their wicked deeds God was now to profane by the sword of the invaders. The Lord through Ezekiel heaped up terms to impress the importance of His ("my") sanctuary. It was their greatest strength and pride—the object their souls loved. Moreover, the children who had been left in Judah and Jerusalem when their parents were taken away in captivity would perish by the sword of the Babylonians. Because of the widespread nature of the calamity and the vast issues involved for God and His people, no mourning would be able to do the occasion justice. Grief would be paralyzed; they would at the most mourn privately. In this manner Ezekiel became a heartbreaking sign to his people. In a real sense his sorrow was a double one: the loss of his wife and the loss of the sanctuary which he shared with his fellow countrymen. God was emphasizing that in a manner He was dissolving the marriage bond with Israel (a Lo-ammi ["not my people"] phase of their national history).

The Change in Ezekiel's Ministry (24:25-27)

The day referred to in verse 25 was the day of the destruction of the temple. Again Ezekiel through the Spirit underlined the worth and beauty of the sanctuary, that stronghold which was considered invulnerable to any enemy because it was God's dwelling place (see Jer. 7:4 ff.). And their children were equally involved in the catastrophe. Concerning the repetition of the day, see 33:21 when a fugitive arrived six months after the destruction of the city, an act which was the fulfillment of this word. Ezekiel was to be afforded an eyewitness report of the very events he himself predicted (for a lapse of time between verses 25 and 26 see Jer. 52:5-7; Ezek. 33:21). For about two years, from the commencement of the siege until the fall of the city, Ezekiel's prophetic utterances were curbed. His warnings had been plain enough. Once he had declared God's final purposes for Jerusalem, there was no further need to keep repeating God's threatenings. The die was cast; there remained only for Ezekiel to await the fulfillment of the predictions already uttered.

With the coming of the fugitive the mouth of the prophet was to be opened. The first mention of his dumbness was in 3:25-27. Until the news came Ezekiel was silent concerning Jerusalem, but he did prophesy concerning surrounding nations (these written revelations begin in chapter 25). Interestingly enough, from the time the word of the calamity arrived Ezekiel's messages were of a more consolatory nature.

"I WILL PROFANE MY SANCTUARY"

No human heart could fathom what this act meant to the heart of God. God had condescended to make Himself known in His temple, accepting godly worship there, ordering the ritual, and protecting the sacred place from foreign intruders. But when sin mars the spiritual value of temporal ordinances, God casts them off, for at greatest sacrifice God always maintains the righteous requirements of His law. That is why Christ died even though it broke the heart of God and Christ. How much does it mean to you and me? Does it command our conformity to His will in every aspect of life?

25

ORACLES AGAINST THE NATIONS

CHAPTERS 25-32 contain prophecies against nations who were in some contact with Israel. Seven nations were singled out for condemnation: Ammon, Moab, Edom, Philistia (chap. 25); Tyre and Sidon (chaps. 26-28); and Egypt (chaps. 29-32). In this chapter (25) the nations were in sequence from northeast to west. The dates vary in 26:1; 29:1, 17; 30:20; 31:1; 32:1, 17. The prophecies against the nations were inserted between predictions before and after the siege of Jerusalem. Thus those of chapter 25 are to be dated soon after 586 B.C. because they presuppose the fall of Jerusalem. The occasion appears to be the delight these neighboring nations had when Jerusalem was made captive in that fateful year.

Though directed against foreign peoples, these oracles were actually part of God's message to Israel. They must never be construed as ventings of national pride, jealousy or revenge. Ezekiel's aim was to set forth God's truth as it related to all nations in order to impress the hearts and consciences of his own coreligionists. To us these portions declare that God ever rules and judges with absolute justice. The principle of I Peter 4:17-18 is pertinent throughout this section. If God judged His own people, in justice He must judge the nations for their sins as well. The principle which is operative in Matthew 25:31-46 is seen as applicable here also: the nations are judged on the basis of their treatment of "my brethren."

Jonah and Daniel addressed their prophecies directly to the foreign nations involved, but it is most probable that the messages of Isaiah, Jeremiah, Ezekiel, Joel and Amos were not directly conveyed to the people concerned. Their primary purpose was for the instruction of Israel. It is remarkable that Ezekiel in his predictions did not mention judgment on Babylon, which was God's instrument of wrath on Israel. In this particular, contrast the extended prophecies in Isaiah, Jeremiah and elsewhere.

JUDGMENT ON AMMON (25:1-7)

The Ammonites lived on the edge of the desert east of the Jordan and north of the territory of Moab, specifically between the Arnon and Jabbok rivers. Their capital was Rabbah, the present Amman. They had joined Babylon against Judah about 600 B.C. (II Kings 24:2 ff.). In 594 B.C., together with Edom, Moab, Tyre and Sidon, they tried to influence Judah to ally against Babylon (Jer. 27:2 ff., ASV). According to Ezekiel 21:18-20 Nebuchadnezzar had set out against Judah and Ammon. But there is no record of an attack on Ammon; apparently it had capitulated and turned against Judah (21:28; Zeph. 2:8-11). Of incestuous origin, Ammon had displayed its hostile attitude toward Judah many times (see Gen. 19:37-38; Judges 10; I Sam. 11; II Sam. 10; 12:26-31; Amos 1:13-15). They sided with the Syrians in the Maccabean War (I Macc. 5:6).

The Lord's controversy with Ammon concerned their joy over the profanation of the sanctuary of the Lord God, which was a belittling of the honor and majesty of God. Their opposition was to the sanctuary and the land of Israel and Judah. They were completely out of sympathy with the manifested grace of God toward His people. Doubtless Ezekiel had also in mind here Ammon's seizure of Gad's territory when the Assyrians took the northern tribes captive (Jer. 49:1). Ammon was to be occupied by children of the east who would consume the produce of the country. Opinions vary as to the identity of the children of the east: some take them to be the Bedouin, the nomadic tribes beyond the Jordan (Judges 6:3); others feel they are the Ishmaelites; and yet others think they are doubtless the Babylonians. Although no group mentioned is automatically ruled out, usage would appear to favor the nomadic tribes of Transjordan. So complete would be the subjugation of Ammon by their enemies that their land would be freely used by the invaders. Ammon would be made to realize the gravity of their offense against the Lord God.

When the hour of Judah's calamity was upon her, Ammon's malicious joy knew no bounds (Lam. 2:15), with hands, feet and soul entering into this unseemly and unfeeling glee. God had taken notice of every action, and His judgment would be staggering. First, He would make them the prey of the nations about them; second, they would cease to be counted among the peoples of the earth; and finally, they would be utterly destroyed. Jeremiah 49:6 spoke of a restoration at a later time, but Ezekiel had no such message for them. Only thus would the Ammonites come to know the Lord, not in repentance but by the powerful and inescapable manifestation of God's wrath.

MOAB DENOUNCED (25:8-11)

The origin of the Moabites is given in Genesis 19:37-38. Their territory was the area south of the Arnon River along the lower region of the Dead Sea. The sin of Moab was that they claimed Israel was like all the other nations, which was scorn and minimizing of Israel's privileged position before the Lord. Israel's fall seemed to point to a failure of the Lord's purpose in her, thus reflecting on the power and honor of the Lord Himself. Now Moab was guilty of denial of God's special dealings and providences in Israel's history. For this insult and impudence the Lord was to open Moab to the depredations of her enemies. Beth-jeshimoth, Baal-meon and Kiriathaim were all sites north of the Arnon River. The side of Moab referred to apparently was the mountains of Moab seen from Jerusalem, with the side meaning literally the shoulder of Moab, for such was the shape of Moab's territory (for a parallel see Isa. 11:14). The phrase "on his frontiers" was literally "in every quarter," that is, in its entire extent. Ammon was joined with Moab in the passage, and the Jewish historian Josephus[1] records that Nebuchadnezzar came to fight against Ammon and Moab in the fifth year after the destruction of Jerusalem. The pronouncement of the Lord was that Ammon and Moab were not to be remembered among the nations. Both were absorbed by the Arabs. As indicated above, Jeremiah foretold the restoration of both Ammon and Moab (Jer. 48:47; 49:6). For further prophecies concerning Moab see Jeremiah 48; Isaiah 15-16; and Amos 2:1-3.

WRATH FOR EDOM (25:12-14)

Edom (or Seir) was related more closely to Israel than either Ammon or Moab (Gen. 25:23; Deut. 23:7). They settled the territory south of Moab from the Dead Sea to the Gulf of 'Aqaba. Conquered and almost annihilated by David (II Sam. 8:14), subjugated by Amaziah (II Kings 14:7) and Uzziah, they won back their independence at the time of the Syro-Ephraimitic (eighth century B.C.) invasion of Judah during the reign of Ahaz. Hostility to Israel was plainly laid to revenge. The phrase "taking vengeance" is literally "revenging with revenge"; it was to be an unrelieved, unabated revenge. For Edom's hatred at the fall of Jerusalem see Psalm 137:7; Lamentations 4:21-22; and Obadiah 10-14. For the hostility through the centuries compare Genesis 27:27-41; Isaiah 34:5-7; Jeremiah 49:7-22; Ezekiel 35:5; Amos 1:11-12; 9:11-12; and Malachi 1:2-5. The visitation of God upon Edom would render it desolate of man and beast, and that throughout the extent of the country, that is, from the south of the Dead Sea to the Elanitic Gulf of the Red Sea. Teman and Dedan cannot now be pinpointed with accuracy, some interpreters placing one in the north of the area and the other in the south, with others judging the reverse. An interesting feature of the prophecy is the statement that the vengeance (recompense in kind) of the Lord would be

[1]Josephus, *Antiquities*, X. 9. 7.

executed by His people Israel. Some students think this prediction was fulfilled when the Edomites were conquered by John Hyrcanus (134-104 B.C.) in 126 B.C. and forced to embrace the Jewish religion (I Macc. 5:3).[2] In this way Herod (an Idumean) was able to become king of the Jews. Now all three nations (Ammon, Moab and Edom) are known by the general name of Arabs. For the time, as Ezekiel foretold, they have faded from history as recognizable national entities.

PHILISTINES DESTROYED (25:15-17)

God accused the Philistines of having been motivated repeatedly by revenge and having carried on a perpetual enmity against Israel. Among the enemies of Israel the Philistines were more often referred to in the Old Testament than any other nation. They gave their name to the entire land although they were able to subjugate to their rule only a small portion on the coast. They constantly harassed and oppressed Israel until subjugated by David, who broke their power after their repeated attacks in the reign of Saul (I Sam. 13:17; 14). They were conquered by Jehoshaphat (II Chron. 17:11); subjugated by Uzziah (II Chron. 26:6); strong under Jehoram (II Chron. 21:16); powerful under Ahaz (II Chron. 28:18); subdued by Hezekiah (II Kings 18:8; Isa. 14:31); and confederate against Jerusalem (Ps. 83:7). Nebuchadnezzar invaded their land (Jer. 47). Other threatening prophecies against them are to be found in Joel 3:4; Amos 1:6-8; Obadiah 19; Zephaniah 2:4-7; and Zechariah 9:5.

When Ezekiel announced that the Lord would cut off the Cherethites, he was playing on words, as "cut off the cutters off." The Cherethites were a part of the Philistines (I Sam. 30:14; Zeph. 2:5). The Philistines originated in Caphtor which is Crete (see Deut. 2:23; Amos 9:7). At one time the Cherethites were part of David's bodyguard (cf. II Sam. 8:18; 15:18; 20:7). This awesome chapter of judgment ends on the reiterated note of God's fearful vengeance. Only thus would the ungodly realize the majesty and glory of the Lord of the nations.

ISRAEL, THE TOUCHSTONE OF THE NATIONS

It is solemn to consider that all four nations of this chapter showed vindictive jealousy and hatred toward Israel. The nations of earth refused to learn that God meant every word in the Abrahamic covenant of Genesis 12:1-3, 7. No nation under heaven could touch Israel for ill without bringing down upon them the wrath of almighty God. The pages of history are strewn with the wreckage of nations who, though great in the eyes and councils of the world, incurred the just wrath of an outraged

[2]Ibid., XIII. 9. 1.

God. While God reserved the right to judge His chosen people for their sins, He also reserves the right to judge those who spitefully treat the Jews, and thus bring reproach on the One who made an everlasting covenant with Israel.

26

THE SIN AND JUDGMENT OF TYRE

THE PROPHECY CONCERNING TYRE covers chapters 26-28. Ezekiel treated Tyre more fully than did any other prophet, the space given to the predictions against Tyre indicating the importance of the subject from God's viewpoint. Tyre was an ancient city of the Phoenicians, appearing for the first time in the Bible in Joshua 19:29. It was a great commercial city in Old Testament times and was prosperous in the Roman period even up to Jerome's day (latter part of the fourth century and beginning of the fifth). Tyre was destroyed by the Saracens during the Middle Ages and has been a sleepy south Lebanese town in recent history. The city was actually composed of two parts, one on the mainland and the other on a rocky island about a half mile from the coast.

During the reigns of David and Solomon Tyre exercised a great influence on the commercial and political and even the religious life of Israel. Hiram, king of Tyre, was a devoted friend of David (II Sam. 5:11), who helped him and Solomon in their building operations (see I Kings 5:1-12; I Chron. 14:1; II Chron. 2:3, 11). Though Tyre and Israel were friendly in the reigns of David and Solomon, they drifted apart later. Tyrians sold Jews as slaves to the Greeks and Edomites (cf. Joel 3:4-8; Amos 1:9-10).

The predictions set forth in chapters 26-28 have been fulfilled with unmistakable literalness (see Isa. 23; Jer. 47:4).

THE SIN OF TYRE (26:1-6)

Ezekiel gave the year and day in which Jerusalem fell (II Kings 25:2-4, 8-9), but the month was not stated. Jerusalem was captured on the tenth day of the fifth month of the eleventh year of Jehoiachin's captivity in 586 B.C. (cf. Jer. 52:12). The prophet directed his oracle of punishment against Tyre, the wealthy capital of Phoenicia which had held a supremacy among the Phoenician cities since the thirteenth century B.C. The Phoenicians were vitally interested in material civilization, were industrious, resourceful, skillful in the arts and crafts, adventurous as seamen; in fact, they were the famous mariners of antiquity. Sidon was the preeminent city at first, but Tyre attained its position in part by her strong natural location, situated as she was on the mainland and on a row of islands not

147

far from the shore. Tyre means rock. She was the commercial center of the Mediterranean world. As to political relations, Tyre sought an alliance with Zedekiah against Nebuchadnezzar in 594-593 B.C. (Jer. 27:1-6). Previously Sennacherib in 701-696 B.C. had taken part of the city on the mainland but did not capture Tyre itself, which resisted the Assyrians for five years. For thirteen years (585-573 B.C.) Nebuchadnezzar tried to take the city, and finally did reduce the mainland fortress, but the island city remained free. It was Alexander the Great in 332 B.C. who took the island city by constructing a road from the mainland to the island.

Tyre's exclamation at the fall of Jerusalem manifested unfeeling exultation over the calamity of Israel, as she looked for self-enrichment through the fall of God's people as a commercial rival (see Prov. 17:5). Tyre rejoiced over Jerusalem's ruin because free passage for her caravans would mean greater prosperity in trade. Taxes were doubtless levied by the Jews, here called the gate of the peoples, on caravans from the north to the south (Egypt). When Judah was strong and subjugated Edom, she controlled the caravan routes to the Red Sea, thus hindering the Phoenician tradesmen from gaining all the profit they hoped for. First and last, Tyre was actuated by commercial greed, and that at a time when far weightier matters were in the balance.

Ezekiel foretold a punishment suited to her situation on an island of the Mediterranean. Wave after wave of invaders were to beat against her to bring about her doom. The prophet could well have had in mind the successive invaders of the city through the coming centuries until it fell at the hands of the Saracens in the fourteenth century A.D. Walls and towers were to be destroyed, as in the invasion of Nebuchadnezzar. Then the dust from her ruined walls, homes, temples and palaces was to be scraped from her, leaving her a bare rock. This Alexander did when he built the road to the island. Rubble from the mainland city served him well when he built the causeway. Spreading of nets was for the purpose of drying them. Such has been the main use of Tyre for centuries. Although a part of the city has been reinhabited, it is desolate for the most part. Mainland Tyre has been so thoroughly devastated that the ancient site can no longer be identified with exactness. The daughters of Tyre (mentioned also in v. 8) were her suburbs or dependencies on the mainland (as well as her colonies) which would suffer the fate of the mother city.

THE PUNISHMENT PREDICTED (26:7-14)

In this portion of the chapter is provided a vivid description of the destruction perpetrated upon Tyre by Nebuchadnezzar. It is made clear from the first that the One who would bring about the fall of the proud city would be the Lord Himself, with the mighty ruler Nebuchadnezzar as His instrument. His name was spelled Nebuchadrezzar instead of the usual form because Ezekiel evidently desired to approximate the Babylonian spelling which has been found on bricks unearthed by archaeologists. The Babylonian *Nabu-kudurri-usur* means "Nabu protect my boundary." In verses 14, 19-21 the beginning of the end for the influential metropolis was set forth. At the time that Ezekiel wrote, the Tyrians were in open revolt against Babylon. The Babylonian monarch was designated king of kings because he had made many rulers subject to him. God had delegated to him universal rule (Dan. 2:37). The invader was seen coming from the north, which was the direction of invasions from Babylon into Syria-Palestine; also, at that time Nebuchadnezzar was at Riblah on the Orontes (see II Kings 25:21; Jer. 52:9).

Coming with a vast host the conqueror would carry out all the details of a well-planned siege. Verses 8 and 9 (ASV) give the usual method followed in the siege of a city. The forts, the mound and the buckler were all familiar features. The buckler or the testudo or roof of shields was used to protect against missiles thrown from the walls. The battering engines were the battering rams employed to breach the walls. The axes, literally, swords, were used in a figurative manner for all the weapons of warfare. Some have considered the first part of verse 10 a hyperbole, but it is not beyond the range of literal fulfillment. Because of the multitude of the enemy's cavalry, they would cover the city with dust upon entering, at the same time shaking the walls with the noise of the horsemen and chariots. Every street was to be commandeered and the people slain with the sword. The pillars spoken of were actually obelisks, and were probably those mentioned by the historian Herodotus[1] as erected in the temple of Heracles at Tyre. One was of gold and the other of emerald, which shone brilliantly at night, and were dedicated to Melkarth, god of Tyre (cf. I Kings 7:15). These impressive pillars would be demolished by the invader.

Commentators have long noticed the change of pronoun from the "he" of the previous verses to the "they" of verse 12. It is rightly understood that Ezekiel was carrying the picture beyond Nebuchadnezzar to other invaders as well who would complete what he began. Especially this would be true of Alexander. The riches and merchandise of Tyre would then be thrown into the sea (see Zech. 9:3-4). The American archaeologist Edward Robinson saw forty or fifty marble columns beneath the water along the shores of Tyre. With the destruction of the city there

[1]Herodotus, II. 44.

would be no occasion for mirth. According to Isaiah 23:16 Tyre was famous for its musicians. The threatening prediction of verses 4-5 was repeated to indicate the desolate condition of the once populous metropolis. Though Nebuchadnezzar did not wreak all his vengeance on Tyre (Ezek. 29:17-21), Alexander did accomplish his objective in 332 B.C. Because the Lord Himself spoke the word, His counsel came to pass.

THE EFFECT OF TYRE'S DOOM ON THE NATIONS (26:15-18)

So important a commercial center as Tyre could not be destroyed without repercussions upon all the nations surrounding her. The isles referred to in verses 15, 18 were the more remote coastlands, her neighbors who would be amazed at and lament over the ruin of the strong capital. Tyre as the mother city sent her priests to her colonies, so there were both political, commercial and religious ties between them. The impact of the news of Tyre's downfall was vividly portrayed by Ezekiel, who probably had the heads of the Phoenician colonies in the Mediterranean in view. They would consider Tyre's fall a world calamity. According to the customs of Oriental mourning (Jonah 3:6) the potentates would descend from their thrones. The Hebrew word can refer to any chair of an official (I Sam. 4:13), not exclusively to the royal throne, although it is used mainly in that connection. The robes and broidered garments were mentioned especially. The elaborateness of the apparel of ancient rulers can be seen from the sculptures of the Assyrian kings in Nineveh.

The usual Hebrew lamentation (kinah) meter was employed in verse 17. The dirge of the princes brought out forcefully the extent of Tyre's influence, her renown and the terror she instilled in the hearts of all (for a similar scene cf. Rev. 18, also with regard to a commercial power of vast influence). The concept of trembling, terror and dismay was repeated with each verse's mention of the isles. The colonies of Phoenicia were in Cyprus, Rhodes, Malta, Spain, Sicily, Sardinia, the Balearic Islands and Africa, with all looking to Tyre as their headquarters, and sending annual gifts to the Tyrian Heracles. Interestingly, the commercial activities of Tyre were not represented as oppressive.

TYRE'S DESCENT TO SHEOL (26:19-21)

So thorough would be the destruction of the once wealthy city that she would be comparable to an uninhabited city. Her desolation would indeed be complete. That the deep would be brought upon her could only mean that the Lord would cause the city's ruins to sink into the depths of the sea (this has partially occurred). She would be brought down to the pit of Sheol (for a parallel see Isa. 14:9-20). For some strange reason some interpreters have understood the people of old time to refer to those of Noah's day (II Peter 2:5), but there is no valid connection between the two concepts. Ezekiel was doubtless referring to those of former generations in general. Emphatically it is stated that the city would cease to exist. The Tyre of Ezekiel's prophecy fell never to rise again. She was personified as going down to Sheol never to return. The last clause of verse 20 has been variously rendered. Those who have followed the Aramaic translation have taken the last clauses of this verse positively, relating them to Judah. Others agree with the Greek Old Testament and relate both clauses to Tyre, rendering them negatively as "that thou be not inhabited, nor set thy glory in the land of the living." It is true that in the prophetic books of the Old Testament the land of promise is designated as the glorious or pleasant land (cf. Ezek. 20:6, 15; Dan. 8:9; 11:16, 41). But any connection with the land of Israel is far-fetched here; the context gives no warrant for its introduction in a passage so wholly given over to the condemnation of Tyre. Nothing in the portion can remotely serve as a transition to this thought. It is probably best to render as the English version has it, but to understand the reference, not to the theocracy, but to the whole earth in contrast to the realm of the dead just under consideration. The last statements of the chapter reinforce the truth that the ancient glory and fame would never be Tyre's again.

History does not state whether Nebuchadnezzar captured the city, or whether he left it unconquered. There are supporters of each position. The more probable is the former, but the silence of the Babylonian cuneiform records on the matter is strange, and the statement in Ezekiel 29:18 is equally mystifying.

A God of Truth and Judgment

In this day of loose thinking, loose living and loose holding of religious convictions, it must be emphasized that the God of the Bible is a God of truth and judgment. He is no respecter of persons, as has been discovered by nation after nation that has contravened His law. The identical principle is operative for individuals as well. Truthfulness is a becoming characteristic in all mankind.

27

LAMENT OVER THE RUIN OF TYRE

THIS CHAPTER IS A LAMENTATION over the loss of Tyre's earthly splendor, written in the kinah (lamentation) measure. The passage dwells on the worldwide trade, commerce and material wealth of Tyre. Throughout the chapter Tyre is likened to a ship, well outfitted, wrongly piloted and ultimately shipwrecked. Ezekiel's description is considered a classic on the nature, scope and variety of the commerce of the ancient world, together with an invaluable geographic list of the chief cities concerned. It has been claimed that, judging from a literary viewpoint alone, chapters 27-28 are among the most beautiful in the entire prophecy. Many feel that the vividness of detail of this chapter places it practically without parallel in the history of literature. The principle exemplified here in Tyre, that of selfish gain, characterizes the world today. To understand the chapter ethnologically one must study it in the light of Genesis 10; to do it justice from the viewpoint of prophecy, Isaiah 13-14 and Revelation 18 must be carefully weighed.

THE GLORY OF TYRE (27:1-11)

Just as the Lord God had expressed sorrow of heart over the sin and defection of Israel, He now through Ezekiel set forth a lamentation (the technical word for dirge, *qinah*) over the illustrious city of Tyre. God's heart is always moved for the destruction of the ungodly. The doom and sentence of Tyre were viewed as already executed. The situation of the metropolis was at the entry (literally, entrances) of the sea, referring to her two harbors, the Sidonian in the north and the Egyptian in the south. Her favored natural position made her the gateway for Mediterranean commerce to Asia. The boast of Tyre that she was perfect in beauty expressed her utter self-complacency, reminding one of the boast recorded at a much later date concerning Laodicea (Rev. 3:17; see also Ezek. 28:1-17 for the same proud flourish of her ruler).

Ezekiel began the description of the city under the figure of a stately ship, indicating the maritime power of Tyre by characterizing her moorings as in the heart of the seas. Her builders were, of course, her leaders and rulers. The aptness of the imagery of a ship is seen from the fact that the city proper, as already mentioned in chapter 26, was an island. The best of wood was used for all parts of the ship; the sidewalls were made of cypresses from Antilibanus, and cedar from Lebanon was utilized for the mast. Senir was the Amorite name for Hermon (Deut. 3:9, ASV), with Sirion the Sidonian designation for the same site. (See I Kings 5:10 and 7:2 for the supplies of fir and cedar given by Hiram of Tyre for the building of the Solomonic temple.) Tyre, beautifully constructed and well equipped, laid tribute on many areas to perfect her singular beauty. The oars of the ship came from the oaks of Bashan, the region east of the Sea of Galilee which still is famous for its oak forests (Isa. 2:13). The deck was constructed of ivory inlaid in boxwood. The use of ivory for ships and homes was developed to a high degree in Tyre (cf. Ahab's ivory palace after his marriage to a Sidonian queen, I Kings 22:39). According to the historian Pliny the best boxwood came from Cyprus. Kittim (or Chittim, v. 6) in this instance may have included not only Cyprus but other areas as well (Dan. 11:30).

Continuing his minute portrayal of the ship, Ezekiel stated that the sail was made from fine linen imported from Egypt. Though such use of this material may seem strange today, state ships in ancient times did utilize it, embroidered in colors also. Byssus (a fine linen) was one of the products for which Egypt was famous (Gen. 41:42; Exodus 26:36). Purple, taken from the murex shells, is found in large quantities near Tyre. Elishah has not been identified with certainty (the name occurs in Genesis 10:4 as that of one of the sons of Javan). Conjectures have identified it with Italy, Sicily and other places, but murex or purple dye was common throughout the Mediterranean region. An area on the Mediterranean coast seems to be indicated. The awning has been understood as the deck of the ship. Sidon and Arvad furnished the rowers for the gallant ship. Sidon was north of Tyre and the oldest Phoenician city (Gen. 10:15). In the poems of Homer the Phoenicians are called Sidonians. Arvad (now Ruad) was on an island north of modern Tripoli. These were the famous mariners of antiquity. The caliber of the crew answered to the splendor of the vessel.

Moreover, every ship in time needs servicing, and the ship of Tyre claimed the services of the old men of Gebal, that is, her rulers or governors. Gebal was the Greek Byblos or the modern Jubayl (Joshua 13:5), which was famous for its builders (I Kings 5:18). The calkers were those who repaired leaks and fissures in the ship. Not one land that carried on commercial and maritime activity failed to deal with Tyre. Barter, the basis on which ancient trade was carried on, went on constantly with all mariners of that day. Now the figure of the ship recedes into the background with the end of verse 9, and is not resumed until verse 25, although throughout the chapter the imagery is still implied. Because the Phoenicians were a commercial people, they depended largely on mercenaries for their army. Persia is mentioned here for the first time in the Old Testament. It was called Elam at first, and was just coming into power. Lud is the Lydia of Hamite extraction (Gen. 10:13). Put or Egyptian Punt (Gen. 10:6) was on the African coast of the Red Sea. The latter two, Lud and Put, were known as mercenaries in the Eyptian army (Jer. 46:9). They were quite at home in the metropolis, for when they were not in service, they hanged their shields and helmets in Tyre. Thus the great city drew mercenaries to her army from all parts of the world, making adequate provision for her defense. Actual defense of the city, however, was not entrusted to mercenaries, but to native Tyrians. The others were on duty on the field. The valorous men (literally, *gammadim*) were perhaps from northern Syria. Certain translations render the word as a common noun—"watchmen" or "warriors" or "valorous men." Being joined with Arvad the word has led some to connect it with a Syrian or Phoenician tribe. It is difficult to decide, but the first view may be preferable. In order to beautify further the illustrious city the warriors decorated its walls with their shields (for the custom at an earlier period see I Kings 10:16-17; for a later time cf. I Macc. 4:57). Tyre thus laid claim on many sources to enhance her beauty, fortify her city and spread her influence. Precisely the same spirit pervades the nations of the world today, but it is without thought or concern for God. Thus their doom is sure, and they only await God's hour.

THE COMMERCE OF TYRE (27:12-25)

With verse 12 began the recital of the commercial glory of Tyre. Notice the different nations, countries and cities plus the wide range of products and merchandise. Ezekiel artfully used a wide variety of expressions. The Tarshish spoken of in this verse, in verse 25, and in 38:13 was probably a town or area in southern Spain, the Tartessus of the extrabiblical sources, a Phoenician colony known for its wealth in silver (Jer. 10:9). Their ships were the larger merchant vessels for distant traffic, and Ezekiel gave a sampling of the metals traded. Next mentioned were Javan, Tubal and Meshech. Javan was the Ionians or the Greeks. The others were tribes from Asia Minor, north of the Black Sea, called the Tabali and Mushki in the Assyrian cuneiform records, and recognized as the Tibareni and Moschi of northeast Asia Minor to the Black Sea. Some think the first group lived southeast of the Black Sea, whereas the Mushki were their European neighbors, but the area referred to appears to be that between the Black and Caspian seas (see Gen. 10:2; Ezek. 32:26; 38:2; 39:1). From this passage, as well as Joel 3:6, the Greeks were described as slave traders. However, the others may be included as engaging in this same traffic. Brass was specifically mentioned as part of the merchandise, although it was actually copper, as throughout the Old Testament, for the alloy, brass, was not known to ancient metal workers.

The Togarmah that traded horses, war-horses and mules was probably Armenia, for the Armenians were a people in the Taurus country noted for horses and mules according to the historians Xenophon, Strabo and Herodotus (cf. Gen. 10:3; Ezek. 38:6). Some suggest Phrygia or Cappadocia, regions famous for horses, but this position is based on no better evidence than that for Armenia. In ancient times the horse was not employed for labor as in later days. Dedan (v. 20 also) is understood as an Arab tribe; another suggestion refers it to the isles of the Persian Gulf or Red Sea. They brought their wares not as tribute but as payment in merchandise. Horns of ivory were the tusks of elephants. Ivory and ebony are products found in India and Ethiopia, but ivory objects have also been discovered in Cyprus. Syria (Hebrew, *Aram*) has been emended by some to read Edom, which would entail the change of the Hebrew letter *r* to *d*. The reason given for the change, apart from the fact that it occurs in the Greek and Syriac translations of the Old Testament, is that Aram (Syria) is not on the way from Dedan and the coastlands to Israel (v. 17). But geographical order is not strictly adhered to in the place-names of the chapter. The handiworks were not those which they brought to Tyre, but rather those which she made. The fine linen was the Syrian byssus, and the costly gems were part of the trade from the north.

But Tyre carried on commercial relations with Judah and Israel as well. The kingdoms to the south traded wheat from Minnith, located in Ammon (Judges 11:33), and pannag, a type of sweetmeats made from honey, together with honey, oil and balm. Tyre looked to Damascus to supply her with her chief export, the wine of Helbon (or Aleppo), a vine-growing region northeast of Damascus. Its wine was mentioned as choice in the Assyrian inscriptions, a wine highly prized by the Persian kings (Hosea 14:7). Vedan and Javan (v. 19, ASV) made their contribution as well. Verse 19 does not begin with "And Dan," for no land or people in the entire list was introduced in this way. Furthermore, it could not mean "Dan also" (AV) for the tribe had been carried into captivity long before and would not be of such prominence to be mentioned separately and specially in this manner. Probably Vedan was a place in Arabia not mentioned otherwise. Some equate it with Aden, as they understand Javan to speak of Yemen. This Javan is hardly the same as that of verse 13; here it is identified as an Arabian city. The bright iron referred to may be the sword blades for which Yemen was noted. Cassia and calamus (aromatic cane) were well-known south Arabian exports.

And so the list of supply sources for Tyrian commerce continued. Dedan, which was associated with the Arabians (not the same as the Dedan of v. 15), traded saddlecloths, which were marks of luxury and eminence. Kedar was probably a nomadic tribe (the name is first seen in Gen. 25:13 as that of a son of Ishmael), with its people known for their large flocks (cf. Isa. 60:7; Jer. 49:28-29). From Sheba in southern Arabia (I Kings 10) and Raamah, which was probably situated on the Persian Gulf (Gen. 10:7), came spices, precious stones and gold. The towns of verse 23 were in Mesopotamia. Canneh has been thought to be a contraction for Calneh (Gen. 10:10), an important commercial city later known as Ctesiphon. Actually, Canneh and Chalmad are unidentified regions, probably in Mesopotamia with Haran. Eden, also an area of Mesopotamia, is the Bit-Adini in Babylonia. Its name is not spelled as the Hebrew name for the ancient Eden in Genesis 2:8 (see II Kings 19:12; Isa. 37:12). Evidently they carried on an extensive trade in yarns from Babylonia (v. 24). Works of art were described also. The description of materials and wares is so precise and detailed throughout this section of the prophecy that the impression is given that Ezekiel had seen the merchants with their merchandise. With the mention of the ships of Tarshish, the great deep-sea ships which sailed to the remotest parts, Ezekiel's sketch of the commerce of Tyre was brought to a conclusion, and there was a resumption of the figure of the ship begun in verse 4. What an array of merchandise, what a variety of wares, what a range of places, and all of it for self and pride! God was in none of it.

THE DOOM OF TYRE (27:26-36)

At the beginning Ezekiel assigns the cause of the downfall of the city of Tyre. Her rowers, that is, those who guided her course or her leaders, were represented as responsible for her ruin, yet Ezekiel maintained throughout that it was God who was the ultimate Judge of the prosperous and wicked city. The east wind, which usually causes great damage because of the violence of its gusts (Ps. 48:7), probably represents Nebuchadnezzar, as some ancient and modern expositors have held. It cannot speak of Alexander for he came from a western direction to attack Tyre in the fourth century B.C. The heart of the seas, which was the place of glory and pride at first, is now the grave of Tyre's greatness. The details of verse 27 were meant to emphasize the thoroughness of the destruction, with both crew and cargo mentioned.

Some claim that to speak of the suburbs as shaking (v. 28) fails to give good sense to the passage. The Latin Vulgate renders it "fleets." With the same verb Isaiah 57:20 speaks of the action of the waves of the sea, so "waves" has been suggested. Judging from the usage of the term in other Old Testament passages, it denotes open places on the mainland which belonged to Tyre. It is not beyond the range of possibility that here it refers to the entire territory of the metropolis. All men of the sea of whatever rank or station would lament over the shipwreck. The different manifestations of grief show how universal would be the lamentation over the catastrophe which would befall Tyre. Making oneself bald was a mourning custom which was connected with pagan superstitions and was forbidden in the Mosaic legislation (Deut. 14:1).

The actual dirge was placed in the mouths of the seafarers, who would be astounded at the city once so splendid but now so desolate. The metropolis that formerly hummed with the bustle and activity of merchants and mariners would be silenced. And again the emphasis was on her natural favorable position in the midst of the sea. The mourners would recount how Tyre had been the source of supply with her wares whereby she enriched many peoples by profitable exchange in trade. She was able to take raw materials and finish them for market. Her riches were famous for Tyrian gold pieces (called Suri) which were well known in ancient times. But when she met her doom, all who held commerce with her would be affected. Both populations and kings alike would be struck with astonishment and fear, so agitated and thrown into confusion that terror would show in their countenances. A final touch was given by remarking that the merchants would hiss at Tyre (I Kings 9:8). There would be elements of scorn, dismay at the calamity and even malicious joy. Fearful and unprecedented would be the downfall of this mistress of the seas; she would not recover from her blow.

RICH WITHOUT GOD

The record of Tyre has a peculiar relevance for our day, for those areas in which she excelled and was the envy of the entire ancient world are precisely the fields in which every modern nation seeks superiority. But Tyre has a message for our age, and it is that riches without God are unable to satisfy the heart of man and often keep many from dependence upon God. Has not this spirit invaded the church, and does it not pervade the lives of too many Christians?

28

GOD AGAINST TYRE AND SIDON

THIS CHAPTER CONCLUDES the oracles of Ezekiel against Tyre. Although it is one of the better known passages of the book, it has been the subject of much divergence of interpretation. Differences appear between those who are liberal in theology and those who are orthodox. Moreover, there are variations in view between expositors who are consistent in interpreting the passage literally and those who at specific points prefer a more symbolic or figurative sense. The chapter should be studied in conjunction with Isaiah 14 with which it has distinct parallels. The prophecy is said to refer to the king of Tyre then ruling, but a fuller realization is intended in an ideal personality according to some, or in a sinister figure, such as Satan or his masterpiece the Antichrist, according to others (see Dan. 7:25; 11:36, 37; II Thess. 2:4; Rev. 13:6).

According to Phoenician annals the king of this time was Ithobal II (called Ithobalus II by Josephus). The prophecy has been dated shortly before the siege of Tyre by Nebuchadnezzar (585-573 B.C.) during the reign of Ithobal II. It was with the spirit of Tyre that Ezekiel is dealing more than with any particular king. The chapter is full of remarkable imagery, and many find it permeated with much irony. It contains many expressions which still seem inexplicable.

JUDGMENT UPON THE PRINCE OF TYRE (28:1-10)

Ezekiel was commanded by the Lord to address the prince of Tyre with words of severest rebuke and judgment. Some think the prince of this verse and the king of verse 12 are the same person, while others find two separate individuals. Some identify the first person with the Antichrist of prophetic times, and the second as Satan. The term "prince" was the regular title of Israelite kings (I Sam. 9:16; 10:1, ASV) and was used interchangeably with "king" (I Sam. 13:14; II Sam. 7:8, ASV). Ithobal II was representative of the pride and self-sufficiency of his people. The application of the passage to Satan was common among leading Christian expositors in the latter part of the fourth century A.D., among them Jerome (cf. Dan. 10 for powers behind earthly thrones). However, the author believes that at this point the main figure was the actual ruler of Tyre at the time. Riches and power so fed his pride that he claimed himself divine; self-deification was his greatest sin. Others whose heads were turned by prosperity were Sennacherib (II Kings 18:33-35), Nebuchadnezzar (Dan. 3:15; 4:30); Pharaoh (Ezek. 29:3); Herod (Acts 12:21-23).

When the king of Tyre claimed to be a god, he was displaying the same spirit as the one who promised Adam and Eve that they could be as God (Gen. 3:5; see parallel sentiments in Isa. 14:13-14; II Thess. 2:4). Kings of Tyre believed they were descended from the gods, but here was an added emphasis of this king's insufferable pride and self-sufficiency. The seat of God referred to was Tyre itself which he considered a divine dwelling place. One suggestion says it was an empty throne in the temple of the god Melkarth at Tyre, which the king is thought to have claimed. According to the writer Sanchuniathon, Tyre was called the "Holy Island." Its maritime power is recognized when it was said to have been in the midst of the seas (v. 8 also). God's rebuke came with withering force as Ithobal was reminded that he was indeed man and not God. Here are both strong rebuke and irony to deflate the ego of the ruler of Tyre. Though he thought and acted as though he were indeed God, this did not alter the facts one iota. Reckoning it so did not make it so.

If Ezekiel meant in verse 3 to indicate that the king was wiser than Daniel in his own estimation, then the language would seem to be ironical, mocking the claim of the ruler of Tyre. But it need not have been ironical; possibly it was a serious statement of what he actually thought himself to be. The text shows how far Daniel's fame had spread by this time, even beyond the bounds of his own people (see 14:14, 20; Dan. 1:20; 2:48; 4:18; 5:11-12; 6:3). When Tyre was besieged Daniel had already been in Nebuchadnezzar's court about twenty-five years. The wisdom of Tyre's ruler was actually displayed only in material things and in the amassing of wealth, not in spiritual matters. The secret referred to, in view of verse 4, was probably the ability to accumulate riches.

Though man has repeatedly been warned not to set his heart on fleeting riches which cannot satisfy the soul (Ps. 62:10; Luke 12:13-21), he cannot in himself resist the temptation, as is all too clear on every side in our day as in other ages. By commercial enterprise and skill in arts and manufacturing, the people of Tyre were able to heap up vast riches. Homer spoke of their wealth in his day. In two verses there are six references to the riches of this commercial empire, which was so minutely depicted in chapter 27. It was this foundation in material possessions that gave Tyre, ruler and people alike, that sense of security, smugness and inaccessibility against which Ezekiel was thundering. The enormity of the presumption that mortal man could be God was repeated before the words of judgment were pronounced.

Though the invaders were not mentioned by name, their character and the punishment they would inflict were stated clearly enough. The strangers were the Babylonians under Nebuchadnezzar (Jer. 27:1-3) who were known and feared for their cruelty (Ezek. 30:11; 31:12). By 585 B.C. Nebuchadnezzar's armies had made their power felt in the ancient world. They were to mar the beauty of Tyre's wisdom. This strange expression seems to point to both Tyre's beauty and wisdom, or the beauty produced by Tyre's wisdom, in other words, the city itself with all its possessions. Claims of deity and superhuman powers would mean nothing to the invaders, for they would be intent on defiling (literally, profaning) the luster of Tyre, which had made such outlandish claims to deity.

Furthermore, utter defeat—as that suffered by those who are conquered in a sea battle—was in store for the Tyrians, as seen in the words "in the heart of the seas" (v. 8, ASV). The death spoken of by Ezekiel would be a violent one (Jer. 16:4), for the intensive plural employed (literally, deaths) expressed the sense of those mortally wounded (the same usage is in Isa. 53:9 when Isaiah predicted the Messiah's violent death). In view of the revealed weakness, would the King of Tyre still dare to claim divine honors and immunities? How would he evaluate his deity in the sad hour when he was found at the mercy of the enemy who would mortally wound him? The final statement of the doom was that Tyre's king would die the death of the uncircumcised at the hand of the Babylonians. This had a deeper connotation than the mere absence of a national custom or rite; it signified those outside the covenant with God. It is true, according to Herodotus' explicit account, that the Phoenicians practiced circumcision (not so the Babylonians), but the force was that the Tyrians would die a death of shame. The strong language was expressive of Hebrew scorn (I Sam. 17:36; 31:4) and was used of those whose bodies were either unburied or cast into the earth without funeral rites. For the Jew it had the same connotation as "barbarian" had for the Romans and Greeks of a later time.

LAMENTATION OVER THE KING OF TYRE (28:11-19)

If interpreters disagree on details in the early part of this chapter, their differences become quite pronounced at verse 11 even though all must agree that Ezekiel still had in mind judgment on Tyre and its ruler. Furthermore, all must concede that the description utilizes highly figurative language, and all who have studied the passage closely must admit there are obscurities and difficulties in any view. However, the importation into the chapter of a foreign mythology or pagan legends must be resisted. And language must be interpreted in conformity with the same rules of common sense that obtain in searching out the meaning of any passage; imagination must not be permitted to run wild. What, then, are some of the lines of interpretation suggested for verses 11-19? It is claimed that Ezekiel has adapted a popular story concerning a primal being who lived in the Garden of Eden and was driven out through pride. It is called by some a mythical tale of Phoenician origin here applied to the king of Tyre. Another view considers that Ezekiel was speaking of an ideal person.

But there are still other positions. The narrative behind the prophecy was supposed to be an adaptation of the paradise story in Genesis. True, it differed in many ways from that narrative, but that was to be accounted for by the addition of a greater amount of crude mythology. In this connection Isaiah 14:4-20 was cited as a close parallel. However, he who has a high regard for the authority of the Scriptures will not accept these explanations. Some feel that the implications of the story point to the first man Adam, the ideal man. The king of Tyre, of course, was compared to him. Still others draw unwarranted conclusions from the historical connection of Hiram of Tyre with the building of the temple in Jerusalem. There was supposed to be a contrast intended between the earlier fellowship with Israel and the later corruption which came in Ezekiel's time. Even the use of irony has not been ruled out in the interpretation of this difficult passage.

The author cannot follow those views which inject without support a foreign and false mythology, a legendary atmosphere or a hypothetical ideal personality. It cannot be conceded that Ezekiel was following a free imagination which admittedly was not usual with him. Instead, he appeared to have the situation of his day in mind with his attention riveted upon the ruler of Tyre, the embodiment of the people's pride and godlessness. But as he viewed the thoughts and ways of that monarch, he clearly discerned behind him the motivating force and personality who was impelling him in his opposition to God. In short, he saw the work and activity of Satan, whom the king of Tyre was emulating in so many ways. Recall the incident in Matthew 16:21-23 where Peter was rebuked by our Lord Jesus. No sterner words were spoken to anyone in Christ's earthly ministry. But He did not mean that Peter had somehow become Satan himself; He was indicating that the motivation behind Peter's opposition to His going to Calvary was none other than the prince of the demons. This appears to be a similar situation. Some liberal expositors admit that it would appear that Ezekiel had in mind some spirit or genius of Tyre comparable to the angelic powers and princes in the book of Daniel who are entrusted with the affairs of nations.

Although the ruler of Tyre deserved the punishment awaiting him, the prophet was commanded by God to take up a lamentation over him. Let it never be forgotten that God does not delight in judgment. It is His strange work (Isa. 28:21), whereas the work in which He delights is salvation and redemption. It must be repeated that the one addressed was not an ideal man expelled from Eden, some mythological figure popularly known or other individual, but the same monarch with whom the chapter began. But behind him stood one with whom he was compared. If Satan, who was far superior to Ithobal of Tyre, received just punishment for arrogating to himself divine prerogatives in the dateless past, then the ruler of Tyre could not escape the outcome of his defiance of the Lord. Because some interpreters are so willing to place this entire description on the human plane, they must surmise that the passage is full of Oriental exaggerations. If these be taken to refer ultimately to Satan, they are eminently intelligible and in place. The full measure of wisdom and perfection in beauty was predicated of the sinister figure behind Tyre. Some hold that in the Near East the king was the re-embodiment of the first man, but no proof is given from Scripture for this position and it is not substantiated here. The description exceeds what we are led to believe concerning Adam in Eden.

Oriental kings made lavish use of precious stones as ornaments, so the portrayal would have been readily understood by the one addressed. It is interesting to compare the nine stones mentioned with the jewels of the high priest's breastplate (Exodus 28:17-20; 39:10-13). Three are omitted in Ezekiel from the list in Exodus, an omission needlessly supplied by the Greek translation of the Old Testament, which varies from the Hebrew in a number of places in this chapter. Parallels of this nature need not be pressed for some hidden meaning. The stones evidently signified the beauties and glories that were bestowed upon him, just as the stones mentioned in Revelation 21 have such a connotation. And it is known that the Babylonians, as well as others, decorated the images of their deities with costly jewels.

What is meant by the tabrets and pipes? One view holds that he was charged with the music and praises of the heavenly hosts. There are reputable interpreters who understand the terms to mean females, that is, the king of Tyre is viewed in his pomp as surrounded by the women of his harem with their timbrels or tambourines. It is sufficient to see here a continuation of the description of the splendor of the angelic personality. The day of his creation cannot mean the day of the king's enthronement or coronation, because joy and celebrations were the order of the day of accession. Where would one find a parallel to this as speaking of the day of one's creation? This is in the realm of conjecture. Moreover, the portrayal is such that it cannot refer to Adam before the fall, and least of all could it be true in any sense of the king of Tyre; for the latter could claim such perfection for himself, but God would not concede it as this passage does of Satan.

Commentators who hold to the view of an ideal man (Adam) inject another figure at verse 14 whom they call the "guardian cherub." It is quite difficult to see the necessity for this here or in verse 16 when the language shows the same person is addressed as in verse 12. The anointed cherub was none other than Satan himself in his position of honor about the throne of God. The line of association, as suggested by some, is not that the cherub of Genesis 3:24 (which, incidentally, is not cherub but cherubim), carried over in Ezekiel's thinking to the cherubim of the tabernacle (Exodus 25:20), which were anointed. The cherubim of the tabernacle and temple which overshadowed the mercy seat were patterned after a heavenly prototype (Exodus 25:9; Heb. 9:23-24). By divine appointment this angelic figure was made the anointed cherub that covered the throne, and was set in a place of special prominence. Mark how Jude 9 attests the power of Satan even when opposed by Michael the archangel. The author fails to follow those who find the cherub's flaming sword (Gen. 3:24) compared with the flash of lightning, and then with God's thunderbolts in order to explain the stones of fire. The association of ideas is strange. Fire is a well-known symbol of God Himself (Heb. 12:29), and the manifestation of His glory is represented under the figure of beautiful stones (Exodus 24:10, 17). Simply stated, Satan originally had continuous and unhindered access to the glorious presence of God.

By what stretch of the imagination could the words of verse 15 be applied to any earthly king? They must be taken to mean prosperity without defect. This too could be valid for the king of Tyre only by exaggeration, and the situation does not necessitate it. Unrighteousness was found in the anointed cherub because he aspired to equality with God (Isa. 14:14); his damning sin was pride (I Tim. 3:6). With verse 16 Ezekiel was beginning his transition from the sinister personality behind the king of Tyre to the monarch himself. The violence might well refer to commercial transactions that led to violence, and the king did not check them but rather aided. Just as Satan primordially allowed his heart to be carried away with pride from the Lord because of his beauty and wisdom, so the ruler of Tyre was following that destructive example. As retribution the Lord, who cast Satan out of His presence in the third heaven, would lay the Tyrian potentate before kings as a horrible example, as a spectacle for both amazement and mockery.

Tyre boasted numerous sanctuaries, and the temples of Tyre were the reason it was called the Holy Island by the ancients. These temples were profaned because the king's sin was the occasion for their destruction. His own sin was the fire which ultimately consumed him (Isa. 1:31). That verse 18 refers to the phoenix, a bird consumed in a fire of its own making, is improbable and has little foundation in the text. The wording of verse 19 parallels that of 27:36.

From Isaiah 23:17 there is an implication of a revival of Tyrian commerce under Persian rule (Neh. 13:16). Two hundred fifty years after Nebuchadnezzar, Tyre was strong enough to withstand Alexander for seven years, having risen to power under the Seleucid kings. The Romans decided to make it the capital of their Phoenician province, and it was a flourishing town in the time of our Lord (Matt. 15:21; Acts 12:20). The geographer Strabo said it had two harbors. The town was in Saracen hands from A.D. 636-1125. Saladin could not capture it in A.D. 1189, but in A.D. 1291 it fell into Egyptian hands. Gradually its strongholds were reduced and it became an obscure site. Present Sur has no ethnic connection with the prosperous Phoenician city of antiquity. The site of the mainland city is uninhabited, as is most of the area of the island city. A few thousand people live on land adjacent to the ancient metropolis.

JUDGMENT ON SIDON (28:20-24)

Because Sidon was the seventh of the enemy peoples surrounding Israel, there are those who feel that the prophecy against her was included in order to complete the number of seven opponents. This is arbitrary and unlikely, but there are good reasons why judgment was due Sidon. Even in the time of the Judges (Judges 10:6, ASV) the corrupting influences of the Sidonians had begun. In Solomon's reign they were still prevalent (I Kings 11:33, ASV). Apparently Sidon was the headquarters of the idolatry connected with Baal, Ashtaroth and Tammuz. Judges 10:12 records a conflict between Sidon and Israel, but the infiltration of idolatry was the procuring cause of their punishment.

Sidon was twenty miles north of Tyre and was probably the parent city. It was founded by Canaan's firstborn (Gen. 10:15). Both Tyre and Sidon were compared to the cities where Christ had wrought His mighty works (Luke 10:13; Mark 3:8; 7:24). The city had been destroyed by fire after a revolt against Artaxerxes Ochus (351 B.C.) but was rebuilt later. The site is now known as Saida, a city of no great importance but a small seaport. The prophecy was general but the reasons adduced above account for the prediction of her doom. The Lord declared He would be glorified and sanctified in Sidon by the judgments which He would inflict on her in His righteousness. Thus would His righteousness be manifested and vindicated before the nations. Ezekiel specified the several forms of visitation which would overtake her. Because from Sidon had come wicked influences and unspeakable degradations in Baal worship, she was likened to a pricking brier and a hurting thorn to the house of Israel. This was a repetition of the thought found in Numbers 33:55. It is interesting to notice that no such thorough judgment was pronounced on Sidon as was uttered on Tyre. God judges according to righteousness and always in proper measure.

ISRAEL IN HER LAND IN PEACE (28:25-26)

As in numerous other passages of the prophetic Scriptures, when the enemies of Israel were judged by the Lord, her restoration and blessing were foretold. Notice how clearly the contrast was given in the famous prophecy of Isaiah 61:2. Ezekiel predicted the Lord's agency in the regathering from all the nations of their dispersion, and it will be accomplished in such a manner that the nations will have it plainly shown them that God's omnipotence has been exerted on behalf of His people Israel. They will no longer be uprooted from their own land but with ease and confidence will live in the inheritance given them by God Himself (cf. Isa. 65:21; Jer. 23:6; Ezek. 34:27; 38:8; 39:26; Amos 9:14-15). It is utterly false and wicked to claim, as some erroneously do, that the land does not belong to Israel, for this is to impugn the clear statements of God. All are to know the majesty and greatness of God. Fifty-four times Ezekiel used the expression or its equivalent "And they shall know that I am the LORD." The thought is that all people must ultimately know that the Lord is the source of all blessings, calamities and overturnings of nations, so that His will may be recognized by all men.

THE PERIL OF PRIDE

As probably nowhere else in Scripture, pride is set forth in this chapter as the destroying sin. It made havoc of the glories bestowed on Satan when he was yet the anointed cherub. Is there not a warning here for us also? There must be a recognition that all privilege and opportunity carry with them great obligation. God has shut up both Jews and Gentiles unto condemnation because of their sins so that He might have mercy upon all (Rom. 11:32). If you have received that mercy, then God expects that through the mercy shown you the gospel may be carried in love and gratitude to the unsaved.

29

JUDGMENT UPON EGYPT

CHAPTERS 29-32 deal with one theme: judgment on Egypt. This is the longest of the prophecies in Ezekiel against any nation. Some find three distinct prophecies in the four chapters (29-30; 31; 32); others, seven. Apart from 29:17-21 (dated 571 B.C.), all the prophecies against Egypt belong to the period 587-585 B.C., shortly before and after the fall of Jerusalem to Nebuchadnezzar in 586 B.C. The time was one in which there was a temporary restoration of Egyptian power, only to be followed by ultimate decline. With the rise of the Persians, Egypt became a Persian satrapy and, in turn, was dominated by Greeks, Romans and Mamelukes.

After the time of Joseph in the patriarchal period Egypt was a constant enemy of Israel except for a short time in Solomon's reign. Egypt periodically urged Israel to rebel against Assyria and Babylon. In Ezekiel's time, as in Isaiah's day, there was a conflict for power in Asia between the empires on the Nile and the Euphrates (cf. II Kings 18:21; Isa. 20:5; Jer. 37:5-10), and Judah became embroiled in the contest.

For a better understanding of the present chapter the historical background must be considered. Pharaoh Necho had been defeated by Nebuchadnezzar at Carchemish (605 B.C.). He was succeeded in 594 B.C. by his son Psammetik II who died in 588 B.C. His son Pharaoh Hophra (Jer. 44:30; the Apries of Herodotus) followed him. He besieged Tyre and Sidon, was unsuccessful against Cyrene and was deposed by Amasis in 569 B.C. Zedekiah, as his predecessors Hezekiah (Isa. 30) and Jehoiakim (Jer. 46), sought Egyptian help against the Babylonians. Ezekiel predicted Egypt would be a poor support in time of need. Isaiah (31:1) and Jeremiah (2:36) before him had condemned Egypt.

THE FIGURE REPRESENTING EGYPT (29:1-7)

The date given in verse 1 is explicit. It was a year and two days after Nebuchadnezzar had invested Jerusalem (24:1-2; II Kings 25:1), and seven months before its destruction (II Kings 25:3-8). The message of judgment was against the Pharaoh of Egypt and all his people. As already stated, this Pharaoh was Hophra, the Greek Apries (reigned from 588-569 B.C.); he was the grandson of Pharaoh Necho who conquered godly Josiah at Megiddo (II Chron. 35:20-27). Zedekiah was looking for help from him against Nebuchadnezzar. The Egyptians did cause the Babylonians to lift the siege of Jerusalem (Jer. 37:5-7), but finally the Egyptians had to withdraw (Jer. 44:30). What had incurred the wrath of God against the monarch of Egypt? The Lord described him as the great monster in the midst of his rivers. The king was spoken of under the figure of a monster, undoubtedly the crocodile, which was worshiped by the Egyptians, and was a symbol on late Egyptian coins (see Isa. 27:1). The rivers referred to were the streams and canals of the Nile. The expression was especially appropriate for the Twenty-sixth Dynasty of Egypt to which Pharaoh Hophra belonged because its capital was Sais in the heart of the Delta. The claims of the king were arrogant indeed (v. 9 also). Actually, instead of his making the river, the river made him, for without it the land would have been a desert. However, his dynasty had carried out improvements of the river and stimulated commerce with her neighbors. A contributing factor to this haughty claim of the king was the annual inundation of the land by the Nile which made the Egyptians feel they were independent of God. Herodotus[1] stated that Apries considered himself so strongly entrenched in his realm that no god could displace him. This boast is analogous to that given by Ezekiel.

The fish spoken of were the followers of the king. The king would involve his people in his fall because of their loyalty to him. God was pictured as capturing the monster by hooks in his jaws. Herodotus claims the Egyptians caught crocodiles with hooks on occasion, although Job 41:1 would appear to question the practical value of this method. But it was certain that the method would be effective in the hands of God for the monster and his fish would be hurled upon the wilderness and the open field, resulting in death for a sea creature. This was a severe rebuke in view of the elaborate preparations Egyptian kings made for burial in terms of mummification, pyramid construction, and endowment for sacrifices to be offered on their behalf. As carrion they would be food for beasts of the field and birds of prey.

The first reason given for the indignation of the Lord against Hophra was his inordinate pride. Here the second reason for the visitation was set forth: Egypt had betrayed and disappointed the confidence Israel had placed in her. Instead of a firm and dependable support to Israel, Egypt had proved to be a staff of reed. The reed was common to Egypt (Exodus 2:3), so the figure was readily understood by the people of Egypt. The characteristics which Isaiah had found in Egypt in his day were still true of the land in the time of Ezekiel (cf. II Kings 18:21; Isa. 36:6 with this

[1]Herodotus, II. 169.

chapter). Their deception had marked them through the years in their dealings with other nations. Any who were unfortunate enough to depend upon shaky Egypt were due for sore disappointment. Instead of security Israel found that in relying on Egypt they were lacerated and shaken. Ezekiel was setting forth the same truth so forcefully enunciated by Jeremiah: "Cursed is the man that trusteth in man, and maketh flesh his arm, and whose heart departeth from Jehovah," and "Blessed is the man that trusteth in Jehovah, and whose trust Jehovah is" (17:5, 7, ASV).

THE PROPHET'S EXPLANATION (29:8-12)

Ezekiel predicted judgment upon Pharaoh, his people and even their animals. History records the violent death which overtook Hophra, who after his defeat at Cyrene was dethroned and strangled by Amasis and his followers. Hophra's conqueror was not named. Devastation and desolation were foretold for the whole land. Only so could they realize who is the supreme Being in the universe, and the extent of His displeasure at the unlimited pride of the Egyptian ruler in claiming the prerogatives of the Creator. Such blasphemous pretensions could not go without answer from God. The ruin of the land was to be so thorough that it would reach from Migdol, the northernmost town, to Syene, the southernmost town in Egypt, thus comprising the entire country. Complete decimation of both population and animal life was declared by Ezekiel.

Because no such forty-year period is known in Egyptian history, some claim a literal fulfillment of the prophecy was never intended and that it is to be taken as hyperbole. But there is nothing in the context that would indicate a shift from the literal to the figurative. The forty years are reminiscent of the wilderness wanderings of their former bondsmen, the people of Israel. The period between Nebuchadnezzar's conquest of Egypt and Cyrus' victory was about forty years, so the forty years are understood as the period when Babylon was supreme over Egypt. Ezekiel, unlike Isaiah (19:18-25), does not relate Egypt to Messianic times.

Again Ezekiel foretold a forty-year desolation for the proud land of Egypt, and such desolation as would show her to be the most devastated and ruined of all the countries. As already indicated, though the monuments and relics of that land indicate nothing of this period, a fulfillment in the past is not thereby ruled out. Was there, indeed, a scattering of Egyptians among the nations and through the surrounding countries? Berosus, the historian of Babylon, states that Nebuchadnezzar, after he had conquered Egypt, took great numbers of the captives to Babylon. Others, undoubtedly, fled to neighboring areas as in similar cases. The

fall of Egypt was to be commensurate with the magnitude of her boast
and defiance of the sovereign claims of God.

THE HUMILIATION OF EGYPT (29:13-16)

Just as the forty years of desolation and captivity for Egypt are not
found in recorded Egyptian history, there is no statement concerning any
return from this exile. This should not concern us unduly, for those acquainted with the records of the ancient Near East realize how loathe
monarchs were to admit their defeats, let alone preserve the record of
them for future generations. Even the statements of Herodotus and the
Egyptian records, which tell of a period of prosperity after Hophra's
reign, need not be considered as disproving the predictions of Ezekiel.
If all the time factors were known, a reconciliation would be readily seen.
The restoration of Egypt would fit well with the known lenient policy of
the Persians toward subject peoples. The return announced here is not
to be confused with that foretold by Isaiah (chap. 19). The explicit prediction was that Egypt would be brought back to Pathros, which is Upper
(or southern) Egypt (see Isa. 11:11). According to many students of
Egypt, Upper Egypt was the original source of Egyptian power. However, it could refer, as a representative part, to the entire country.

But though they would be restored, they would remain a base and sub-
servient kingdom, shorn of former power and greatness. Egypt did suffer
from Nebuchadnezzar's invasion, and its rule over the nations was broken
and never regained. They declined under the Persians, the Ptolemies and
Rome. Egypt has been a weak country in the centuries since except for
a momentary revival of power during the Middle Ages. While Egypt is
taking on more life and prominence in our time, this is a far cry from the
might of her glorious days. This revitalization is paving the way, however,
for the realization of other prophetic utterances (for the future of Egypt
see Dan. 11:36-45). When Egypt was a world power to be conjured with,
the temptation was ever present in Israel to play her off against enemies
from Mesopotamia to Israel's discomfiture. But with the diminution of
Egypt's influence and the silencing of her voice among the councils of the
mighty nations, Israel would not be inclined to misplace her confidence
and trust in the broken reed of Egypt. God alone would be exalted in that
day.

NEBUCHADNEZZAR'S CONQUEST OF EGYPT (29:17-21)

This prophecy was given about seventeen years after that in verses
1-16 and is the latest recorded prophecy of Ezekiel, dated 571 or 570 B.C.
The prediction was evidently uttered at the end of the thirteen-year siege

of Tyre by Nebuchadnezzar. History is silent as to the outcome of this conflict, but this passage reveals that the conquest of Egypt was literally carried out by Nebuchadnezzar (585-573 B.C.). Ezekiel's statement in verse 18 has been taken to mean that Nebuchadnezzar was unsuccessful in his campaign against Tyre, but this is not the significance of the prophet's words. He is rather stating that the thirteen-year siege had not been materially successful. The army, wearing helmets and carrying materials for the siege, had no reward for their arduous labors. The Tyrians were able to send off their wealth, according to the statement of Jerome, out of the reach of the Babylonian army. Without booty the Babylonian commander could not pay his army, so he turned to Egypt to take its wealth. The kings of the Twenty-sixth Dynasty had engaged in commercial enterprises and had accumulated wealth. Nebuchadnezzar was thus unconsciously the instrument of God against Egypt; he was also doing God's work against Tyre, even though unwittingly.

The last prophecy of the chapter has been variously understood. Because of the mention of "that day" and "horn" the passage has been taken to refer to the day of the Lord and the raising up of the Messiah (Luke 1:69). Thus the prediction would be Messianic in the broad sense, and a revival in Israel would appear to be indicated. To say the least, this would be quite an abrupt change from the subject just under discussion, and how would it fit with the concept of Ezekiel's grant of the opening of the mouth in the midst of Israel in his own day? It would seem more consonant with the context to understand that Ezekiel is using a well-known figure of the budding forth of a horn, in short, the ancient glory of the nation would be quickened. With the fall of Egypt the affairs of Israel would rise. With such fulfillment of his prophecies Ezekiel's message would be all the more heeded. He may have felt constrained before this because of the unbelief of his people, but now he could command confidence and boldness in speaking for God to the people. Prophecy was meant to glorify God, to warn and comfort the people, and to minister to the servant of God at the same time.

A BROKEN REED OR THE ROCK OF AGES

What Ezekiel declared Egypt to be to Israel, disappointing her hopes and betraying her confidence, is what every prop is that man can muster to help him physically and spiritually. Man's efforts to please God are doomed to failure because, no matter how alluring, they all turn out to be but a broken reed, a mockery instead of a support. One sure foundation exists through the ages; it is the rock of ages (Isa. 26:4, ASV). All other ground is quicksand.

30

EGYPT'S DOOM NEAR

In marked contrast to the prophecy in 29:1 this chapter does not date its prophecy. However, the subject of the denunciations, namely, the land of Egypt and her rulers, is the same. There is no chronological data to determine the date of this chapter's prophecy. Some expositors divide the first portion (vv. 1-19) into four divisions on the basis of the words "thus saith the Lord" (vv. 2, 6, 10, 13) and the contents of the paragraphs. Since Egypt was a world power, her circumstances and experiences influenced the world about her.

Judgment on Egypt and the Nations (30:1-5)

One cannot understand the full import of the prophetic message of the Scriptures until he realizes that the prophets of God took God's standpoint in the matter of uttering judgment. Though wrath might be pronounced upon the enemies of the Lord and of His people, nevertheless the prophets fulfilled their commission with compassion and concern for those upon whom the stroke was to fall. If this principle is not given due consideration, the prophets may be made to appear as narrow nationalists who rejoiced in the calamities of their political foes. This is to misunderstand the prophets and to do them an injustice. As Ezekiel looked on to the hour when Nebuchadnezzar was to chastise Egypt, he saw it as a day of distress and mourning, of wailing and lamentation. Twice he proclaimed that the day of reckoning was near. The human heart is ever prone to put off the judgment of God, easily finding solace in the unfounded thought that if God's visitation be postponed long enough, it may never occur at all. The day was designated both as the day of the Lord and as the time of the nations. We dare not interpret the phrase "the day of the Lord" as though it were unrelated to the other important references to this time made by the Old Testament prophets and the New Testament writers (cf. Isa. 13:6, 9; Joel 1:15; 2:1, 11; 3:14; Amos 5:18, 20; Obad. 15; Zeph. 1:7, 14; Zech. 14:1; I Thess. 5:2; II Thess. 2:2; II Peter 3:10).

Some have interpreted the significant phrase to mean any time in which God's judgments are experienced on earth. Although such an interpretation will allow for all the references to be included under it, nevertheless it empties the words of their well-known eschatological force. They do speak of events in the far future when God will consummate His plans for Israel in the earth. The reference here is best taken as God's judgment on Egypt identified in principle with that day when He will call all nations to account. It will doubtless be objected that this gives the phrase little or no meaning for the hour in which Ezekiel lived. This is not necessarily so. Egypt's judgment was the commencement of worldwide punishment on all nations, especially those around the land of Palestine from whom Israel had suffered much. Nebuchadnezzar's victories prepared the way for the realization of the universal empire of the Gentile monarch. The day of clouds, that is, of calamity and distress, in that hour was but a link in the chain that will ultimately lead to the climaxing judgment of all time.

In the hour of Egypt's catastrophe others would learn the impotence of man before the scourge which the Lord sends against him. Ethiopia would be terrified at what would transpire in Egypt, for lesser nations have a way of looking for security to stronger peoples. Not only would many fall slain in the midst of Egypt, but great numbers would be deported and taken captive from their land. As a building Egypt would be overthrown. Everything upon which she relied would be swept away from her, with every support failing her in the hour of her greatest need. Of the confederates and provinces of Egypt mentioned in verse 5 (ASV), the first three have been before us in the prophecy of Ezekiel, whereas the last three are difficult if not impossible to identify with certainty. Ethiopia was referred to in 29:10, and is known into modern times. Put and Lud (see 27:10) were mercenaries in the Egyptian forces (Jer. 46:9, ASV). But who are the mingled people? The reference is so general that a positive identification cannot be made. They have been understood to be the foreigners who served in the Egyptian army as mercenary soldiers (cf. 27:10; Jer. 25:20, 24; 46:9, 21). Extrabiblical sources confirm the fact that Egypt made great use of hired soldiers from various nationalities. This is a possible, perhaps even a probable, interpretation of Ezekiel's meaning.

Furthermore, those who seek to emend the Hebrew text on the basis of the Greek translation will find themselves far afield. It is better to admit that Cub is unknown to us rather than to omit it or alter the text to conform to some preconceived notion. The identity of the children of the land that was in league has been a matter of some discussion. The original text will allow the rendering "the children of the land of the covenant" (ASV marg. and the Greek translation). Jerome and others have understood the reference to be to the Jews, for Jews had gone from Palestine and settled in Egypt to escape the troubles of their own country (see Jer. 42-44, especially 42:22; 44:14). In short, Egypt with all her confederates would perish under the rod of God.

DESOLATION OF THE LAND OF EGYPT (30:6-9)

Man is ever slow to realize that in the hour of extreme need, the arm of the flesh is always disappointing. Egypt would find that every ally and every human confederate would be unavailing when God brought her into judgment. "From the tower of Seveneh" (v. 6, ASV) may be read as "from Migdol to Seveneh," indicating the northern and southern limits of Upper Egypt. The visitation would be thorough, leaving no area of the country untouched. Ezekiel by emphatic repetition portrayed the utter desolation of the land, with the picture one of unrelieved devastation and waste on every side. Fire is a common figure in the Scriptures for war and its ravages (cf. vv. 14, 16; 15:5; 39:6). Just as fire is all-consuming and irresistible, so the visitation of God would do its work of extermination and extirpation. Again it was stated that Egypt's supporters would be of no help to her. Throughout her history she had made much use of the force and arms of her allies, but in the crucial and all-determining hour they would be useless to her. The Ethiopians dwelt without anxiety because as allies of Egypt they continually looked for protection from that quarter. With the fall of Egypt they would realize their own impending visitation. It is taken to mean that the Egyptians would flee by ship to Ethiopia. The terror and consternation of Egypt in that hour can only be likened to the time of Egypt's judgment when Israel was delivered from Egyptian servitude in the exodus (see Exodus 15:12-16).

GOD'S INSTRUMENT OF PUNISHMENT (30:10-12)

If the earlier part of the chapter has dealt with the judgment of Egypt in more general terms, now the passage treats of particulars and specific agents. It was the mighty Nebuchadnezzar of Babylon whom the Lord had chosen as the instrument of His wrath upon Egypt (cf. 29:17-20). The invader would decimate the population of the land, filling the land with casualties. It is with ample reason that Nebuchadnezzar and his people had come to be known as the terrible of the nations (see 28:7). Notice throughout this portion that it was the Lord Himself who was the motivating Personality. Nebuchadnezzar and his followers were merely agents in the omnipotent hands of an outraged God. When Ezekiel spoke of the rivers of Egypt, he was referring to the branches of the Nile in the Delta. The threat to dry up the rivers of Egypt was not a figurative expression but a grim possibility (cf. Isa. 19:4-6; 44:27). Apart from the Nile Egypt was nothing more than a barren wilderness. The worst calamity that could have befallen Egypt would be the desiccation of her river, for her life depended on the annual inundation of the land by the Nile.

VISITATION ON EGYPT'S IDOLATROUS CITIES (30:13-19)

In this portion Ezekiel mentioned specifically the principal cities of Egypt that were to be demolished. Some of them belonged to Lower Egypt, while others were in Upper Egypt. Ezekiel revealed a minute acquaintance with the topography of Egypt. The stroke of God would fall heavily upon the idols and images of Egypt, idolatry being the great sin of Egypt from earliest times. The Greek historian Herodotus related how Cambyses of Persia, son of Cyrus the Great, took Pelusium by setting before his army cats and dogs, sacred to Egypt, which the Egyptians would not attack. Fear instead of confidence would fill the land, and there would be no more independent rulers in that country. Pathros, Zoan and No were singled out for judgment. The first was the usual name for Upper Egypt; the second was probably the land of Goshen where the people of Israel settled (the Tanis or Zoan of Num. 13:22); and the last was No-Amon or Thebes, the ancient capital of Egypt. So many cities were mentioned in this section to show how universal the judgment would be. Sin or Pelusium, called the key of Egypt, was situated on the northeast frontier of the country. Though a mighty stronghold of the land, it would be brought low by the invaders.

Moreover, the enemy would feel so assured of victory that in the armed attacks to breach the cities, they would take no precautions for concealment as would be afforded by a night attack. Some render the last word of verse 16 as "all the day," which is a possibility. If taken in this sense, the passage conveys the thought that the enemies of Memphis would accord her continuous harassment. Aven, called Beth-shemesh (Jer. 43:13) or Heliopolis where sun worship flourished, would also feel the lash of the sword and suffer captivity with Pi-beseth. The latter was Bubastis where sacred cats were mummified. The cat-headed goddess was Ubastet. Herodotus claims that annual festivals there witnessed gatherings of about 700,000 people. How senseless is man in his perverseness about worship; he will worship even the lowest creatures rather than the blessed Creator. The young men referred to may have been those in training for the priesthood at these cities.

Finally, to complete the list, mention is made of Tehaphnehes, the Greek Daphne (see Jer. 2:16). This city, named after the Egyptian queen, Tahpenes, was a residence of the Pharaohs (Jer. 43:7, 9). It was the same as the Hanes of Isaiah 30:4. Darkness as a sign of approaching calamity would settle upon the city (see Joel 2:31; Matt. 24:29). The long-endured tyranny of Egypt would at last be broken. A cloud of distress and calamity would descend upon the once favored city, and her daughters would be taken captive. The reference could be taken figuratively of her towns, but the analogy of the young men of verse 17 would appear to favor literal daughters. Why such a lengthy and repeated recital of the visitation of the Lord? It was to underscore the uniqueness of the Lord. The divine purpose and glory were never lost sight of. This dominant theme must be stressed and reinforced again and again. No prophet does it more consistently or emphatically than Ezekiel.

PHARAOH BROKEN BY NEBUCHADNEZZAR (30:20-26)

The eleventh year of verse 20 dates back to 587 B.C., three months after the oracle in 29:1. Since the arm is the normal figure for military power, it figures largely in this last portion of the chapter. The breaking of the arm of Pharaoh may refer to the unsuccessful attempt of Egypt to help Jerusalem in the invasion of Nebuchadnezzar (see Jer. 37:5 ff.). But the defeat of Pharaoh Hophra may not be all Ezekiel had in mind; allusion could be made here as well to the defeat which Pharaoh Necho suffered at the hands of Nebuchadnezzar at Carchemish (cf. II Kings 24:7; Jer. 46:2). There would be no way to reverse the outcome of the conflict, and Egypt would be rendered powerless for any armed encounter. Her first reverses would not have been overcome before added and more severe defeat would be her lot. Because of the complete helplessness and defenselessness of the Egyptian population the people would be scattered abroad (see v. 26 for the same prediction). In the strongest possible terms the Lord foretold in verses 24-25 that it would be He who would use Nebuchadnezzar as His agent of destruction, and would make his military strength invincible. At the same time He would make certain that the power of Egypt came to nought. When will men learn that God alone is sovereign in the affairs of earth? When God arises to judge, neither the forces of heaven, earth or hell are able to stay His hand. At whatever cost, men must learn that God is Lord.

THE DAY OF THE LORD

When one collates the number of references to this awesome day in the Bible, he is struck with the fact that in a coming day God will no longer be silent in His government of the universe. He will take over and intervene manifestly in the consummation of the world's affairs. How is it with your spiritual house? Is all in order?

31

PHARAOH'S FALL

THIS CHAPTER IS CLEARLY AN ALLEGORY and resembles in content and purpose the portion on Tyre in chapter 27. Certain expressions ("garden of God" and "Eden") are reminiscent of chapter 28. Throughout the chapter there is a mingling of the symbolical and the real. There are also parallels to Isaiah 14:3-20. The Babylonians had brought the Assyrian Empire to an end, and they would be the instruments to do the same in Egypt.

THE GREATNESS OF PHARAOH (31:1-9)

The eleventh year referred to was that of Jehoiachin's exile, calculated to be June, 586 B.C., less than two months after 30:20, and about two months before the fall of Jerusalem. Obviously Ezekiel was addressing not only the Pharaoh of Egypt but his followers and subjects as well. The same wording closes the chapter in verse 18. Nor can we restrict the reference to the multitude to the army of the Egyptian monarch; it must include the people of Egypt. The question implies that his greatness could not be duplicated nor matched. Others think the answer should be that he was like the king of Assyria who was overthrown by the power of God through the Babylonians, just as Egypt would be. But the first view appears preferable in the light of the context.

Verse 3 begins with an attention-arresting call to direct the minds of the hearers of the message to fallen Assyria in order that Egypt would learn the futility of pride and self-exaltation against God. The Assyrian was not the name of a tree, as some have supposed, but that nation of Mesopotamia was compared to the lofty cedar. The figure of a tree was later used of Babylon under Nebuchadnezzar (Dan. 4), and by Christ in the parable of the mustard seed (Matt. 13:31-32). God was in effect saying to Pharaoh and his people, "If you are inclined to pride yourself on your glory as a mighty empire, just consider what happened to Assyria, described under the figure of a cedar." To read *Asshur* as *te'asshur* ("pine tree") is neither necessary nor more harmonious with the context than to allow the Hebrew text to remain without emendation. Some claim that the Assyrian has nothing to do with the discussion here; that is, the word is the name of a tree. However, the author contends that the Assyrian

177

was introduced by the figure of the cedar as a warning to Egypt. Others maintain that only the Assyrian was in view, but verse 18 indicates clearly enough who was the ultimate object of the prophecy. Besides, at the time of Ezekiel's prophecy, the Assyrian power had come to an end.

Because the cedars were as much as eighty feet in height and beautifully symmetrical, the Assyrian was likened to a cedar in Lebanon. Lebanon was mentioned because it was the region noted for cedars. As to literal fact neither Assyria nor Egypt was in Lebanon. By virtue of the thickly interwoven branches, the cedar afforded a forestlike shade. The top of the tree was covered with thick boughs. Another reading of the Hebrew text renders the words "among the thick clouds," but this is scarcely in harmony with the description of the majestic tree. All was meant to convey the idea of majesty and loftiness in nature to be compared and carried over into the realm of the political and governmental. Moreover, the cedar grew to such unusual height because it was so profusely watered. The waters and rivers referred to the Tigris River with its branches. But figuratively Ezekiel meant that the surrounding and lesser nations contributed to Assyria's prosperity, which in turn was channeled out to the peoples in her sphere of influence who were on friendly terms with her. With such factors contributing to her growth and increase it was small wonder that the Assyrian Empire flourished, expanded, outstripped all its neighbors and was unusually magnificent.

When Ezekiel referred to the birds of heaven and the beasts of the field in connection with the stately cedar, he was continuing to use figurative language. The last part of verse 6 shows the nations were intended (for the same symbolism see 17:23; Dan. 4:10-12; Matt. 13:32). All the nations that surrounded Assyria in the day of her glory were granted her protection and support in some measure. Again Ezekiel underscored that the unprecedented growth previously enjoyed by the Mesopotamian power was brought about by the many helpful and contributing causes which the Lord permitted to come into its national life. In verse 8 by four different expressions Ezekiel stressed that the glory of Assyria was unique. None could compare with her, and none could outstrip her. Why was the garden of God introduced here? It is very doubtful that the reference is like that in chapter 28. It must be remembered that Assyria was in that area of the Near East where the Garden of Eden was situated. The writer's purpose appears to be to compare Egypt's greatness with that which is indeed extraordinary. If nothing could be compared to Assyria in beauty, and Egypt is throughout this passage the other element of comparison, then it is clear that Ezekiel meant to underline the vastness of the power of the Pharaoh of Egypt. Finally, over and above all that natural factors contributed, God Himself bestowed greatness on Assyria. The other nations of her day were jealous of the favored condition and position of Assyria. What more could Assyria have asked for?

THE FALL OF THE KING (31:10-14)

Ezekiel was speaking in this portion in retrospective fashion. The subject was the judgment already experienced by Assyria through the Babylonians under Nebuchadnezzar. With the interchange of pronouns between "thou" and "he" it is evident that the prophet was mingling the figure with the reality. The lifting up of the heart explains literally that pride was meant by the unusual stature of the cedar. Assyria's great offense was pride, as it is of so many powers and individuals today. God hates pride because it always robs Him of His rightful glory (cf. 28:6; Isa. 14:13-14; Dan. 11:12). The human instrumentality which God used in bringing about the destruction of Assyria was called the mighty one of the nations, a reference to Nebuchadnezzar. It was the Lord who delivered the one power into the hand of the other, resulting in the complete expulsion of the Assyrian whose wickedness was his undoing.

The blow fell upon Assyria when the armies of Nebuchadnezzar had come to be known among the nations as a terrifying force to contend with. Carrying the passage back again to the figure, Ezekiel described the great trunk of the tree as covering the land and filling the watercourses. There is something sad about the felling of a stately and majestic tree; how much more is this true when the reality represented is a mighty nation with its many people. Those nations that had formerly looked to her for sustenance, encouragement and protection realized soon enough the futility of expecting any help from that quarter. In spite of their previous dependence upon Assyria, the nations that viewed her fall were ready to take advantage of her ruin. Like vultures upon carrion they were prepared to make the most of the downfall of that very power which had so recently been their mainstay and reliance.

With verse 14 the figure merges into the reality. God had an educative purpose in the fall of Assyria: to teach the nations the folly of striving for earthly might. The ultimate objective of the judgment was to deter others from the same disastrous course. The verse refers to all kings and rulers. Those "that drink water" is a poetic expression for trees that are fed by water and, in this instance, has the significance of a reference to the nations of earth with their respective governmental heads. Now, with the statement concerning the nether parts of the earth and the pit, the scene shifts from Eden, the garden of God, to Sheol.

THE DOOM OF EGYPT (31:15-18)

The Prophet Ezekiel not only described the condition and activities of Assyria during its power and earthly existence, but he also followed the ruined power after death. The aim of the writer was to present the effect of the judgment of Assyria and, through it, the more immediate subject of the impending judgment on Egypt and the rest of the nations. Just as mourners cover their heads when they are in mourning, so the Lord Himself inaugurated the mourning over the fall of great Assyria. The rivers and the great waters referred to were the canals and tributaries of the land of Assyria, representative in this context of the nations which were tributary to the Mesopotamian empire. The picture of the drying up of the water sources is in keeping with the figure of the tree. There is a subtle play on words in making Lebanon, which is literally the white mountain, to mourn or to be made black, for such is the meaning of the Hebrew original for the verb "mourn."

Furthermore, the great trees, speaking of the mighty nations of earth, took strange consolation from the companionship in misery. Thus is portrayed the effect of Assyria's fall on those in the nether regions. What about those who were allies and confederates of Assyria in the days of her prosperity? Could they render any assistance in the hour of disaster and calamity? Unfortunately those who were her support in her tyranny and were protected by her, were utterly useless in the hour of need, for they underwent the same fate. The question of verse 18, somewhat enlarged over the original mention in verse 2, would imply that Assyria had no equals. Now comes the application of the whole parable to Egypt. It is the answer to the query of verse 2, and indicates whom Ezekiel had in mind throughout his denunciation of Assyria and his description of her woes. The reference to the uncircumcised is especially forceful because the Egyptians did practice circumcision and were amazingly meticulous, as the pyramids show, about proper burial, so this placing of them on the level of those mentioned was the deepest disgrace possible to them. To the Egyptians those in this condition were outside the range of the civilized world. The entire phraseology was used of those slain by the sword and buried in a promiscuous way without regard for the proper dignities (see 28:10; 32:19, 21, 24). Ezekiel concluded with a most effective thrust, saying to Pharaoh Hophra: "Thou art the man!"

THE SIN OF PRIDE

It requires no special powers of discernment to realize in reading this bill of particulars in the indictment of the Spirit against Egypt that God is unalterably opposed to man's pride. He will not brook it in any of its numerous ramifications, for He loves humility. Let us ask God to humble us under His mighty hand that He may exalt us in due season.

32

FINAL LAMENTATION OVER PHARAOH

THIS PROPHECY, the final one in this section on Egypt, was delivered almost two years after that of chapter 31, about eighteen months after the fall of Jerusalem in 586 B.C. The chapter, one of Ezekiel's most vivid prophecies, begins with a description of the fallen king as in other prophetic lamentations. Viewed as a whole, the passage contains two lamentations (vv. 1-16, 17-32), one over the fall of Egypt, and the other over the burial of the king and his subjects. Only two weeks elapsed between the two prophecies (see vv. 1, 17). The first prediction is dated February, 585 B.C., eight months after the fall of Jerusalem. The twelfth year, the twelfth month, and the first day of the month was nearly two months (33:21) after Ezekiel heard of the destruction of Jerusalem through a fugitive.

JUDGMENT ON PHARAOH (32:1-10)

The subject of this prophecy is not in doubt, for Ezekiel was told at the outset that his lamentation was directed to the king of Egypt. The Pharaoh was likened to a lion, a well-known figure in Scripture for a powerful and invincible ruler. On land Pharaoh was as a lion; in the waters, as a sea monster. He was feared both on land and sea. Certain students of the Scriptures are quick to read into the words a mythology foreign to the nature of the Bible, finding here an echo of a chaos monster, reminiscent of a conflict between Tiamat and Marduk found in Babylonian accounts. But the passage supports no such concept. The monster is not a mythological creature but the crocodile of the Nile (see 29:3-5). Not the hippopotamus but the crocodile is seen as the representative sea creature for Egypt. The verb translated "break forth" (v. 2, ASV) is employed of the coming forth of an infant from the womb (Ps. 22:9), or of ambushers rushing from their hiding place (Judges 20:33). Here it describes the manner of the crocodile to plunge suddenly into a stream

182

and stir up the mud. The Egyptian king disturbed the even tenor of the life stream of the nations around him.

The figure of the net has in mind the capturing of lions because sea monsters are taken by hooks. God was the moving Personality throughout, for twice He referred to the net as His. The enemy (the "company of many peoples" being the Babylonians) was only an instrument of God's judgment. The threat to leave the sea monster on the land implies that it would be rendered powerless, as a fish is out of water. Moreover, the birds of heaven and the beasts of the whole earth would feed on the carrion (cf. predictions in Matt. 24:28; Rev. 19:17-18). If Egypt had any confidence in her size or power, this would prove to be no deterrent to the visitation from the Lord upon her. The flesh of Egypt's slain would cover the mountains, and her multitudes would only fill the valleys with more corpses.

The mention of blood in verse 6 is a possible allusion to the first plague of Exodus 7:19 (cf. Rev. 8:8 for the time of the tribulation). The "land wherein thou swimmest" should probably be rendered "I will water the earth with the outflow of thy blood" or "with thy outflow from thy blood." The land in view was, of course, Egypt. If Ezekiel's statement seems exaggerated, compare the parallel in the words of Tiglath-Pileser I: "The corpses of their warriors I heaped in heaps upon the mountains; the blood of their warriors I caused to flow over the clefts and heights of the mountains."

The figure now changes from that of a river monster to that of a great luminary in the heavens. There appears to be here a more general darkness than the one over Pharaoh's own country (cf. Rev. 8:12-13). Some understand verses 7-8 to be explained by verses 9-10. It has been suggested that Ezekiel was speaking figuratively of the political sky, but there could be an allusion intended to the judgment of darkness in Exodus 10:21-23. All creation feels the shock when one so mighty meets his doom. Notice that the figure is also employed in connection with the day of the Lord in Joel 2:10. The overthrow of Egypt was a prelude, as it were, to the destruction of world rule in the last days. Pharaoh, represented as a bright star, was to be completely darkened. When he was darkened, the others lost their brilliance in sympathy with him. The emotions suggested in verses 9-10 are grief, anger, dismay and terror. It is not just that the news would reach the nations, but that it would occur among the nations so that they would behold it. The results of Pharaoh's fall would be felt by people beyond the range of his knowledge. For similar reactions at the fall of Tyre see 26:16 and 27:35.

Babylon's Role in Egypt's Fall (32:11-16)

Both Jeremiah (46:26) and Ezekiel (21:19; 29:19) had already foretold that the king of Babylon would be the rod of God's chastisement on
Egypt. Now it is unequivocally stated again. The pride of Egypt would
be brought low by those who are vividly designated as the terrible of the
nations, a characterization of the Babylonians employed in 28:7. The
many waters referred to are those of the Nile and its canals. Neither the
foot of man nor the hoofs of beasts would trouble the waters any longer,
because both man and beast would be destroyed. Egypt would no more
be a source of disturbance to the nations surrounding her, for her doom
would be complete (cf. Zeph. 1:3).

When God promised to make the waters of Egypt clear, the passage
literally meant "cause their waters to settle"; with the settling of the mud
the water would clear. When waters are no longer trampled, they settle
and run smoothly. The allusion was to the words of verse 2. The rivers running like oil were figures of prosperity and life-giving blessing which
would issue after Egypt's usual power was removed. Some understand
this passage to refer to the Messianic age, but it probably does not look
that far into the future. Again the Lord emphasizes that the ultimate
purpose in His dealings with Egypt, indeed with all nations, is that all
may realize His supreme authority, power and deity. Since women in the
Near East were hired as mourners, the statement concerning their lamentation is especially appropriate (cf. v. 18; Jer. 9:17-18).

Egypt's Hosts in Sheol (32:17-21)

Verses 17-32 have been characterized as "the most solemn elegy over
a heathen people ever composed." This portion is a remarkable confirmation that beings have existence and identity after this life. It also proves
beyond a shadow of a doubt that after death destiny is fixed; there is no opportunity given to reverse decisions made in life. The month indicated
is assumed to be the same in verse 17 as that in verse 1, so the time was
then two weeks after the lamentation recorded in verse 2. The prophet
followed Egypt and her multitude beyond the grave (see Isa. 14:9-11).
It is not Ezekiel writing in the style and spirit of Dante (quite an an-
achronism!), but the reverse. Ezekiel is credited with doing that which he
prophesies, which underscores the certainty of that which is stated by
divine command. Pharaoh and his followers were to be cast into the pit
(v. 31). God's word is alive with power, so Ezekiel's utterance was
said to accomplish what God wills. Whatever excellence Egypt may have
imagined herself to possess would be as nothing, for her body would be

consigned to the grave as with all the rest. She was to be delivered up by God and drawn away to her deserved judgment. It is as though the command were addressed to her enemies. The king of Egypt was seen as descended into Sheol where the other nations would address him, speaking to him to taunt him because now he is on the same plane as they. The soul is conscious in Sheol for, as already indicated, there is existence beyond the grave and not extinction. Those designated as helpers of Egypt were auxiliary nations, but their help was unavailing in the hour of her extreme need.

ASSHUR IN SHEOL (32:22-23)

Next appears an enumeration of the prominent nations that would receive Egypt into Sheol. Some of those named had not yet disappeared from the pages of history, but their doom foretold of God was nonetheless sure and was viewed as having occurred. The nations may be divided into two groups—the greater, more remote nations, then the smaller ones near at hand. Asshur or Assyria was first because of the prophecy in chapter 31, and because her fall was still a recent event in world history at the time of Ezekiel's writing. Sheol was seen under the figure of a huge cemetery, where the nations that had been so dreadful in their history on earth had become helpless and despised in its depths. Notice how often these nations were described as having undergone a violent death, slaying by the sword, indisputable evidence that they were the objects of God's righteous judgment. The company referred to may indicate the many nationalities in the Assyrian Empire. Those who caused such widespread terror had become objects of horror and dread.

ELAM IN SHEOL (32:24-25)

Elam was already an independent kingdom in the time of Abraham (cf. Gen. 14:1). It was subjugated by Ashurbanipal of Assyria about 645-640 B.C. When it recovered its power, it became the heart of the Persian Empire after the Babylonian exile of Judah. Elam was destroyed by Nebuchadnezzar as foretold by Jeremiah (Jer. 49:34-38). The bed spoken of is her sepulcher. The repetition of phrases throughout the section emphasizes the dirgelike monotony. Though Semitic peoples generally practiced circumcision, these were described as uncircumcised to bear out the concept of their pollution and defilement.

MESHECH, TUBAL AND THEIR FOLLOWERS IN SHEOL (32:26-28)

Interpreters are not agreed on the identity of the people called Meshech and Tubal. Some regard them as remnants of the old Hittite people who were driven into the mountainous country in the eastern region of Asia Minor. Others identify them with the Scythians, seeing them as one people. But the Old Testament knows of no invasion of Palestine by the Scythians. Still others understand them to be the wild tribes who at times broke into the Fertile Crescent from unknown regions in the Caucasus Mountains. It is suggested that those meant were the northern nations, the Moschi and Tibareni between the Black and Caspian seas.[1] When it was stated that they would not lie with the mighty, the sense is that they would not have separate tombs but be buried in a common and promiscuous manner. Others would have a more honorable burial, so that these were not worthy to lie beside them. Those accorded an honorable burial would have their weapons of war with them in keeping with the custom of burying soldiers with their arms (I Macc. 13:29). Ancient Latin writers also attest this practice which was a token of respect for the dead. To declare that their iniquities would be upon their bones is to indicate that their sins would rest upon their own heads. The prediction closes with a direct address to Pharaoh concerning his certain doom.

EDOM, THE PRINCES OF THE NORTH, AND THE SIDONIANS IN SHEOL (32:29-30)

The same end would overtake Edom with her kings and princes (literally, chiliarchs) who were the heads of the leading families. In addition to her kings Edom had princes or dukes (see Gen. 36:40). Coming from Isaac, they were circumcised, but they would share the same fate as the foreign uncircumcised. Along with them the kings of northern Syria and Phoenicia would experience the righteous wrath of God.

PHARAOH'S DOOM (32:31-32)

When Pharaoh would see the great array of departed ones in Sheol, he would be comforted over his own multitude, his strange comfort coming from seeing that he was not alone in his misery and doom. His would be the dismal comfort of knowing others were companions in his misery. "My terror" in verse 32 is that which the Lord would impose on Pharaoh's followers. The scene of their actions was the land of the living, especially the land of Judah. In concluding the chapter, we need to remember the prophecy of blessing for Egypt in Isaiah 19:23-25.

This concludes the series of oracles against foreign nations. Those prophecies in chapters 35, 38 and 39 which denounce foreign powers have as their main emphasis promises to Israel. The chapters against foreign

[1]Cf. Herodotus i. 106; iii. 94. He speaks of them as a defeated people under Darius Hystaspes.

nations were uttered while Ezekiel was silent toward his own people. As already stated, Egypt was conquered by Nebuchadnezzar. The silence of the Greek Herodotus is far from decisive in this matter, for he was unable to read the Egyptian sources and received his information through secondary sources. Furthermore, the Egyptians were adept at covering their disasters. For example, Herodotus did not even mention the important Battle of Carchemish. Some consider the prophecy as completely fulfilled. Sin carries with it its own destructive power.

THE MONOTONY AND CALAMITY OF SIN

In reading this chapter, one cannot fail to be impressed with the monotony of the oft-reiterated punishment from the Lord on one nation after another. There is nothing beautiful in the matter of sin, for it is sin then judgment, just as effect follows cause. And think of the boundless and unrelieved calamity of it all. Such awaits every soul out of Christ.

33

THE PROPHET A WATCHMAN

CHAPTERS 33-39 are a unit and progressively unfold some of the most vital truths in Ezekiel's prophecy. Chapter 33 is similar to chapters 3 and 18; the repetition is doubtless for emphasis. It is erroneous to see here conditions of grace which prevail today; the setting of the passage is the age of law. One portion of the chapter describes human responsibility toward God's law; another section, the necessity for repentance (cf. 3:16-21). The passage may be considered as a preface to the prophecies of comfort and salvation which follow.

The only date in chapters 33-39 is that in 33:21, the fall of Jerusalem in relation to the reception of the news by Ezekiel. The fall of the capital city marked a turning point in Ezekiel's ministry. The prophet had anticipated and waited for the fulfillment of his prophecies some seven years; now they were realized to his sorrow. This chapter in a sense may be considered as Ezekiel's recommission for his prophetic task. He had not been in a state or period of suspended animation, as has been suggested, but was silent relative to the people of Israel while he uttered the threatening predictions of chapters 25-32.

THE DUTY OF THE WATCHMAN (33:1-6)

It was customary to place a watchman on the city wall in the time of a threatened attack from an enemy (for the function of the watchman see II Sam. 18: 24-25; II Kings 9:17; Jer. 4:5; 6:1; Hosea 8:1; Amos 3:6; Hab. 2:1). Though this chapter's discourse begins with a hypothetical case, yet it is clear that the directing Personality is the Lord who directs the affairs that touch His people. But also implied is the care necessary in choosing a watchman whether in the temporal or in the spiritual realm (cf. I Tim. 5:22; I Peter 5:2 for the N.T. counterpart). The command to speak is significant in view of the fact that Ezekiel had been forbidden to speak to his people from 24:26-27 until Jerusalem was captured and the news reached him. In the meantime, as we have seen, he had been proph-

188

esying concerning foreign nations. The watchman concept explains in a sense why Ezekiel had to predict so much concerning judgment, and why his earlier messages were warnings. The trumpet call was the signal of danger (see I Cor. 14:8).

Once the watchman performed his assigned duty, then it was the responsibility of all who heard to act accordingly. If the warning went unheeded, the faithful watchman who had done his prescribed duty was not to blame. All responsibility would rest upon the one warned. The figure of the blood on the head was taken from the sacrificial animals, where the offerer placed his hands on the victim so that the guilt in question might be transferred to the sacrifice. There is no question here that the captive was given ample warning, but he chose not to heed it, thus manifesting his own guilt. Had he obeyed the warning, there is no doubt that he would have escaped the invading scourge.

Whereas in verse 2 it was the Lord who would bring the enemy, doubtless because of Israel's sin, there is no specific reference to agency in verse 6. Now the case was one where negligence and remissness were on the side of the watchman, and his dereliction of duty was indeed costly. There is a sense in which the victim was taken in his own iniquity, for in a time of war and threatened invasion there is an obligation to watchfulness on the part of everyone. His negligence was designated as iniquity. But the watchman was also culpable, and the ancient law of Genesis 9:5 made him guilty of the blood of his brother.

The Function of the Watchman (33:7-9)

There is scarcely a new appointment intended in these verses, but a reaffirmation of the position he had held as indicated in chapter 3. In distinction to the setting on the part of the people of the land, God called His watchman. Ezekiel's obligation outweighed that of any earthly watchman because the area of his specific interest was the spiritual realm. When he transmitted the message given him by God, it was made clear that the sinner could meet with a violent death in case there was no repentance. Notice the appeal was directly to the wicked man. God's dealings are personal, and they were not to think that they were lost in the mass regardless of their individual spiritual condition. Once the warning was sounded, the watchman would have delivered his soul and be free of the guilt of bringing about the death of his countryman. In the spiritual realm this was the confidence of Paul in Acts 20:26. As for Ezekiel, he had in fact done this in his ministry to Israel, though Jerusalem fell in spite of it.

THE RESPONSIBILITY OF THE HEARER (33:10-20)

For a parallel to this portion of the chapter compare the teaching of chapter 18. The principle was set forth that no one was to think of himself as in a hopeless condition because of failure to obey God's law. Upon repentance, mercy would surely follow. Contrariwise, no man was to feel he could glory in his own righteousness, and thus become careless after living in obedience to the law. The people were complaining that they were pining away (literally, rotting) in their transgressions and sins. In view of this despondency it was difficult for Ezekiel's message to have any effect. Since their calamities were unusual (cf. Lam. 1:12; 2:13, 20), they felt that their doom was sealed and complete destruction awaited them. At first they would not believe his prophecies; now that they had been literally fulfilled, in despair they asked if there was any hope for them.

How Ezekiel pleaded with his people to turn to the Lord and live! God's answer to their despair of life was that He desired that men live, and the past was not irrevocable. Here is a reaffirmation of the truth of 18:23, 32 (see II Peter 3:9). In verse 11 appears a beautiful blending of compassion with the demands of God's holiness, exhibiting both a yearning and a tenderness on God's part toward Israel. Should death issue as a consequence, it would be the result of their own will and not God's. Repentance and forgiveness were available to all. But God's law requires continued, not sporadic, obedience to its precepts. The question of the eternal salvation of the soul is not in view here. A man's destiny will be determined on the basis of his conduct at the time of judgment, and the judgment under consideration is, of course, one in this life alone. The chapter is not dwelling on matters after death. Moreover, no man can presume on past good deeds as granting him license for evil. When Ezekiel spoke of living, he was stressing the thought of having the favor of God and the external benefits manifesting it.

Here as in chapter 18 Ezekiel contrasted the wicked and his ways with the previous example of the outwardly righteous (cf. 18:21). Examples of what a return to righteousness involved are given in Exodus 22:1-2 and Numbers 5:6-7. When Ezekiel referred to statutes of life, he had in mind those principles of conduct wherein a man should live. The inability was on man's part; there was no weakness or defect in the law itself (for the same concept see 20:11; Lev. 18:5). Further revelation was needed, and it was given to Paul, to show how the weakness of the flesh prevented meeting the requirements of the law (cf. Rom. 7:10, 12; 8:3; Gal. 3:21; Heb. 7:19).

Because many in Israel did not comprehend God's principles of operation, they blamed Him for the calamities that had overtaken them, complaining that His moral dealings were not equitable. How often we hear unthinking men accuse God of unfairness. Actually, they were being judged for their own sins. As in every case where the Lord's justice was questioned, Ezekiel was quick to vindicate God's dealings. When sinful man sits in judgment upon God, there is immediate evidence of the partiality and unfairness of his own actions.

The prophet summarized in verses 18-19 the principles enunciated in the passage. Again it is imperative to stress that he was speaking of a judgment on this side of the grave and not of judgment in an eschatological or final sense. His concluding remark in this portion was to remind them of their defiant indictment of God's ways and the certain judgment that awaited each individual involved.

THE FALL OF JERUSALEM ANNOUNCED (33:21-22)

In these verses appears the record of the fulfillment of the promise to Ezekiel in 24:25-27. For years he had been warning his people that Jerusalem could not stand against the Babylonians because God was not with them to protect them. At last God's predictions were fulfilled, and Ezekiel was informed of the fall of Jerusalem by those who had escaped the disaster. Here was the confirmation of all his prophecies. The date of the fall of Jerusalem was 586 B.C. The Syriac version and some Hebrew manuscripts read eleventh instead of twelfth year, which would allow six months rather than a year and a half for the news of Jerusalem's fall to reach the exiles, and many accept this date. The captivity referred to was that of Jehoiachin (see 1:2). The Hebrew word for "one that had escaped" could be a collective noun and no doubt refers to a number of fugitives (cf. Isa. 15:9; Jer. 48:19; Amos 9:1). If the noun be taken as a collective, then it would have required time to assemble the escaped remnant, which could have consumed the time indicated. Some feel Ezekiel could not have received the message earlier than a year and five months after the fall of Jerusalem. There were confusion, difficulty in travel with the burden of their belongings, hesitancy and fear to enter the enemy's country, and other causes to hinder speed and progress. Now Ezekiel was free to carry on a work of reconstruction and hope. Evidently before the escaped of Jerusalem had come to Ezekiel, the prophet had been greatly agitated in his spirit in preparation for the message he was to hear the next day. By revelation he knew of the fall of the city before the message arrived. It was more than a case (as some have suggested) of telepathy when the expression of the hand of the Lord upon Ezekiel is followed through the book. The opening of his mouth took place the night before the fugitives arrived. The message received (v. 21) gave him confidence to speak further to his fellow exiles. He was at liberty again to denounce Israel's sin in order to bring them to the place of blessing under God's prospering hand.

PROPHECY AGAINST THE REMNANT IN JUDAH (33:23-29)

There is no date attached to the prophecies from 33:23—39:29. Chapters 40-48 are dated more than twelve years after 33:21-22. The first message after the fall of Jerusalem was one of rebuke of the people's carnal confidence. The unrighteous were to have no part in the land of Israel but were to experience God's judgment. The prophecy was directed against those who remained in the land of promise after Jerusalem's fall. Ezekiel had predicted the destruction of the city of Jerusalem because of their sin, and it happened; he then warned the survivors that their continuance in sin would bring certain judgment upon them. The truth of verses 24-29 follows the message already stated in verses 1-20.

By some strange logic they reasoned that if God gave Abraham the land when he was alone, surely the land would be more firmly theirs because of their great number. Even under Gedaliah and in the midst of desolation— the evidence of God's fulfillment of His threatenings against their sin— they were still confident and hopeful of deliverance, even though they had not turned to the Lord in repentance. It was known that the land was given to Abraham for his descendants to possess and, though decimated through war, they still were many compared to the single individual Abraham. They were actually arguing on the basis of the promises of God to Abraham, which they felt had to be fulfilled in spite of the disaster that had befallen their land (for a similar spirit see Matt. 3:9; Luke 3:8; John 8:33, 39). They were basing their claim on quantity instead of quality.

Men in all generations seek to substitute considerations of heredity for heart obedience to God. They felt the land must be theirs in spite of the desolation of Jerusalem because of the covenants of promise. They overlooked the fact that occupation of the land depended on certain well-defined conditions. Sadly enough, their voice was not the voice of faith. Ezekiel repudiated their claim with force, and specified the basis of his statement. They were eating flesh with the blood, even though flesh was to have the blood drawn away before they were permitted to eat it. Breaking the neck was insufficient (see Gen. 9:4; Lev. 3:17; 7:26-27; 17:10; 19:26). The survivors in the land continued in their former sins, their sinful lives precluding their inheriting the land.

Moreover, they gave themselves to shedding of blood, relying upon and putting their confidence in violence. They supported themselves by force and not upon right. It has been suggested that this statement shows that news had reached Ezekiel of the assassination of Gedaliah, the governor of Judah, but this cannot be verified. The abomination referred to is mainly applied to idolatrous worship and practices, which were accompanied by the basest forms of immorality. Furthermore, the fact that they were spared thus far was no guarantee that they were beyond God's chastening hand. All types of judgment would overtake them, with the very object of their confidence, the sword (v. 26), becoming the means of their undoing. So it happened; some fell by Ishmael, whereas others by the retributive action of the Babylonians for the assassination of Gedaliah, whom Babylon had appointed governor (cf. Jer. 40-44). Desolation would reign on every hand and, because of the fear of disease and wild beasts, there would be no travelers through the land. The section ends with a virtual signature of the Lord, as so often throughout this book.

REBUKE OF THE EXILES (33:30-33)

Ezekiel had a word not only for those left in Judah, but for his own companions in exile. The last portion of the chapter describes the status of affairs at Chebar. Though the exiles seemed so eager to hear Ezekiel's words, as though willing to obey, they had no intention whatever of obeying. Since they would not take his ministry seriously, their apparent interest in his preaching was no indication of a sincere desire to obey the message. By the walls, that is, secretly, and at the doors of the houses, that is, openly, the people spoke of Ezekiel and his message. Their realization that his prophecies were true, accounts for his popularity. But their interest was not deep nor heartfelt. Perhaps the new note of hope and promise fascinated and pleased them, a natural reaction after so much of threatening prediction. Their outward actions would lead one to believe that their desire was to learn the will of God to do it, but their ultimate concern was their own advantage and self-advancement. They heard and did not.

They enjoyed and delighted in his new message of restoration and blessing for Israel and predictions against hostile nations, but they would not obey the moral implications of the prophecies which were prerequisites for personal participation in the blessings. They had no concern for the subject of it. The melody meant everything to them, the words or meaning, nothing. But their reaction to the message would not hinder its fulfillment which was eminently certain. The clear office of a prophet was to interpret history in the light of God's purpose for Israel. Time authenticated the word of the servant of the Lord, so that the people finally knew by bitter experience that all Ezekiel had foretold was not man's speculations or words, but the assured word of the living God.

WATCHMEN ARE WE ALL

Ever since Cain insolently asked the Lord whether he was his brother's keeper, the unsaved have been strangely unconcerned with the greatest need of the human heart. But this attitude must never characterize the child of God who is always to consider it his primary concern that the spiritual needs of others be met. Time is short and the need was never greater.

34

THE WICKED SHEPHERDS AND GOD'S SHEPHERD

From this chapter on, Ezekiel's prophecies are mainly consolatory to Israel, telling of God's grace toward His people and His faithfulness to His covenant promises. Before the destruction of Jerusalem the Prophet Ezekiel (as Jeremiah) dwelt on messages of judgment; once the judgment had fallen, the prophecies center about promises of blessing. The prophecy is undated and is an elaboration of the message in Jeremiah 23:1-8.

The Wicked Shepherds of Israel (34:1-10)

The chapter is God's rebuke against the false shepherds of Israel who served only for personal gain. The passage presents a vivid contrast between Israel's shepherds in the past and the Shepherd of Israel of the future, with the history of the nation and their bright future given under the allegory of a shepherd and a flock. Kings, prophets and priests were all designated as "shepherds" or "pastors." Here the message was directed against the rulers (see Jer. 2:8). For the figure of the shepherd in the Old Testament compare Psalm 78:70-72; Isaiah 44:28; 63:11; Zechariah 11:4-14; 13:7. The Lord Himself is beautifully portrayed as the Shepherd of His own (see Ps. 23:1; 80:1; Isa. 40:11; Jer. 31:10; John 10:1 ff.). The New Testament reveals a rich reward for faithful shepherds (I Peter 5:1-4). When we think of "pastor" or "pastoral," it is with the spiritual emphasis foremost (as prophets and priests of old), but the concept in this chapter applies to the kings (as in Homer as well as in Jer. 23:1-8). Just as the Lord chose fishermen to be fishers of men, He appointed David the shepherd to shepherd His people, and other rulers after him.

The fourfold mention of shepherds in verse 2 served to emphasize those against whom the prophecy was directed. In Assyria and Babylon a king was designated the "shepherd of his people." Here they were the preexilic rulers of Judah. The figure was well known in Israel, having been in use from David's time (cf. II Sam. 5:2). The duty of the shepherd was to protect and provide for his sheep, but Ezekiel's indictment showed

that the shepherds of Israel had a concern only for their own profit and
benefit. The bill of particulars was presented in verse 3, with the forms
of the verbs in the Hebrew original indicating that the faithless shepherds
were continually doing these acts. The emphasis was that the shepherds
had but one objective in mind, namely, their own enjoyment and pleasure.
The sheep were so downtrodden and frightened that they became an
easy prey to their enemies. Five classes are mentioned in verse 4, whereas four are specified in verse 16. Instead of receiving consideration and
tender care, the sheep were violently driven away, cruelly treated and left
to care for themselves. What a contrast to the work of the blessed Shepherd of Luke 15:4-5.

The passage moves on the premise of God's love and compassion for
them in their sufferings. This is not to exonerate the people whose sins
Ezekiel had vividly brought before them, as attested in the earlier portion
of the book. They were scattered, an experience they knew during the
period of the exile in Babylon. Furthermore, they had no shepherd
worthy of the name to oversee their interests (for an echo of these truths
see Matt. 9:36). When it was stated that they had become food to all the
beasts of the field, Ezekiel meant their Gentile oppressors and foes like
the Syrians, the Assyrians, Ammon, Moab and others.

Again it was stressed that the sheep were scattered. The passage is one
of tremendous pathos. God still called them His sheep, for He had never
relinquished His right to any undershepherd of the flock. The high hills
were introduced because they were the sites where idolatries were particularly carried out under the sanction and encouragement of their rulers.

After the indictment was set forth, the sentence (the "woe" of v. 2) was
pronounced in the form of the word of the Lord. According to his custom
Ezekiel rehearsed in verse 8 the dereliction and guilt of the shepherds.
The demand of the prophet in verse 7 was renewed in verse 9 to achieve
great force and ultimately greater receptiveness on their part. It was no
idle threat that the Lord would require the treatment of His flock at the
hand of the rulers. God had done so in the case of Zedekiah, who was deprived of his sons and his sight, and in the case of the other princes of
Judah (Jer. 52:10). The main objective of the Lord was the deliverance
of the sheep and their well-being.

THE LORD, THEIR FUTURE SHEPHERD (34:11-16)

The faithless, perfidious ways of the shepherds of Israel have strikingly
and vividly been brought before us. Now the contrast is presented between men's faithlessness and the faithfulness of God. Whereas human
leaders had no concern for their charges and subjects, the Lord will seek

and search out His sheep. The picture is one of taking charge with deep affection. The only solution to the failures of the monarchy clearly will be the establishment of the theocracy. The same truth is expressed by our Lord Jesus in John 10. Again the emphasis is on the scattering of the sheep, but this will not deter in the least the recovering ministry of the Shepherd of Israel. The cloudy and dark day was figurative of the time of Israel's national distress (see Jer. 30:4-7); it was the time of their dispersion and not God's judgment on the wicked nations.

In beautiful and unforgettable words Ezekiel predicted a literal return and restoration of the people of Israel to their own land. Notice it will be a regathering from worldwide exile and dispersion. It is both unnecessary and impossible to spiritualize these promises. If the scattering were literal, and no one is foolhardy as to deny this, then the regathering must be equally so. Having brought them back to the land of promise, the Lord will not intend that they shall suffer want in any respect. He will supply their every need in provisions, protection and peace. The words of verse 15 are reminiscent of Psalm 23. A rabbinic source[1] comments: "He who is on the watch for [the Messianic] salvation, the Holy One, blessed be He, will make to lie down in the Garden of Eden, as it is said in Ez. 34:15." The lying down will not be in the Garden of Eden but in the renovated and cleansed earth of the millennial reign of the Lord Jesus Christ, Israel's Shepherd. The Lord's treatment of His flock is diametrically opposite to that of the wicked shepherds (v. 4). But there will be judgment on the rich of the nation who oppress the poor. Prosperity, as so often happens, will cause forgetfulness of God and His goodness, so the fat and the strong will have to be visited with punishment. Not only will the love of God be displayed in His care of His flock, but His righteous character and government will also be upheld. There is a fine and exact balance in the exercise of God's wondrous attributes, and the believing heart rejoices in all God's ways.

GOD'S JUDGMENT BETWEEN THE SHEEP (34:17-22)

Once the Lord has dealt in proper fashion with the rulers, there must be a judging between the individuals in the flock. Not all have the reality of faith; some are only professing, their works revealing their actual identity. This passage anticipates the judgment so clearly given in Matthew 25:31-46. Some think Ezekiel turns here from the kings to lesser officials who had mistreated their fellow countrymen. God will judge between one class (the weak and the helpless) and another (the strong and the oppressive). We can only understand that the strong followed the op-

[1]*Pesikta R.* xxxiv.

pressive measures of their rulers in trampling underfoot their poorer brethren.

If there be any question as to whom Ezekiel had in mind, such doubt is removed by the words of verse 18, which refer to the wealthy who oppressed their poor brethren. After they fed themselves bountifully from a good pasture, they insolently and unfeelingly ruined what could have been of benefit to the rest. Thus the weak and downtrodden knew only the dregs of existence and deprivation as the ordinary course of their life.

By an unerring judgment the Lord Himself will do the work of adjudication between His sheep, manifesting the true and the spurious. The ruthless tactics of the oppressors are depicted, as is the manner in which they had accomplished the utter discomfiture of the helpless flock, whereby the sheep were scattered abroad. The deportation of Babylon was but one instance of this dispersion. So for the immediate present of Ezekiel's day the Lord would grant a measure of deliverance for the needy, but the full realization of the prediction of verse 22 must be in the future in Messiah's reign. How much is to be accomplished in Messiah's kingdom! Is it any wonder that the godly in Israel have always looked with longing and faith to that hour of blessed consummation?

GOD'S SHEPHERD, THE MESSIAH (34:23-31)

In satisfying contrast to the numerous incompetent and ineffective shepherds in Israel's past, will come one Shepherd whom the Lord will set up. There is doubtless allusion to the former separation of the nation into two kingdoms (cf. also John 10:16: "one flock, and one shepherd"; see also 37:24). Not only is there the contradistinction to the many before Him, or the need of only one Shepherd for a united nation, but the fact that others will not be needed in view of His eternal rule. Twice it is stated that He will feed them. This is not a gathering of all believers into the church through Christ. The reference to God's servant David is to be understood as David's greater Son, the Lord Jesus Christ. The verb "set up" (v. 23) does not imply the resurrection of David himself, but the appointment of Another (cf. the language of II Sam. 7:12 for the same verb; see Jer. 23:5; 30:9; Hosea 3:5;—in the last two references He is already called David). If this were the literal David, it is strange that there is no introductory word concerning his resurrection. Kimchi, the great Jewish commentator, stated: "David is the Messiah who shall arise from his seed in the time of salvation." It is the antitypical David, the Messiah. Messiah is referred to as David in Isaiah 55:3-4 as well, which refers to the name of the dynasty (cf. II Sam. 20:1; I Kings 12:16). And the goal of all God's dealings with them is that they may recognize that He and none other is their God.

The prophets were one in declaring that when Israel is finally in the place of obedience before the Lord, they will experience the fulfillment of blessings on earth. Millennial conditions are in view in verses 25-28, which picture some of the features on the physical side of the covenant in Jeremiah 31:31-34. The evil beasts (v. 28) were not figurative of the neighboring nations, but this is how actual beasts will behave (for the original promise see Lev. 26:6; also later confirmations in Isa. 11:6-9; 35:9; Hosea 2:18). In His hill of Zion the Lord will restore the former and the latter rains (v. 26); it is from this verse that we have the gospel song "There Shall Be Showers of Blessing." The physical elements presuppose in Israel the indispensable spiritual foundation. The former rain falls in the Holy Land in October or November; the latter rain from the middle of December to March. Israel will in turn be a source of blessing to the surrounding nations (cf. Zech. 8:13). Moreover, the refreshings of the Spirit are often compared to a shower (see Isa. 44:3). The literal is the primary concept with the corollary of spiritual elements. It is interesting to compare with the "showers of blessing" the mention of "the times of refreshing" of Acts 3:19-20. The curse will be lifted from the earth.

Having spoken of the showers of blessing, Ezekiel then pictured the fruitfulness of the land in order to show also the desirability of the land for those living in it. Neither natural forces nor human foes will disturb their peace. In contrast to all the preceding centuries when life hung in doubt so constantly, then all will be safety and security. Some understand the plantation (v. 29, ASV) or plant of renown to refer to the Messiah (cf. Isa. 11:1; Jer. 23:5), because the verb "raise up" is the same as that used for the Messiah. However, the context stresses the fruitfulness of the period, and there appears to be a reference to the fruit that will be famous. There will be great fertility and growth of vegetation. It is the truth of Amos 9:13.

Unquestionably the climax is the conversion of Israel when they will recognize the Lord as their God and experience the blessedness of the acknowledgment of them by the Lord as His people. It is the same theme as that of Romans 11:25-27. The final verse leaves no doubt as to the literal subjects of the parable. Think of the greatness of the divine condescension in setting forth the promises. The great gulf between God and man was yet to be bridged by the one Shepherd of verse 23, the God-Man, and the accomplishment of all that is predicted rests ultimately with God.

THE SHEPHERD OF ISRAEL

The picture of the sheep which Ezekiel portrayed on the physical side gives some idea of the condition of Israel on the spiritual plane. Sheep are quick to go astray, and the lost have departed from their God and been scattered. Reread the chapter and see how many times it is stated that the sheep are scattered. But the condition is not hopeless, for the same Word informs us that the sheep can be returned to the Bishop and Shepherd of their souls (I Peter 2:25).

35

CONDEMNATION OF EDOM

THIS THREATENING PROPHECY is against Edom, called Seir (see Gen. 32:3; 36:8). Israel and Edom were at enmity from their beginnings (cf. Gen. 27:41). Israel was commanded not to fight against them on their way to the land of Canaan (Deut. 23:7), and Edom had many times manifested a hostile spirit toward Israel, rejoicing in their misfortunes and at other times allying themselves with Israel's enemies. Not only Ezekiel but Isaiah, Jeremiah and Obadiah denounced Edom.

The prophecy in 25:12-14 is elaborated here. Why a second oracle against Edom? It has been suggested that in the meantime Edom had aggravated its offenses against Israel. It may appear at first as though the present prophecy belongs to the oracles against foreign nations, but it is probably here as a point of contrast to chapter 36, that is, wrath for Mount Seir contrasted with blessing for the mountains of Israel. The sins of Edom were (1) her aid to Babylon (v. 5); (2) her attempts to annex Israel's territory to her own (v. 10); (3) her vengeful joy over Judah (v. 12 ff.); (4) her perpetual enmity (v. 5; 25:15; Amos 1:11).

In the light of Isaiah 34:5 and 63:1-4 is there evidence to take Edom as representative of Israel's enemies in general in whatever place or time? Arguments have been advanced on both sides of the question. This much cannot be denied: Edom was considered Israel's most bitter and inveterate enemy (see Obad. 10; Ps. 137:7; Mal. 1:2-5). His enmity was ultimately against God, hence its seriousness.

THE DESOLATION OF MOUNT SEIR (35:1-4)

The complete prophecy, which has been viewed as a corollary of that in chapter 34, goes from 35:1–36:15. Mount Seir covers the mountainous area settled by the Edomites between the Dead Sea and the Elanitic Gulf. The threat against the land involved, of course, the people living on it. Seir included the highlands east of the Arabah from the Dead Sea to the Gulf of 'Aqaba (see Deut. 1:2). The main cities were Petra and Teman, which now lie in ruins. The prediction has been literally fulfilled. Edom was first subjugated by Babylon, then Medo-Persia, and then in 126 B.C.

by John Hyrcanus the Hasmonean, who compelled them to become Jews. There is no trace of the Edomites now, although their desolate cities can still be identified, as predicted by Obadiah (v. 18) and Jeremiah (49:13).

EDOM'S PERPETUAL ENMITY TO ISRAEL (35:5-9)

Ezekiel then further elaborated on the sin of Edom, which consisted of a perpetual enmity which was the root of antagonism to the chosen people through the centuries of their conflict (see Gen. 25:22 ff.; 27:41). They had given over (literally, poured out) the people of Israel to the power of the sword. Israel was thus compared to water, which the Edomites so heartlessly poured out. The time of the iniquity of the end may refer in some contexts to the final punishment of iniquity. Here the phrases are explained as the time of their national calamity, that is, the iniquity which was punished by the end of the state. The reference was thus to the destruction of Jerusalem (cf. 21:29). Edom was indeed exemplary among the nations for her hatred and animosity toward Israel. The fact is found in the Law, the Prophets and the Writings of the Old Testament.

When the Lord warned Edom that He would prepare them unto blood, the meaning was that He would give them over to universal slaughter. Edom had not hated blood, for to hate blood is to have a dread of murder. Twice it is stated that blood would pursue them. This is retribution in kind (see for this principle Ps. 109:17; Matt. 7:2; 26:52). The four occurrences of blood (Hebrew, *dam*) in verse 6 constitute a play on the name of Edom (red). Because Edom had cut off the needy in Israel (Obad. 14), the Lord would cut her off by war. The result would be that none would traverse her land. The designation was for all groups, especially the caravans, for Edom's tribes were the channel of commerce between India, the East and Egypt. This was the source of Edom's wealth.

The height of indignity in the Orient was not to be properly buried. The slain of Edom would be found in the mountains, hills, valleys and watercourses, all without benefit of burial. God's sole and final answer to perpetual enmity was perpetual desolation. Unrelieved desolation was decreed on this hostile power. It was then, as it is now, a fearful thing to fall into the hands of the living God (cf. Heb. 10:31).

EDOM'S COVETOUSNESS OF ISRAEL'S LAND AND BLASPHEMY AGAINST THE LORD (35:10-15)

When Israel was conquered, Edom thought it was the hour for her to subject the land of promise and unite the two nations. Most commentators understand the two nations and the two countries to refer to Israel and Judah with their territories. Either view makes sense in the passage. It would seem, however, that the ultimate design of Edom was to gain a definite advantage territorially for herself. But there was one element upon which Edom had not reckoned: it was the Lord who was there. This shows the enormity of the sin, for it was actually a design against the Lord Himself. It was not as though the land was without an owner, for the Lord was there. See the promise for the future in 48:35. The Lord was there in Ezekiel's day in spite of the corresponding truth of 11:23. After Jerusalem's fall Edom moved into Judean territory, holding land as far north as Hebron. In 126 B.C. the Maccabean John Hyrcanus retook this area called Idumea (I Macc. 5:3, 65).

The principle of recompense in kind was again set forth, for Edom would receive from the hand of the Lord in direct proportion to her anger, envy and hatred against Israel. She could not expect mercy who had shown none to others (see Amos 1:11 for Edom's behavior). By His visitation on Edom for their sins the Lord would manifest to Israel His zeal for His people and His land. This vindication of God's purpose would be displayed to Israel and all other nations. Even the sneers and derogatory mouthings of Edom against the land of promise had been taken into account by the Lord. The mountains of Israel (v. 12) stood for the land of Israel, just as Mount Seir stood for the land of Edom.

In reviling Israel the Edomites had actually belittled God and His workings among them, for the Lord was completely identified with His people (for a similar situation see Matt. 25:40, 45 at the judgment of the nations). With verse 14 Ezekiel leaped over the intervening centuries to speak of the time when God's kingdom will be realized on earth. At that time when the whole earth will rejoice, Edom will have no part in the earthly kingdom of Israel's Messiah. There will be a complete reversal of the former positions, with joy for Israel and the earth, and desolation and woe for Edom. Some take the words "whole earth" in the restricted sense of all the land of Edom, but if so, this is no stronger statement than has already been made more than once in this chapter. Though lexically possible, contextually it is not strong nor acceptable.

Again it was emphasized that there were lasting consequences of hatred of Israel. The great powers of earth were under orders from God to chastise Israel from time to time. But there was a distinction to be made in the manner and spirit whereby these commissions were carried out. Examples are plentiful in Scripture: Jehu and Ahab's house (Hosea 1:4); the Assyrian and Israel (Isa. 10:7; 14:25); Nebuchadnezzar and Israel (Isa. 47:6-8). So it was here with Edom but, with this difference, that they had not been delegated by God to punish Israel. The chapter closes with the statement which was virtually the signature of the Lord throughout Ezekiel's prophecy.

PERPETUAL DESOLATION FOR PERPETUAL ENMITY

This chapter is inseparably connected with the covenant of Genesis 12:1-3. Edom could not escape the application of the Abrahamic covenant, which explains the strong language and the irrevocable judgment on her. When a nation gives itself over to perpetual hatred of Israel, then there is no other alternative than perpetual desolation from God. Nation after nation has experienced this in the past, and some have done so in modern times.

36

THE CONVERSION OF ISRAEL

CLEARLY AND FORCEFULLY this chapter presents the prerequisite regeneration which Israel must experience before they can enter nationally into any of the blessings God has indicated for them. This portion was doubtless in mind when the Lord Jesus spoke to Nicodemus (John 3) concerning the new birth. Throughout the early section of the chapter there is a studied contrast with what is stated of Edom in chapter 35. As indicated in the previous chapter, verses 1-15 of this chapter are connected with chapter 35 as one continuous prophecy. The passage gives the opposite of that which was warned in chapter 6.

The chapter contains the most comprehensive enunciation of the plan of redemption to be found in this book, setting forth all the factors that comprise God's plan of salvation. In fact, Ezekiel's presentation is so orderly and unified that he has been called "the first dogmatic theologian." In analyzing Ezekiel's doctrine of the salvation of Israel, the salient factors are as follows: (1) The preeminent motive in their redemption is the glory of God (vv. 22, 32). (2) Israel will know ultimately that their God is the Lord (v. 38). (3) There will be an abhorrence of their sins (vv. 31-32). (4) Forgiveness of their sins will be realized (v. 25). (5) Regeneration will be effected (11:19; 18:31; 36:26-27). (6) The gift of the Holy Spirit will be granted (v. 27; 37:14). No prophet before him assigns the ministry of the Holy Spirit in regeneration such a precise place as Ezekiel does. (7) Included is obedience to God's laws (v. 27; 11:20).

This chapter constitutes the acid test for those who would explain prophecy any other way than literally. It must be admitted, even grudgingly, that the chapter is speaking of a literal Israel, a literal land and a literal regeneration experience. Those who suggest the passage may be expounded in a typical or figurative fashion do not make a convincing case; first, they give no valid reason for departing from the literal, commonsense interpretation, and second, in their comments they are forced to treat the promises as literal ones.

ISRAEL'S LAND TAKEN BY THE ENEMY (36:1-7)

Ezekiel directly addressed the mountains of Israel and the land so the people would understand God's plan for it in the coming days. The mountains thus represented the people as well as the land. The enemy referred to was Edom in particular (cf. 35:10 with 25:12), but others were not thereby excluded. The mention of ancient high places was not in the usual sense of idolatrous areas, but of the mountain land of Israel which has had a long history behind it (see Deut. 32:13; II Sam. 1:19, 25). The boast of the enemy had been that he was in full control of the land of promise. Ezekiel was so passionately stirred that he repeated the word "therefore" five times (vv. 3, 4, 5, 6, 7). The enemy intended to swallow the people of God, the verb meaning literally to pant or snuff up, a figure from the panting of wild beasts, as a wild beast ravenously smells after prey to devour it (see Ps. 56:1-2). The residue of the nations refers to those not conquered and destroyed by the Chaldeans, that is, the Ammonites, Moabites and Philistines. Israel was the subject of the conversation of idle talkers. The "lips of talkers" (v. 3) is literally the "lip of the tongue" or "the lip of a man of tongue," thus a talker or talkers in general. They were slanderers and defamers. This had been foretold already in Deuteronomy 28:37 and Jeremiah 24:9.

The multiplication of particulars in verse 4 served to show God's care over the land whereby He observed all. The mountains of the land were seen in relation to the people as the leaders were to the people. Whenever the Lord's will and holiness were infringed upon, His reaction was characterized as one of jealousy. This was His zeal in wrath to vindicate His holiness and truth. The residue of the nations was involved because they also had viciously rejoiced at the desolation of Jerusalem and the land. The greatness of God's wrath was explicable on the ground that they were plotting and devising against His land. Therefore, the inhabitants of the land were cast out as a prey.

Because Israel had borne the contempt both in words and deeds (vv. 3-4), of the nations, the latter would bear their own shame. To emphasize the seriousness of the matter the Lord had sworn (literally, lifted up the hand) that the godless nations would experience retribution in kind. It would be shame for shame and reproach for reproach. It is vital to remember that such action on God's part does not reveal in any sense a partiality toward Israel. It is rather a vindication of God's glory and will, for He has condescended to link His purposes on earth with the people of Israel.

THE FUTURE FRUITFULNESS OF THE LAND (36:8-15)

Ezekiel predicted that the land to which Israel will be restored will be productive, populated and peaceful. These prophecies, especially those in verses 12-15, could not have been fulfilled in the return from Babylon. The promise of productivity was addressed directly to the mountains of Israel themselves. The present great reforestation projects in the State of Israel, amazing as they are, are only harbingers of the reality to come. The conditions depicted here are clearly millennial. When Ezekiel stated that they were at hand to come, he did not mean Israel, but the blessings just promised. From Ezekiel's viewpoint these promises were near at hand. Thus many take the primary reference to the return from Babylon. But the prediction will not be completely fulfilled until the future restoration, of which the return from Babylon was a foreshadowing.

Because the Lord is exercised on behalf of Israel, the land will be rejuvenated in order to be ready for occupation by those returning from worldwide dispersion. But the productivity of the land would be useless unless there were men to enjoy and use it, so Ezekiel foretold the great increase in population and even of the animals of the land. There will then be an approximation in the land of those conditions which existed in the days of Israel's prosperity, in fact, they will be better than in the halcyon days of Solomon. Ezekiel elaborated on the theme of the occupancy of the land by the people of Israel; it is they who will walk again upon the mountains of Israel. No longer will the land bereave the nation of its inhabitants (see Jer. 15:7).

The land was called a devourer of men because of the many wars that repeatedly decimated the population in times past (cf. the report of the spies in Num. 13:32). It is possible that the reference was to famine (v. 30). In a sense the land of promise was a bereaver of the nation, for it was subject, through the chastisements of God, to droughts (Jer. 14:1; Amos 4:7), to blasting and mildew (Amos 4:9), locust (Joel 1), and famine (Hag. 1:10-11; 2:17). Although the word "bereave" is used in verse 13, it is felt that in verse 14 it is employed in a play on words (necessitating the transposition of only one consonant in the original) with the Hebrew word meaning "stumble." However, such a change is not at all necessary. Ezekiel was presenting the land as in some sense the instigator of Israel's sin and downfall. But now by a fivefold statement Ezekiel was declaring that the land will no more experience the shame of the nations because of occupation of their land by enemies, as well as the accompanying destitution. Of course, all that is promised the land relates directly to that which the Lord is yet to do for His people Israel.

GOD'S LONG-SUFFERING FOR HIS NAME'S SAKE (36:16-21)

Once more Ezekiel gave a backward look to underscore why Israel had suffered the past judgments at the hands of the Lord (see Lev. 18:28; Num. 35:34). This portion of the chapter constitutes one of the great passages of the book and sets forth the basic principles of God's dealings with Israel and of Ezekiel's outlook on the history of his people. It was solely because they had defiled the land by their sins that the Lord determined to purge it by their removal from it. In Israel a woman was not permitted to enter the sanctuary until her purification (cf. Lev. 15:19; Isa. 64:6). Idolatry was the condemning sin which plagued them throughout their national history. When the prophet spoke of blood poured out, he was probably referring to murders, judicial violence and even child sacrifice in the worship of idols (see 16:36; 23:37). For such enormities in the civil and spiritual realms they were scattered from their country.

In an intensely interesting manner Ezekiel pointed out that Israel, because they had brought the exile upon themselves by their sin and were directly responsible for the low regard the nations held for their God, had profaned the holy name of the Lord. Israel's exile itself was a profanation of God's sacred name, as though He could not have prevented their expulsion from their homeland. In the eyes of the heathen the fortunes of a nation and its deity were inseparable. It is well for us as believers today to realize that God is concerned how He is represented before the unbelieving world by our words and actions. Do we properly represent Him or misrepresent Him? Do our lives manifest the grace that saved us, or are they a disgrace to the grace that redeemed us? And God has a supreme concern for His manifested excellence. His chief consideration is for the glory of His name, then for the welfare of His people upon whom His name has been placed. To act otherwise would be impossible for and unworthy of God, the moral Governor of the universe.

THE CONVERSION OF ISRAEL (36:22-31)

In unmistakable language Ezekiel made clear that the basis of all God's dealings in grace are never predicated on man's merit, but rather on His holy character and name. This is designed to humble all pride (see Deut. 9:6; Isa. 48:11). One's name stands for all that an individual is or does. God's name is both great and holy. For that reason He could not allow His wonderful name to be profaned in any sense among the nations because of Israel's sin and punishment, which did not properly reflect the blessed character of their God. In place of the former profanation of His name the Lord will see to it that His glorious name is sanctified. God is said to be sanctified when His character is made evident to the world, especially in and through those who are in covenant relationship to Him.

Now Ezekiel set forth chronologically the method whereby the Lord will set His name in the proper light before the peoples of the earth. The first step God will take in the vindication of His name among the nations will be to institute a worldwide regathering of His people from every country in order to settle them in their own land. From verse 24 it is difficult to see a near reference here in view of the comprehensiveness of the terms and the lasting nature of the transactions under consideration, namely, eternal issues.

The next verses in the chapter are among the most glorious in the entire range of revealed truth on the subject of Israel's restoration to the Lord and national conversion. After Israel's regathering by divine activity the Lord will cleanse them by sprinkling clean water upon them. Here is an allusion to the Mosaic rites of purification (see Num. 19:17-19; Isa. 4:4; Zech. 13:1; Ps. 119:9). There is a reference to the washing of water by the Word. Through their idolatrous practices they had contracted moral uncleanness (v. 17). For the concept of sprinkling in cleansing see Psalm 51:7, 10; Hebrews 9:13; 10:22. The sprinkling symbolized purifications by water generally and collectively (Lev. 14:5-7), for they all prefigured removal of uncleanness. Justification, and not sanctification, is in view here. The Lord will perform for Israel in actuality what the law pictured by sprinkling with clean water (cf. John 3:5).

What was stated in figurative terms in verse 25 is now presented in literal phraseology. The gift of the new heart from the Lord signifies the new birth, which is renewal by the Spirit of God. The promise was first given in 11:18-20. The heart stands in Scripture for the whole nature. In 2:4 and 3:7 Ezekiel had described the previous condition of their heart. The spirit indicates the governing principle of the mind which directs thought and conduct. A stony heart is a stubborn one bent on doing its own will. This verse is the rabbinic proof text for the view that the evil inclination (*yetser hara'*) will finally be removed by God. This passage is parallel to Jeremiah 31:31-34 on the new covenant.

In addition to the gift of the responsive heart the Lord will grant the gift of His Spirit to willing ones in Israel. This is the coming of the Holy Spirit upon Israel in the future, not that at Pentecost. The gift of the Spirit is frequently connected with the coming of the new economy for Israel (see 39:29; Isa. 44:3; 59:21; Joel 2:28-29; Acts 2:16 f.). As in other prophetic portions it is declared that the new life within is reflected in a new and godly walk according to all God's laws. Furthermore, when Israel is in right relationship with the Lord, He will see that they are in possession of their promised land (see 28:25; 37:25). When Israel is in reality the people of God and He is their God, there will be the complete nullification of the judgment of Hosea 1:9.

The sequel to Israel's conversion is the blessing of God upon all nature on their behalf. Just as in Genesis 1 plants and animals were called into being by God's command, so He will call for the grain to make it grow, so that there will no longer be famine (cf. 34:29). And the verse beautifully links their spiritual salvation with their material prosperity, and in just that order. Supernatural fertility of the land is one of the accompaniments of the kingdom (see v. 35; 47:1-12; Isa. 35:1-2; 55:13; Zech. 8:12). When Israel is thus surrounded by irrefutable proofs of God's grace and goodness to them, they will be melted into further repentance by the abundant mercy of their infinite God.

GOD'S GLORY THE SOLE OBJECTIVE (36:32-38)

In the light of coming blessings there was a call to repent. Far from procuring such blessing, their past history was only a source of shame and confusion when meditated upon. Again, the closest possible relationship is indicated here between their restoration to the Lord and their restoration in blessing to their land. With verse 34 there is a backward glance to verse 9. In fact, the great prosperity of the land in the time of fulfillment can only be compared to that of the Garden of Eden, which is the ultimate comparison. Notice the emphasis in verse 36 on the first personal pronoun; it is the Lord who is moving throughout. He is determined that the nations, or rather the remnant of the nations (v. 3), shall know His purpose and His power. Since the judgments of God have not fallen upon them, it is clear that they are godly.

There had been a day when the Lord refused to be inquired of by His disobedient people (14:3; 20:3), but now the Lord would be accessible for their turning to Him in genuine repentance and would grant their requests. The purpose of all prophecy is to stir up to godly action. The implication is that they would be heard by the Lord. The last verses refer to the increase in population, which is the reversal of verse 12, and the repetition of the promise in verses 10-11, 33. Ezekiel closed this blessed and vital chapter with a vivid comparison for tremendous growth. When the male population (Deut. 16:16) went to Jerusalem during the pilgrimage feasts, tremendous numbers of animals were brought for sacrifice (see Micah 2:12 for the figure of a flock). How large these offerings were can be readily seen from the practice in the time of David (I Chron. 29:21), Solomon (II Chron. 7:5), Hezekiah (II Chron. 29:33), and Josiah (II Chron. 35:7-9). Some prefer to think of the feast of Passover in particular (II Chron. 35:7), but there is no good reason to limit the sense.

Those interpreters who accuse Ezekiel of being ritualistic, formal, legalistic, external, etc., owe him a genuine apology on the basis of this chapter alone. Ezekiel has shown himself to be not one whit behind the most emphatic of the prophets in the matters of spiritual conversion and spiritual life. The doctrines of Ezekiel are, indeed, those of Paul as well: forgiveness (v. 25), regeneration (v. 26), the indwelling and ruling Spirit of God (v. 27), the spontaneous keeping of God's law (v. 27; Rom. 8:4); the inseparable connection of Israel's history with God's self-revelation to the nations (vv. 33-36; Rom. 11); and the conversion of the nation Israel (vv. 24-31; Rom. 11:25-27).

ISRAEL GLORIOUSLY REDEEMED

The words of this chapter should fill us with joy. Is there not something the Lord wants you to do to work toward the day of Israel's deliverance and glory?

37

THE NATION RESURRECTED

THIS PASSAGE, part of a series of revelations received during the night before the messenger came with news of the destruction of Jerusalem, was to dispel the gloom of the people over the sad news. The main aim of the vision was to counteract the despair and pessimism which had laid hold of the despondent nation (v. 11). The passage reveals how well that generation knew the doctrine of the resurrection. Otherwise, Ezekiel's figure would have had little meaning for the people (see I Kings 17; II Kings 4:13-37; 13:21; Isa. 25:8; 26:19; Dan. 12:2; Hosea 13:14).

The church Fathers and most orthodox commentators have taken the passage in verses 1-10 to be a *locus classicus* for the doctrine of the resurrection of the dead. But their views vary as to the specific meaning of the vision itself. Some see here a general resurrection of the dead in the last day, while others relate it to Israel's awakening to life from death in the Babylonian captivity. Jerome took the first view. Still others find here only a political revival of the nation. There appears to be general agreement among students of the passage that conversion of the soul of an individual is not in view here. The entire vision in a sense was suggested by the saying among the people in verse 11. It is not a literal prophecy of the resurrection of individuals in the nation, but of the nation as a whole (the figure was already employed in Hosea 6:2). Isaiah 25:8; 26:19 and Daniel 12:2 prophesy a physical resurrection of individuals. The chapter points up the spiritual condition of Israel during the many centuries of her dispersion throughout the world. The main divisions of the portion are (1) the national resurrection and restoration of Israel, and (2) the reunion of the nation from its two kingdoms.

THE VALLEY OF DRY BONES (37:1-6)

The mention of the hand of the Lord indicates prophetic ecstasy and inspiration. Ezekiel was brought out in the Spirit of the Lord, that is, in vision, and set down in the valley of 3:22. The unusual and instructive feature about the valley was that it was full of bones, which were evidently not in heaps, but scattered about. The Talmud states that the bones were just those of Ephraim, but they were surely of all Israel, as

212

indicated in verse 11. Many of the people had been slain by the sword (v. 9, "these slain"). There was no evidence of spiritual life whatever. They had been dead for a long time, and the bones had been bleaching for a considerable period. In order to emphasize the hopelessness of the situation from the human point of view, the Lord asked Ezekiel whether these bones could live. Ezekiel's answer revealed that it would require a power beyond man's to bring this about. It was an answer of reverence, not giving a positive or negative response.

However, the matter was not left at this point, for God had the answer and the solution. There was a clear indication that only the miraculous power of the life-giving word of God could accomplish the impossible task. The prophesying was in the sense of speaking on God's behalf, which is the basic and primary sense of all biblical prophecy, and not here with the concept of prediction. Nothing could be more emphatic than that the agency for effecting the purpose of God in the resurrection of the nation was the powerful word of God. The bringing of the dead bones to life by two separate acts was reminiscent of the creation of man in Genesis 2. Breath was mentioned first in verse 5 because it was the most important element in the transaction. "Breath," "wind" and "spirit" are renderings of the same Hebrew word, with the context deciding in each case. With the breath of life infused into them, the dry bones would live (see Ps. 119:25; John 6:63). Every operation set forth in verse 6 was so that the lifeless and useless bones might again live as human beings.

THE RESURRECTION OF THE DRY BONES (37:7-10)

Though prophesying over dry bones would appear to the worldling as the height of folly, Ezekiel obeyed without cavil or doubt. At his prophesying there were reactions in the realm of physical nature. What a shame that creation, even inanimate, is so responsive to God's word, and man, the only intelligent creature of God besides the angels, is so often rebellious. In the midst of the thundering and earthquake the bones began to move. As though superintended from a higher intelligence, they came together in exactly the right way and proportion to form normal human bodies. This was nothing less than a miracle from any angle considered. Never minimize the power of God's utterance.

However, there was one element lacking, and it was of paramount significance, namely, breath. As stated above, the restoration of the dry bones was depicted in two stages, reminiscent of the creation of man in Genesis 2:7. Apparently the reference to the absence of breath in the bodies indicated that when Israel will be returned to the land in the latter days, they will be unconverted. Surely the general tenor of the prophetic

Scriptures points in this direction (see Zech. 13:8-9). Otherwise it is difficult to see how a covenant could be made nationally with such a godless one as the Roman prince of the end times (cf. Dan. 9:27). The "four winds" (v. 9) is a Semitic expression for the four corners of the earth, which definitely implies that Israel will be regathered from the four quarters of the globe (see Isa. 43:5-6; Jer. 31:8). It is important to repeat that Ezekiel was not speaking of a physical resurrection of the dead but of the revival and restoration of Israel to spiritual life. With his final word of prophecy the entire valley, strewn with an innumerable quantity of desiccated bones, was transformed into a vast battlefield, as it were, filled with an unusually large army. What a transformation for God to turn a valley of dry bones into a strong army. Such is the boundless power of the word of the living God.

THE MEANING OF THE VISION (37:11-14)

This section gives the explanation of the vision so that there could be no excuse for misunderstanding the meaning of God. The bones represented the whole house of Israel, that is, both Judah and Ephraim, as the latter part of the chapter attests. The fact that the dry bones were seen as speaking was another indication that the passage was speaking in figurative language of great spiritual truths. The bones were singled out because they were the seat of physical force and energy. Their hope of resumption of national life seemed out of the question. They complained that they were clean cut off, literally, "we have been cut off for (or to) ourselves," that is, cut off from the source of power and left to ourselves. "It is all over with us" has been suggested as the force of the statement.

By a change of figure the bones were then seen buried in graves instead of scattered and strewn upon a valley. God's bringing them into the land of Israel is further evidence that the passage is speaking figuratively of the resurrection of the dead nation, and not of a physical resurrection of dead persons. Besides, there is no teaching in the Scriptures that the resurrection of anyone from physical death will take place in stages, such as is stated here for the dried bones of the people of Israel. Every phase of the transaction was separately declared again so that there would be no mistaking that all emanates from the mighty power of God and attests to His incomparable grace. What He has spoken, He has performed. Our God is altogether irresistible in His working.

THE UNITED AND CONVERTED NATION (37:15-23)

This section treats the symbol of the reunion of the tribes of Israel, the explanation of the symbol, and the sanctification and blessing of the nation in the Messianic reign. Many interpret this portion not as a literal return of Israel to their land but as the gathering of converted Israelites into the kingdom of God as seen under Old Testament imagery. But the earlier part of this chapter, to say nothing of other passages in this book and other prophets, has already shown that God will restore and reestablish the nation in their own land. It was now to be made known that when the dispersed will be brought back to their country, they will no longer be divided and disunited as they have been since the days of Rehoboam. Ezekiel was commanded to picture this by the symbolism of the two sticks. The sticks are here equivalent to scepters, reminiscent of those in the days of Moses (see Num. 17:1-2 ff.). "Judah, and . . . his companions" (v. 16) showed that the southern kingdom included, in addition to Judah, the greater part of Benjamin and Simeon, the tribe of Levi, and godly Israelites who had come at different times from the northern kingdom with its idolatry and false priesthood into the kingdom of Judah (cf. II Chron. 11:12 ff.; 15:9; 30:11, 18; 31:1). Incidentally, these same scriptures show the folly of the Anglo-Israel delusion with its position of ten lost tribes. In connection with the other stick Joseph was mentioned. In all probability he was chosen because the house of Joseph, comprising the two powerful tribes of Ephraim and Manasseh, formed the main body of the northern kingdom.

After Ezekiel had carried out his commission to join the sticks, the people eagerly questioned him as to the meaning of his actions. This presupposes that Ezekiel performed this publicly. The use of the plural "them" in verse 19 is a construction according to the sense, for the rod represented the ten tribes. Again the explanation underscored the prediction that the scattered nation will be duly regathered to their land first. In a threefold way the Lord promised that there will be one nation in place of the long-dismembered commonwealth of Israel. Underlying all prophecy concerning Israel is the presupposition of a united people, a healing of the breach in the commonwealth of God's people (see Isa. 11:12-13; Jer. 3:18; Hosea 1:11). One God, as well as one Shepherd and King, requires a counterpart of one nation. The prophets all recognized the northern tribes as still in existence and knew of no such error as "lost" tribes (cf. Isa. 43:5-7, "every one"; 49:5-6; Jer. 3:12-15).

The Davidic King and the Sanctified People (37:24-28)

After the Lord had defined in minutest particular that the nation will be completely cleansed of all defilements and corruptions, making them thus in truth the people of God, then He disclosed once more (see 34:23-24) who their Sovereign and Ruler will be in the days of the fulfillment of their national history. Some have understood the words "David my servant" to mean David literally, but the consensus of prophetic testimony decides in favor of applying it to Christ alone. Apart from the fact that God would not design a culminating age with two supreme rulers on earth in a sort of coregency, a concept foreign to Old Testament prophecy and the repeated mention of the numeral "one" in connection with their final king, there is no inherent reason why David must rule again. There was no such implication in the original Davidic covenant of II Samuel 7. That unconditional promise stated only that David's final Heir would rule forever, not that he himself would do so. Apart from the undisputed fact of the standing jealousy between Ephraim and Judah, the division of the kingdom came about because of the apostasy of Solomon, a son of David. This disruption can only be reversed by the righteous rule of the Son of David, the Messiah.

Notice how often "for ever" is employed in this context. The first usage in verse 25 is exactly as literal as the second reference. Also notice the number of references to perpetuity in the remainder of the chapter: occupation of the land is forever; the kingship of David's Son is forever; the sanctuary will be in their midst forever; and the covenant of peace will be in force forever. Their dwelling in the land was repeated for emphasis (see Isa. 60:21; Joel 3:20; Amos 9:15). The covenant of peace is none other than the new covenant of Jeremiah 31:31-34. It will be an everlasting covenant as well, because it will be grounded in God's grace. Many have denied that this refers to a physical building and sanctuary, but this seems pointless in view of the last nine chapters of the book, which are treated at length. Just as it pleased God to dwell in a tabernacle when Israel departed from Egypt, so He will tabernacle among them in their converted condition (cf. Exodus 25:8).

In the final verses of this important chapter the Spirit of God began to prepare the mind for the revelation of the manner in which God will have a sanctuary in the midst of His people and will dwell with them (for the same concept see Zech. 6:12-13). According to the Old Testament view of the future, man is not taken to dwell with God in heaven, but God condescends to dwell with man, whereby the earth is gloriously transformed (47:1-12). Without question chapter 37 takes its deserved place among the significant documents of revealed truth relative to Israel's future.

"Can These Bones Live?"

One finds himself loaded down with abundant disclosure of God's truth in this beautiful chapter because so much is promised for God's beloved people. But nothing is guaranteed for time or eternity to Jew or Gentile apart from simple faith in the Lord Jesus Christ. Can the dead bones live? Any who are dead in trespasses and sins can live through faith in the life-giving One.

38

THE PROPHECY AGAINST GOG

IN THE LAST GREAT DIVISION of Ezekiel's prophecy the themes are distinct and significant. Chapter 34 emphasized the rulers; chapter 35, the enemies; chapter 36, the nation converted; chapter 37, the nation resurrected; chapters 38-39, the land; and chapters 40-48, the sanctuary. Chapters 38-39, it is generally recognized, constitute one prophecy. They tell, if interpreted literally, of a coming northern confederacy of nations about the Black and Caspian seas with Persia and North Africa, who will invade the promised land after Israel's restoration to it.

However, there are these different views as to the time of the prophecy: (1) any time in the church age, but probably toward its close; (2) during Daniel's seventieth week after the rapture of the church: (*a*) at the commencement of the period; (*b*) in the middle of it; (*c*) at the end of it; (3) after the visible return of Christ to the earth and a short time before the inauguration of His Messianic kingdom; and (4) after the millennial reign.

The first view would appear to be scarcely tenable in view of the number of time expressions used that point to the latter days of Israel's age (38:8). Furthermore, it is clear God is dealing again with Israel nationally (39:25, 27). The second position, placing the conflict in the tribulation period, is the one which best harmonizes the prophetic scheme of the eschatological passages of the Old and New Testament. The beginning or middle of the period is not favored because the final war, of which Ezekiel 38-39 are a part, will require a period of preparation which will be climaxed by "the latter time of the indignation." The third interpretation is not acceptable because, although Christ will institute proceedings to cleanse the land (Matt. 13:41), the events of this chapter would demand a longer period than that just before Christ's investiture in the kingdom. The fourth view appears to rest on the similarity of names—Gog and Magog in Ezekiel 38-39 and in Revelation 20. This is insufficient basis for an acceptable position in view of the indicated time factors involved.

Thus the writer favors the end of the tribulation period before Christ is visibly manifested to the world (see Zech. 14:1-4). The armies of chapters 38-39 would appear to be included in the universal confederacies seen in Zechariah 12 and 14. Ezekiel 38-39 are actually an amplification of the prediction in 37:28. The invasion will take place after Israel has been restored to their land, a fact set forth prominently in these chapters. Notice that twice it is stated (38:17; 39:8) that former prophets foretold this invasion (Ps. 2:1-3; Isa. 29:1-8; Joel 2:20; 3:9-21; Zech. 12:1 ff.; 14:2-3).

Modern criticism claims chapters 38-39 are inserted here, probably by another author as the result of a combination of materials. However, the admission has been made that the theory is not a happy one. There is the opinion that the prophecy is against Babylon. But, although it is remarkable that Ezekiel nowhere prophesies against Babylon, these chapters cannot be twisted to speak of her.

Those who object to a literal interpretation of the chapters present the following arguments: (1) The ideal character of the name Gog, the nearest to it in Scripture or secular history being Magog. (2) The nations mentioned are not contiguous to Israel or one another, so they would be unlikely to act together, such as the Persians and Libyans. (3) Israel's resources would never be an enticement to so large a host of the enemy (38:12-13). (4) The estimated number of corpses to be buried in seven months would be 360 million, to say nothing of the dangers of pestilence from the unburied corpses. (5) The scene of the controversy differs from that in Isaiah 34:6, where it is Edom. (6) The carnality of the presentation of God's dealings with His enemies does not fit into Messianic times.

All these arguments are said to demand a nonliteral interpretation, for this passage is considered as a prophetic parable. Some suggest a "generally literal" interpretation where the details are not necessarily so. The writer cannot allow himself such liberties in interpreting the plain statements of the prophetic Scriptures. It is either the grammatical, literal, historical interpretation or we are adrift on an uncharted sea with every man the norm for himself. There is not a syllable at the beginning of this chapter to alert us to explain the passage in any other than the literal method.

THE GREAT COMPANY OF INVADERS (38:1-6)

The four main divisions in chapters 38-39 are seen in the four commands to the prophet: 38:2, 14 and 39:1, 17. The five names—Gog, Magog, Rosh, Meshech and Tubal—of verse 2 (ASV) have occasioned lengthy discussion and a wide variety of opinion. It is not worthy of the prophecy to make identifications merely on the basis of similarity of sounds. The first name that appears in the text is Gog, which has been suggested as an

ideal name for the Antichrist, but for this there is not a shred of biblical
or nonbiblical evidence. Another suggestion is that the name was arbi-
trarily derived from the name of the country, Magog, but this is not valid
because Gog appears in I Chronicles 5:4. The Tell el-Amarna Letters
found in Egypt speak of a Gagaia as the home of barbarians, but there is
no certain connection with the biblical figure. There was a Lydian king
named Gyges, but again there is no assured relationship with this passage. The Gog of Ezekiel's predictions was the leader from the land of
Magog. The name Magog is not found outside the Bible. It does not
appear to be a variation of Gog, for this would not make a strong statement. Jerome stated that the Jews of his day held that Magog was a general designation for the numerous Scythian tribes. The name is found as
early as Genesis 10:2, where it refers to a descendant of Japheth. Josephus
identified the name with the Scythians.

Gog was said to be the prince of Rosh, Meschech and Tubal (v. 2,
ASV). Of the first name, Rosh, it must be admitted that it is often found
as a common noun, meaning "head." But most interpreters understand it
to be a proper noun. Byzantine and Arabic writers mentioned a people
called Rus inhabiting the country of Taurus and reckoned among the
Scythians. There have been many writers who connected the name Rosh
with the Russians, but this is not generally accepted today. Apparently
the Greeks very early included under this name all the nations of the
north.[1] Meshech and Tubal have been identified as Phrygia and Cappadocia. They appear to be the Moschi and Tibareni of the classical writers
(see Gen. 10:2). They lived in the neighborhood of Magog. Against this
sinister leader Gog the prophet was commissioned to utter this threatening prophecy. The Lord was arrayed in His wrath against this powerful
leader.

Moreover, with reference to this enemy of God and His people, the
Lord had a threefold program and strategy. First, He would divert Gog
from his planned program and method of attack. The ideas of coercion
and unwillingness are present. As a wild beast is turned about from his
natural desire for prey, so Gog would be deflected from his initial purpose. Second, the placing of hooks in the jaws indicates the enemy would
be powerless to pursue his original objective; divine restraint would hold
him in check. Finally, the Lord would see to it that Gog did engage himself initially in his venture of madness. The directing force was ascribed
to God, but Satan was the secondary motivating power as in II Samuel
24:1 and I Chronicles 21:1. When Gog advanced, it would be with an
excellently equipped, skillful and numerous army. The mention of horses

[1]*Iliad*, xiii. 5-6.

and horsemen is not to be taken to mean that the army would consist entirely or primarily of cavalry.

The nations specified in verse 5 are the Persians from the east, Cush or Ethiopia (with the possibility of some about the Euphrates River in Asia), and Put or Libya in North Africa. Included are nations in the extreme north (v. 6), east and south of the promised land. Many think these names militate against a literal interpretation of the passage because the nations and countries mentioned are so distant from Canaan, but such considerations do not trouble armies to that extent today. Some have found great difficulty in the references to armor, buckler, shield, sword and helmet, but even in our day of advanced weapons of warfare it is interesting to learn that in some parts of the world conflict is going on with primitive weapons. (And how else could an ancient writer have described warfare? He knew nothing of planes and guns.) It is our concern only to understand what the commonsense interpretation of the passage indicates.

Finally, the list of participants was completed with the reference to Gomer and Togarmah. The former are the hordes of the Cimmerians, tribes that settled along the Danube and Rhine and later formed the Germanic people. The latter are the Armenians, already mentioned in 27:14. It is clearly stated that all these hordes will issue from the far north of the promised land and will be numerous indeed. If ever an invasion could succeed because of superior numbers, this will be it. But the entire story has not been told.

THE INVASION BY GOG (38:7-9)

With consummate and telling irony Ezekiel urged Gog to be fully prepared for the encounter, and to see to it that all was in readiness as far as his confederates were concerned. He was to be a guard—actually, their leader and commander—to them all. With verse 8 there is an abundance of important details. First, the notation of time indicated that the attack of the enemy would not take place for a long time. The events here predicted were not to be expected in the lifetime of Ezekiel or his contemporaries. Second, the occurrences set forth constituted a visitation from the Lord. The verb is the usual one for a visitation either in blessing or in punishment, as here, but some have preferred a rendering like "for a long time thou art missed," or "after a long time thou art made leader." Actually, neither rendering is very forceful for so common a verb, nor is it warranted from the context.

Third, the time element was distinctly stated as "in the latter years," which is equivalent to "the latter days" of verse 16. No student of prophecy can afford to overlook this phrase in the Old Testament or its parallel in the New Testament. A wrong interpretation here will result in confusion, and color the entire picture. When used by the Old Testament writers, it has reference to Messianic times, that is, the era in which Israel's national history will find its fulfillment and climax. For the importance of the time notation see 38:8, 16; 38:14, 18; 39:8, 11.

Fourth, there was mention of the enemy's invasion of a specific land (this is hardly the place for figurative exposition), whose people had been restored from the effects of the sword. Ezekiel was speaking of the nation as exiled by the sword (representative of all the weapons) of the enemy. Fifth, this beleaguered nation had been gathered out of many nations. This cannot refer to the Babylonian captivity but to worldwide dispersion. Sixth, the place of the conflict was pointed out as the mountains of Israel, which have been a continual waste. This had in view a period of time longer than that of the seventy years in Babylon. Seventh, there had been a supernatural agency exercised on their behalf, so that they had been brought out from among the peoples of the earth. Finally, they were viewed as living securely, all of them, without fear of invasion or deportation.

Just when least expected and without the slightest warning, the enemy will swoop down on the returned exiles, as an unheralded storm. The land will be covered and smothered by the vast multitude of Gog's followers, just as a cloud blankets a land below it. Gog will see to it that he has plenty of allies and enough mercenaries to carry through his satanic scheme. But thus far the purpose of the enemy or his desired objective has not been stated. These follow immediately in the record.

THEIR INTENTION TO PLUNDER (38:10-13)

What is it that will allure the coalition of nations to descend upon and invade the Holy Land? Will it be a desire for territorial expansion, greater markets, national prestige or even revenge? The plan will be devised because of one important feature of Israel's occupation of their ancestral home: their wealth. The people will consider themselves eminently secure. How much we hear today on all sides of national security, social security and financial security. Men's minds are occupied with plans for security; so Israel in that day will be living without fortifications, without military installations and without barriers of any kind against easy access to their land. Thus the enemy will see the opportunity of the day to invade, overrun with ease and come off with a handsome prize, for the returned people will have come with much wealth (cf. Isa. 60:5-9). The enemy, greedy of Israel's wealth, will embark on a campaign of conquest for gain. It is now common knowledge that the deposits of mineral wealth in the Dead Sea are the greatest in the world. The envious eyes of the foe will not be denied longer; the hour when Israel lives without fear of attack will be considered the most auspicious for the invasion and plunder. World opinion will mean little to the adversary when superior might can be called upon.

An interesting phrase is employed to define the place where God's people will be dwelling. It is called the middle (literally, the navel) of the earth, as explained in 5:5. The land of Israel is in the center of the earth as far as God's purposes for the world are concerned (cf. Deut. 32:8). Rabbinic literature states:

> As the navel is set in the centre of the human body, so is the land of Israel the navel of the world . . . situated in the centre of the world, and Jerusalem in the centre of the land of Israel, and the sanctuary in the centre of Jerusalem, and the holy place in the centre of the sanctuary, and the ark in the centre of the holy place, and the foundation stone before the holy place, because from it the world was founded.[2]

In addition to the nations mentioned in verses 1-6, three were added. Sheba and Dedan were Arab peoples. Tarshish has been identified with Great Britain, but not on good grounds. It may be either Spain or Sardinia, for there was a Tartessus in both areas. Some interpreters have inferred from verse 13 that these nations will befriend Israel and come to her defense, but this cannot be maintained with certainty. The questions asked may be ironical to point up the enormity of the venture upon which the invading nations will have embarked. The young lions of Tarshish are taken to mean either strong leaders and princes or greedy rulers of these commercial communities. Since there was a figure intended in verse 4 when hooks in the jaws of the enemy were mentioned, lions and prey are coordinate elements of another figure.

ISRAEL A PREY

Through the centuries Israel has time and again been the prey of one nation after another. Yet in every case the visitation of God in wrath has been unmistakable upon the ones involved. But the nations have not fully learned their lesson as far as hatred of Israel is concerned and will try yet once more. Satan will urge them on yet again to their doom, so that all may see that God curses those who curse Abraham's seed. Let us be found among those seeking their good and their blessing.

In the earlier portion of this significant chapter Ezekiel had been explicit concerning the nations involved in the final invasion of the Holy Land, their motivation, their intention and objective, as well as the clear

[2]Midrash Tanchuma, Qedoshim.

demarcation of time in the prophetic events. Thus far the activity of God has been stated in quite minimal terms. Elaboration has been on the human side and the human participants, as though the Spirit of God would lay bare to the fullest the enormity of the godless plans of the wicked nations of the end time. Now it was time for the Lord God to make known His ultimate purpose, which Ezekiel did with customary clarity and forcefulness.

God's Intention (38:14-16)

The Lord addressed Himself again to the leader of the hostile confederacy that had already made plans for the plundering of restored Israel in their land. It is important to notice the emphatic repetition of the time element. Again the attention was focused on the fact that Israel will be living in imagined security. The question is doubtless a rhetorical one. The Lord knew full well that Gog will have already acquainted himself with the fact of Israel's political condition in order to be sure of his attack. The Lord revealed His knowledge of every hidden purpose and motivation. The area of origin was again stated as out of the uttermost parts, the farthest reaches, of the north. It is well known who has been dominant in this region of the world ever since the end of the last global conflict, an area which has actually kept the entire world in turmoil constantly. Russia is a power that must be reckoned with now, and surely will figure largely in the events that lie ahead, especially when the church is raptured to her risen Lord. Once more the full retinue is passed in review. Do not fail to notice "my people" in verses 14 and 16, and "my land" in verse 16. The godless nations have had little idea how involved God is in all that concerns His people and His land. This has been true throughout their national existence but will be made all the more evident when God finally decides to intervene decisively into the affairs of men in the consummation of the prophetic program for the earth.

Nowhere in the Scriptures will it be found that God instills in the heart of any man any evil purpose or device. He is the Promoter of good and never evil. However, the Old Testament presentation is always intended to show that God is the sovereign Ruler and Overruler of all. Thus it is stated that God will bring the enemy against His land. He actually will bring these nations to the doom which will already be in their wicked hearts. It is a parallel to the condition of Pharaoh of Egypt in the time of the exodus. God does not and He did not implant stubbornness in the heart of the Egyptian king, but He did allow him to be surrounded by circumstances which called forth the wickedness in that heart. When God states that He will be sanctified in Gog, the thought is not that the earthly ruler in any way will add to the character or attributes of God. But in the Lord's dealings with him, the God of all the universe will be recognized as holy. Just as circumstances lay bare the wickedness and godlessness of men, so the same conditions reveal in a blaze of glory the blessed God whom we delight to worship in Christ our Lord.

THE ANNIHILATION OF THE ENEMY (38:17-23)

Verse 17 has been variously interpreted. Because the statement is couched in general terms, it is claimed there is evidence here that Ezekiel intended no definite series of events. Rather, he was speaking of Gog and his confederates as representative or typical of all the enemies of the people of God; in short, the portrayal is of that now lengthy conflict between good and evil, the kingdom of God and the powers of darkness. Another view is that, since the things prophesied are far away in the future, the reference is to Ezekiel's own prophecy of these events. Neither of these views is acceptable. The first does not do justice to the abundance of geographical and other detail. The second does not square with the fact that the passage speaks of prophets (plural) and the time setting is "in old time," that is, counting from Ezekiel's day.

Actually, it is difficult to point to a definite utterance of earlier prophets that can be construed as predicting specifically the activities of Gog and the northern confederacy. One interpretation equates Gog with the Assyrian of Isaiah 10:5-16 and Micah 5:5, but this is a weak position. On what grounds are Gog and the Assyrian to be identified? Geographical considerations need further substantiation. Yet others see a reference to all that the earlier prophets have foretold of God's judgment on the ungodly nations of the world, citing passages such as Numbers 24:17-24; Jeremiah 3-6; Joel 3; Daniel 2:44-45; Zephaniah 1:14; 3:8. It is possible that there is no direct reference to any specific group of prophecies but to a general concept that permeates prophecy. Earlier prophets, in speaking of eschatological times, foretold catastrophic events and God's judgment on Israel's enemies, though the specific name of Gog did not appear in their prophecies. The expected answer to the question of verse 17 is an affirmative one.

The reaction to the audacity and effrontery of the invasion of Gog and his forces was stated in bold terms and a vivid anthropomorphism (see Ps. 18:8). The picture is of the breath which an angered man inhales and exhales through his nose. God's patience would be exhausted with the repeated attempts of Israel's enemies to annihilate her. The Lord Himself will undertake the destruction of Israel's enemies, choosing to use no secondary agent, for this is to be a final and irrecoverable judgment. The order will be, first, earthquake, then anarchy, pestilence and natural disasters. God's violent shaking of the earth will affect every area of nature, both animate and inanimate. All creation will be convulsed at the same time, and the higher creation, man, will be thrown into confusion and civil strife (for similar manifestations connected with the coming day of the Lord, see Zeph. 1; Isa. 2; Jer. 4:23-26). Supernatural panic will complete the picture of distress for man. The judgments, though so general and widespread that they must relate to the end of Israel's age, were taken from the pattern of the destruction of Sodom and the plagues of Egypt. Throughout the recital the supreme purpose was always clearly stated and constantly emphasized. God does not delight in judgment, and He states fully why He must visit man with wrath. By the unusual manifestations of His power obtuse man will come to realize the nature of the great God and Sovereign of the universe.

The details of the vast visitation are given in chapter 39, but the groundwork has been carefully laid to show the human provocation for such sweeping visitation in wrath upon wicked men. Ezekiel did not prefer the prediction of judgment on puny men, but he kept his eyes riveted on the goal of the glory of the Lord in all the earth.

39

THE JUDGMENT OF GOG

CHAPTER 39 is inseparably connected in thought and form with the previous chapter. This is not another invasion by Gog, as some scholars have claimed, but the same one described from a different viewpoint. If there have been those who have denied the literal character of chapter 38, there has been an equal number who oppose a literal interpretation of this chapter.

Some of the arguments advanced against a literal explanation are these: First, it is maintained that the name Gog is merely an ideal name derived from the historically attested name of Magog. Second, it is claimed that the nations involved are too far from the land of promise ever to confederate in military action. A third factor that is said to argue against literality is the great number of armies involved. It is maintained that the land invaded could not sustain such a large number of soldiers for even a day.

A fourth item of difficulty is pointed out in the results of the victory. That there should be wood for fuel for seven years and that Israel should be occupied in burial of the dead for seven months, are said to be fantastic and impossible. It is held that a million men would have to be so occupied, and that for the one hundred eighty days of the seven months, if each person buried two bodies in a day, the total would be three hundred sixty million corpses. This is to say nothing of the putrefaction and odors of the slain before burial. A fifth argument is even more serious, for it claims that the literal interpretation introduces disagreement among the prophets. In this chapter the struggle is on the mountains of Israel; in Isaiah 34 the conflict is on the mountains of Edom; in Joel 3:12-14 it takes place in the Valley of Jehoshaphat; and in Zechariah 14 and Revelation 20 it is in the neighborhood of Jerusalem. A final argument has it that, since the occurrences relate to the final epochs of the world and Messianic times, the passages must have a nonliteral interpretation.

These arguments can be refuted as follows:

Argument one: It is arbitrary in the extreme to single out one proper name in a group of several in this chapter and claim it is an ideal name. There is no proof for this statement.

Argument two: The same argument was leveled against the historicity of Genesis 14. Eminent archaeologists are firm in the position that the biblical account there is reliable. So here; no a priori negative argument can stand scrutiny.

Argument three: On what basis does this objection rest? How can it be substantiated? Who knows fully how future armies may be sustained in the field? To point out difficulties in a passage does not of itself disprove a statement. The supernatural working of God cannot be ruled out.

Argument four: Every position here is built on inferences and conclusions which are not valid. If the account is to be taken nonliterally, why the abundance of details and even specific numbers? The literal interpretation alone does justice to the text.

Argument five: The student of the prophetic Scriptures will realize that these locations are not mutually exclusive, for the final conflict will occur in more than one stage. The same type of argument here would make a shambles of the resurrection accounts found in the Gospels.

Argument six: It is a serious *non sequitur* to hold that all occurrences of the final stages of human history demand nonliteral interpretation. This is a plea for a dual hermeneutic in Scripture and is palpably false.

Those who have attempted to refer these chapters to specific conflicts in the past have arrived at widely different results. One view places it in the conflict of the Maccabees with Antiochus; another in the invasion and overthrow of the Chaldeans; and still another in the temporary victories and final overthrow of the Turks. All these are equally unsatisfactory because the passage is clearly set in the future, in the time of Israel's consummation. The time is still before the return of the Lord in glory. It will be seen that the serious and fatal weakness of the enemies of Israel will be their reliance on numbers, and their confidence that Israel's weakness means their strength and ultimate victory. They fail, as always, to take God into account. But notice the three ways employed to indicate the vastness and severity of Gog's overthrow: (1) the wood for fuel (vv. 9-10); (2) the long period for burials (vv. 11-16); and (3) the sacrificial feast on the carcasses (vv. 17-20).

GOG'S JUDGMENT DESCRIBED (39:1-10)

This chapter begins, as 38:3, with an unequivocal assertion of the divine displeasure against Gog. The repetition is intended for emphasis. The statement concerning turning Gog about (v. 2, ASV) carries with it the idea of compulsion. Some translate the Hebrew verb "lead thee on" (v. 2, ASV) as "leave but the sixth part" (AV), "strike with six plagues," or "draw with a hook of six teeth." But the first rendering is probably best.

It is surely overdrawn to see in the six the number of the beast in Revelation 13:18. Some interpreters take the geographical notation to identify Gog with the king of the north of Daniel 11:40-41, 45. The Lord will render the enemy powerless for the conflict by striking from his hands both bow and arrows. Warriors from the north were known in ancient times to be skilled bowmen.

Ezekiel was explicit as to the place of the encounter taking place near the city of Jerusalem on the mountains of Israel. This was the testimony of Joel (chap. 3) and Zechariah (chap. 14) also. Because of the amount of carnage, burial will not be the order of the day. The Lord has determined that the carcasses will fall to the ravenous birds and beasts. Such absence of burial was especially abhorrent in the Near East. This picture in verse 4 anticipates what is stated at greater length in verses 17-20. The fire threatened is that of war and, more generally, that of destruction from the Lord (see 38:22; Rev. 20:9). The isles referred to are the coastland and islands of the Mediterranean. Though the judgment on the enemies will occur in Israel, the catastrophe will extend far out to the ends of the earth to accomplish the purpose of God. Once more the Lord will relate His purpose in Israel to that for all the world. It is the concept of concentric circles where that which is accomplished at the very center reaches out irresistibly to the farthest confines of the circumference. God is the Lord of the nations. His true character will appear in its proper light as both righteous and mighty. Such emphasis is made of this thought throughout the book of Ezekiel because this is the design of God in all history, and there is no more important concept in all the universe. That which gives stability and worth to life on earth is the determining truth that a God of holiness, wisdom, love and truth is working out His blessed will throughout the universe and among created intelligences.

There may, indeed, be some who think that matters may be altered or fashioned to their liking. To them the word comes that there is no escape from what has been predicted, for it is as good as done. When God predicts, He makes it manifest that He can also perform that which is foretold. Israel will use the weapons of the invaders for fuel. In our day the word concerning fire does not sound so strange as it once did; wooden weapons are not without the range of use. The hand staves mentioned are those with which animals were usually driven, but here probably employed in warfare. The number seven expresses completeness, but it also points up the fact that the numbers of the invading forces will be vast, and that Israel's zeal will be aroused to keep the land cleansed from all pollution. And what a turning of the tables on the enemy! The plunderers will be plundered and the robbers will be robbed. What the enemy will intend for Israel (38:12) will be visited upon them, another vivid example of the law of recompense in kind.

PURIFICATION OF THE LAND (39:11-16)

Ezekiel first brought out the vastness of the forces of the enemy by showing the length of time involved and the quantity of material to be burned at the destruction of the enemy forces. Then he underscored the same truth from the angle of the time needed to accomplish the burial of all the slain, indicating that the place of Gog's burial will be the valley of the Jordan above the Dead Sea, which is further explained by the words "on the east [literally, in the front] of the sea." Gog's burial will be east of the Dead Sea. The valley will be so clogged with the corpses of Gog's hosts that the way will be impassable for travelers. The valley ends in a blind alley because the farther extremity is closed and sealed off. Instead of all the spoil on which their heart will be set, they will find the place of their doom and burial. Ironically, although they will only intend to pass through in their campaign for plunder, they will find here the place of their undoing. So great will be the carnage that Gog will give his name to the valley, which will receive a new name commemorating God's victory over Israel's adversaries.

Moreover, death will come so suddenly to so many that it will take the better part of a year to finish the burying. All facts emphasize the vast proportions of the catastrophe. There will be need of cleansing because bloodshed defiles a land (see 36:18; Num. 35:33-34). The occupation of interment will engage the entire nation, and all the while they will be impressed with the thought that they have been witnesses of God's judgment on His and their enemies. God will be glorified in victory over the invading enemy. The final verses of this section seek to convey the zeal of the nation in seeing that the land is thoroughly purged. The ones referred to will be appointed to care for any bones that may have been overlooked. A memorial of the disaster will be left in the name of a city which will remind of the vast multitudes who will be involved in the invasion. Numbers will be no assurance of success if the venture be undertaken against the will and people of God.

THE FEAST OF THE BIRDS AND BEASTS (39:17-20)

Now there is presented the third emphasis of the greatness of the invasion and the subsequent slaughter at the hand of the Lord. Incidentally, the figure gives a clue as to the time setting for the entire passage. It is the same scene as that of Revelation 19, the great supper of God, and the chronology is clear. The events will transpire at the end of the great tribulation and just before the millennial reign of the Messiah of Israel. A word of caution is in order here. Because the time factor is explicit in Ezekiel and Revelation, there is no ground to equate the Gog of Ezekiel with any individual or group mentioned by John. The concept of the Lord's sacrifice was already found in Isaiah 34:6; Jeremiah 46:10; and Zephaniah 1:7-8.

But why should there be a sacrificial feast at all? It will be impossible to complete the burial all at once. The animals mentioned are figurative of the different ranks of the slain men. In verse 18 the actual or literal passes over into the figurative with the reference to princes, then rams. Bashan was famous for its fine pastures and well-fed cattle (cf. Deut. 32:14; Ps. 22:12; Amos 4:1). In the law of Moses the fat and blood of animals, considered the most holy portions, were offered to God and were not allowed the worshipers (see Lev. 3:11-17; Ezek. 44:15; for the same idea of sacrifice, cf. Isa. 18:6; Rev. 19:17-18). The sacrificial feast mentioned in verse 19 is referred to as "my table" (v. 20) because it is the Lord who will hold the feast. It is a vivid figure to bring out the idea of vast carnage, deserved judgment and irrevocable doom.

GOD'S OVERRULING PURPOSE (39:21-29)

Some feel that verses 21-22 are not directly related to the themes of chapters 38-39. When Ezekiel here reverted to the near future and the conditions of his day, he was in a sense recapitulating the truths of chapters 34-37. Furthermore, he was still setting forth principles of God's dealings which are as applicable to Israel as they are to others. If the people of Israel could discern the working of God among the nations, then it is equally true that the nations of earth could learn the character and will of God from His relationships with His chosen people. In short, both segments of the human family are an object lesson for the other, displaying the infinite holiness and love of the universal God. The visitation of the Lord upon the rebellious nations will first have significance for Israel. Contrariwise, the nations will then realize that Israel suffered captivity and defeat not because of any inherent weakness in God, but because of their sinful ways which He punished in this manner. The withdrawal of God's favor from Israel, far from being a result of any caprice, was occasioned by their unrelieved opposition to the will of their God.

Verses 25-29 teach that the complete return of Israel will occur after the defeat of Gog and his confederates. Ezekiel summarized his prophecies of hope and restoration. When he stated that God will have mercy upon the whole house of Israel, he had in mind that all previous restorations were partial. Now a universal and final restoration will take place.

It was God who allowed them to go into captivity; it is He who will see to it that they are regathered; indeed, it is He who will insure that not one is left out of the land. Mark well how often it is stated that Israel and the nations will recognize the only true and sovereign God; this is one of the dominant themes of the book—God manifested and magnified in the history of His people. In conclusion, to summarize all the benefits promised, Ezekiel spoke of the outpouring of the Spirit upon the house of Israel (see 36:25-31; Joel 2:28 ff.; Zech. 12:10).

GOD'S GLORIOUS PURPOSE

Throughout Ezekiel, as in the rest of the Bible, the major theme is the purpose of God to bring glory to His name. To this end God wrought His plan of salvation at Calvary at infinite cost. It is good spiritual exercise to examine whether His purpose is being fulfilled in our lives.

INTRODUCTION TO CHAPTERS 40-48

THE LAST NINE CHAPTERS of this prophecy form an inseparable unit. Along with certain other key passages of the Old Testament, like Isaiah 7:14 and 52:13–53:12 and portions of Daniel, the concluding chapters of Ezekiel form a kind of continental divide in the area of biblical interpretation. Students of the Scriptures have scrutinized carefully and written voluminously on this crucial section of the Word of God. It is one of the areas where the literal interpretation of the Bible and the spiritualizing or allegorizing method diverge widely. Here amillennialists and premillennialists are poles apart. Moreover, neither camp is homogeneous in interpretation; there are many varieties of opinion within each school of thought. Many cover the entire portion with certain generalizations and leave it at that. But this is unworthy of the book and the Author behind the text. When thirty-nine chapters can be treated detailedly and seriously as well as literally, there is no valid reason a priori for treating this large division of the book in an entirely different manner. There must be compelling evidence that such a disclosure should be handled in such a way. Some may think it not germane to enter upon such a discussion, and would counsel to proceed at once to the exposition of the sacred text. This is possible, but lays the writer open to the charge of arbitrariness. Great issues are at stake; good and sincere men differ widely in their interpretations; wisdom would dictate that time be allotted to some discussion of the views which are so determinative for such a long section of the Word of God.

Several approaches have been suggested for these last chapters. According to a broad classification they may be identified as the literal and figurative views. But these in turn have other subdivisions and ramifications. One interpretation holds that the portion is a description of Solomon's temple, but this is difficult to substantiate or defend because the details are quite different between Solomon's temple and that of Ezekiel. Another position claims that Ezekiel gave a lofty ideal or pattern for the exiles in their building of the restoration temple. However, it is more than strange that there is no reference whatever to such a temple in any postexilic book. A third view has been espoused by some Jewish commentators who hold that the Messiah will build the temple and will inaugurate the ritual. As will be seen later, this explanation is not restricted to Jews and their theological position; it will be treated at greater length.

A fourth approach taken by some Christian commentators parallels the view just stated by believing in a literal temple, sacrifices and priesthood during the millennium. These objections have been leveled against this view: First, it is pointed out that the atonement of Christ nullified Old Testament sacrifices (see Heb. 9:11-15; 10:1-4, 18). Second, the system of the old economy was provisional and not to be restored for believers (cf. Gal. 3:23-25; Col. 2:16-17). Third, all believers are Abraham's seed (Gal. 3:7, 16, 29) and members of the "Israel of God" (Gal. 6:16). There is now no middle wall of partition. Fourth, the New Testament refers to the church as the new Israel (see I Peter 2:3-5, 8-10). The promises to Israel of old now include the worldwide church (cf. Rom. 15:9-12). Fifth, all believers now are priests (see I Peter 2:5, 9). Sixth, the Apostle John uses these chapters to describe the church of Christ (Rev. 21:9–22:5), removing the Jewish elements.

Lest the discussion get too far removed from these objections against the literal interpretation of the chapters, here are answers to them: First, no Christian would think of denying that the redemptive work of the Lord Jesus Christ on Calvary brought Old Testament sacrifices to an end for us all. It may be a poor expression to speak of them as nullified by the atonement of Christ, for it must be recognized that Old Testament sacrifices never had any redemptive efficacy (see Hebrews 10:4 for a significant and determining and permanent principle of God's working). But just as the Old Testament sacrifices could have value in pointing forward to the death of Christ, why may they not have equal value in pointing back to the death of Christ as an accomplished fact? The celebration of the Lord's Supper through the Christian centuries has added not one infinitesimal particle to the efficacy of the work of Christ on the cross, but who will dare to deny that it has value for the believer, since it is enjoined upon us as a memorial?

Second, it is not denied that the legal economy was provisional and that the old covenant was to be displaced by a new covenant (Jer. 31:31 ff.). But how is it possible to miss the teaching of Scripture that the church age is not the only or last era of God's operation in time? Because certain conditions do not obtain in our age is no guarantee that God has not indicated their presence in an age that follows ours. The opposition, with a false view of what God is accomplishing in time, wrongly makes our age the last one before the eternal day. This necessitates some strange handling of Scripture to fit all the remaining parts into our epoch of world history. It cannot be done without definite wresting of Scripture and a change of interpretive principle in midstream.

Third, we do not deny that all believers are Abraham's seed, but this is in the spiritual realm. A Gentile believer *never* becomes Abraham's seed by nature. The Lord charged the natural seed of Abraham with many ordinances. Are these binding on us as the spiritual seed of Abraham? To ask the question is to answer it. The position is actually not relevant to the interpretation of these important chapters. To claim that all believers are the Israel of God is to fail to realize the meaning of Galatians 6:16 and to lose sight of the climax of Paul's argument throughout Galatians.

It is asserted that the New Testament refers to the church as the new Israel. Neither Romans, I Peter nor any other book of the New Testament teaches this view; it is read into the passages that are cited. Because Peter speaks of believers today as a spiritual house, the inference is not that we are the house of Israel. When he mentions that the saved are a holy priesthood, it is not to be taken that we are an Israelite or Aaronic priesthood. If we offer up spiritual sacrifices, the reference has absolutely nothing to do with those of the tabernacle or the temple except in a typical manner. If we are called an elect race and a holy nation, the conclusion to be drawn is certainly not that we are the Jewish nation. The promises given to national Israel in the Old Testament have not been transferred lock, stock and barrel to believers of the New Testament. This is the same approach that is careful enough to assign the curses of the Old Testament to the literal Israel. But where is there a scintilla of warrant to treat the Scriptures in this fashion? Try it on Romans 11 and see what inescapable havoc is wrought.

To maintain that all believers are now priests does not invalidate the truth that there was a past priesthood before the formation of the church, as there will be an authorized priesthood after the completion and rapture of the church. Again the error must be refuted which holds that this age is the consummating age in God's earthly program.

An assertion that cannot be allowed is to state that the Apostle John utilized Ezekiel 40-48 in his descriptions of the church in Revelation 21-22 after he had removed the Jewish elements. What are the points of similarity, and how great are the features of dissimilarity? Identity must rest on more than general factors. Details must be taken into consideration, and it is precisely the Jewish elements used by Ezekiel that reveal he had something different in mind than the message of John.

Reverting once more to the various approaches to these crucial chapters, a fifth view holds that Ezekiel was only interested in presenting a figure of the redeemed of all ages worshiping God in heaven. But what of the many earthly details of the vision? Yet a sixth view is called the symbolico-typical or allegorical view, favored by the church Fathers and the Reformers. They saw in these chapters Christ and the spiritual endowments of the church in the Christian era. This is entirely too subjective and would mean nothing for either Ezekiel or his contemporaries. A seventh approach maintains that the section is a prophetic parable, that is, spiritual truth is pronounced in the thought categories of Ezekiel. Those who adhere to this position find comprehensive principles of God's presence with His people. Again, this interpretation does little justice to the abundant detail of the chapters. Was it not true that the many details of the tabernacle of Moses embodied comprehensive spiritual and prophetic principles? Did they thereby lose their literal significance? Was the tabernacle actually built in Moses' day or was it not? Was it purely idealistic or ideational? One reading of the pertinent Old Testament passages settles the question for all time. The analogy holds true for the passages now under consideration.

Jewish and Christian commentators have been generally agreed as to the Messianic character of Ezekiel's final chapters. However, this has not meant ease in the task of interpretation, whether in general or as to details. On the basis of chapters 40-48 Ezekiel has been called "the father of Judaism." Yet the Talmudic rabbis despaired of ever interpreting the portion, claiming the discrepancies with the Pentateuch could only be explained by the Prophet Elijah. The different names for the views of these chapters indicate in themselves the wide diversity. One is called the historico-literal, which holds that the portion was fulfilled in the temple of Solomon, so these chapters aim to preserve the memory of that magnificent structure. The difference between Solomon's temple and Ezekiel's are so patent as to need no further elaboration. Another is termed the historico-ideal, which believes that the chapters predict vaguely some future good. But others explain the position as maintaining that the temple is the one that should have been built after the captivity, but because of the unbelief and disobedience of the people it never was realized. It is pointed out that there were features impossible to the returned exiles: the method of distributing the land and the river coming from the temple. This approach is unsatisfactory from a number of angles, but chiefly because it bases all on a naturalistic foundation without due recognition to the supernatural features inherent in the chapters.

A third view is the Jewish or Jewish-carnal theory, which states that the ideas were actually carried out by Ezekiel's successors on their return to the land of promise, insofar as they were able. However, since it was imperfectly done, the Messiah will fulfill it to the letter. It should be pointed out that this position has had the support of some Christian interpreters as well.

A fourth position has been designated as the Christian-spiritual or Christian-allegorical. This view, held by Luther and the Reformers, sees the chapters as symbolic of future blessing for the church in the age of the gospel. But even a passing acquaintance with the great principles of dispensational interpretation of the Bible would rule out this approach. Any view of the Scriptures which confuses Israel with the church, or mingles them into the same category, is suspect.

The final view, known as the literal, declares that the prediction speaks of the restoration and establishment of the people of Israel in their own land in the last days of their national history, their conversion to the Lord through faith in their long-rejected Messiah, and the manifest presence and glory of the Lord in their midst. This view has to its credit that it takes into account the broad context of the book of Ezekiel; it is consonant with the prophecies of the Old and New Testament; and it permits the historico-grammatical method of biblical interpretation to have its rightful exercise, allowing the context in each passage to be the determining factor.

Why is there so much objection here to the literal view? It is held that it was not part of a prophet's ministry to give specific directions for the building of the temple. But Ezekiel was also a priest. Furthermore, Moses was a prophet and he was given ample instructions for the building of the tabernacle; Solomon was a king and yet built a temple to the Lord. Who is to determine when the Lord shall entrust any task to any individual? Second, it is argued that the literal interpretation destroys any connection with the series of Ezekiel's prophecies after the destruction of Jerusalem, which are not legislative in character. But we shall see that these chapters are connected with the preceding chapters and form the fitting climax to Ezekiel's magnificent prophecy. Third, it is held that the symbolical view is favored by the form used, namely, a vision. But even in a vision there are literal features which are demanded by the context. Finally, the symbolic character of the section is said to be confirmed by the dimensions of the temple. This is an argument which can be treated either way, for the dimensions have been conceded by architects to be entirely within the realm of feasibility.

Though the majority of expositors favor a symbolic or figurative explanation, there is sounded from time to time a word of caution. Some admit that there are serious and grave difficulties in the allegorical or symbolical approach. For one thing it can be easily discerned that Ezekiel enters too minutely into details of architecture for a symbolical interpretation to satisfy the requirements of the case. Furthermore, he expected these plans to be carried out in detail, so it is useless to find here a symbolic description of the church's worship. The chapters do not pretend to describe natural, but rather supernatural, conditions. Equally unsatisfactory is the attempt to employ a "double fulfillment," one for Israel and one for the church. Although a double fulfillment is not impossible (see Hosea 11:1), it can only be introduced as a last resort, and there is no good reason to utilize it here. Even some expositors who explain the chapters as symbolical are prepared to warn against the temptation to allegorize the prophetic picture and thus evaporate either the natural or the supernatural elements. Such a procedure, we are told, must be resisted firmly, because it contradicts all reason.

Moreover, it must be admitted that no one can assure that any state of affairs may not be fulfilled in the future. So-called physical improbabilities or difficulties do not preclude a literal interpretation, for the obstacles may be apparent rather than actual. The more one studies the detailed measurements of the chapters, the more the conviction grows that Ezekiel was speaking of a literal plan which is meant to be literally implemented in future times.

The literal position has been at times accused of inconsistency in interpretation, but the opposing camp is not free of such. A notable example is that of an honored expositor who considers all the chapters symbolical of the kingdom of God, yet spends 254 pages to give an exposition of chapters 40-48 in detail. What is his point of departure? He is convinced that the river of Ezekiel 47 is precisely that of Revelation 22, which belongs to the heavenly Jerusalem of the new earth. His basic theological error is that he believes that from the destruction of Jerusalem in the first century A.D., there has been no longer a congregation of the Lord in Israel outside the church of the Lord. In all fairness it must be admitted that the expositor is consistent, but he is also in error. The promises to Israel in the Old Testament, and in the New as well, cannot be so lightly dismissed.

In conclusion, it must never be forgotten that the details in chapters 40-48 concerning a future temple in the land are not intrinsically more difficult to comprehend than those of the tabernacle in the wilderness. Both are predicated upon the supernatural wisdom and power of God.

A word should be said concerning the interesting and instructive omissions in this portion. Pentecost is not mentioned among the great feasts, perhaps because of its so distinctive fulfillment in Christian times. Second, there is no reference to the ark of the covenant, because God's glory fills all. Jeremiah 3:16-18 will be realized in that age. Third, no high priest is spoken of, for Christ is the High Priest (see Zech. 6:12-13). Last, no king is referred to, for the Lord is King (cf. Zech. 14:9, 16-17).

GLORY AHEAD FOR ISRAEL

To read the last nine chapters of Ezekiel in their literal force is to learn that God has glorious plans in view for Israel and through them for all the earth. But such predictions of blessing never carry with them the assurance that there will be blessing for individuals anywhere apart from personal response in faith to the invitation of the Saviour.

40

GOD'S GLORIOUS HOUSE

IN MANY WAYS these chapters may be considered the most important in the book. They assuredly form the climax and crowning experience in the life of Ezekiel. His book begins with a vision of God's glory (chap. 1), and concludes with a vision of the same. These chapters are the fitting sequel to the series in chapters 33-39. Though they contrast greatly with Ezekiel's earlier prophecies, they are explained on the ground that he was a priest as well as a prophet. Apart from this fact the Spirit of God is wholly sovereign in such matters. The last section is separated from the earlier part of the book by an interval of thirteen years. The last dated prophecy was 32:17. The emphasis throughout the portion is on the holiness of God. The movement is from the sanctuary outward to the people and the land, just as had been the case with the presentation of the tabernacle. The last nine chapters may be divided as follows: (1) the new temple, 40:1–43:12; (2) the new worship of God, 43:13–46:24; and (3) the new apportionment of the land among the tribes, 47:1–48:35.

THE MAN WITH THE MEASURING ROD (40:1-4)

Notice that verse 1, most explicit with its notations of time, is dated as to the captivity in which Ezekiel found himself—the day, the month and the year—as well as its relationship to the fall of the city of Jerusalem. Obviously the subject matter to be disclosed is of great significance. This first chronological statement points back to 1:1 and 33:21. As to the exact year, estimates vary from 572 to 574 and even 575 B.C. Also, there is some difference of opinion as to the meaning of the first of the year. It is held among Jews that the new year began on the tenth day of Tishri (the seventh month) in the fall of the year, according to one understanding of Leviticus 25:9. Later the new year was changed to the first day of the seventh month, and the tenth day became the Day of Atonement (Lev. 23:24; Num. 29:1). Actually, there are no good arguments against taking this as the ecclesiastical year which began in the spring of the year (see Exodus 12:2). The month, then, would be Nisan. The civil year, commencing in the seventh month, appears to have been a later arrangement.

The tenth day was the time when preparations for the Passover were begun. The destruction of the city of Jerusalem, which was the culmination of Israel's sin, as well as the confirmation of Ezekiel's predictions, forms now the somber background for the delineation of God's glory and His coming kingdom on earth. On that memorable day, so clearly delimited, Ezekiel was transported in vision to the city of Jerusalem.

Because of the mention of visions of God some feel Ezekiel's vision should not be taken too literally, any more than the symbolic presentation of Jerusalem in Revelation 21. But, throughout the portion it will be seen that the natural and the supernatural are intertwined. There is a resemblance between the beginning in chapter 1 and that in chapter 40. The characterization of the prophecy as a vision in no wise detracts from the literal reality of what is depicted here, any more than it does in Daniel or Zechariah.

The very high mountain is not identified; it may be Mount Hermon. However, there is more reason to believe it is Mount Zion (cf. Isa. 2:2; Micah 4:1; Ezek. 17:22; 20:40).

Ezekiel's approach was from the north, so the Hebrew text ("on the south") is to be preferred to the Septuagint ("over against"), although the Greek necessitates the change of one consonant only. The vision of the building and consecration of the new temple is in contrast to the desecration and destruction of the former temple (chaps. 8-11). When Ezekiel reached his destination, he saw a man who has been taken by some to be the interpreting angel as in Zechariah and Revelation. By a comparison of Scriptures it is best to understand Him to be the Angel of the Lord (see 44:2, 5) since He is called Lord. Such Old Testament appearances of heavenly creatures as men paved the way in men's thinking for the incarnation of the Messiah.

The brass was actually copper with the symbolic significance of strength (I Kings 4:13; Job 40:18), unwavering steadfastness (whether in good or evil, Jer. 1:18; 15:20; Isa. 48:4), and judgment (Deut. 28:23; Lev. 26:19; Micah 4:13). The line of flax was for the longer measurements; the reed was for the shorter. The task of measuring was important (cf. Zech. 2:1; Rev. 11:1; 21:15). Some interpret the work as the pronouncement of God of His title to all that is involved, but the emphasis in each instance appears to be a delineating of that which belongs to God. The Man with the measuring rod spoke to Ezekiel to alert him to use his eyes, his ears and his reflective faculties (the heart), all of which indicated the importance of what was to be revealed. What was to be disclosed would require the concentration of Ezekiel's every faculty. Surely no less is required of us in order to comprehend the vast themes set forth in the ensuing chapters.

THE WALL, GATE AND LODGES (40:5-16)

The competent opinion of architects who have studied the plan given here is that all these dimensions could be drawn to scale to produce a beautiful sanctuary of the Lord. The wall was meant to convey the concept of sacredness, the fundamental idea being that of separation because is was too low to serve as a bulwark against an attack of an enemy. The surrounding wall was not new to the ancient world, for in the great Babylonian temples the courts were surrounded by massive walls with great gateways, giving the impression of a huge fortress. The same was true of Egyptian temples.

Since the measuring factor runs throughout this section of the book, these are the lengths of the measuring units: A cubit is about eighteen inches long (see Deut. 3:11). Some suggest a longer cubit was used, but there is no proof either way. The handbreadth varies because it was derived from parts of the human body. If the Hebrew cubit were nearly twenty-one inches, and the handbreadth about three and one-half inches more, then the entire measurement would total about two feet, and the rod about twelve feet.

The buildings of the east gate were presented first because this entrance was in the direct line of approach to the temple. The lodges were accommodations for the ministering priests and were actually guardrooms where temple officers were located to keep order and to care for the house. In verse 10 reference was made again to the eastward gate, which was in some ways the most important of all, for through it the glory of God would return to the sanctuary (chap. 43). It remains closed thereafter because God had entered by it. The prince was permitted to eat in the gate before the Lord; however, he had to come in by the porch and leave in the same manner; there was no passing through the gate (44:1-3).

The guardrooms and intervening spaces were provided with windows, which would suggest that the whole was roofed over. Regarding the closed windows, they were latticed because they had no glass. The palm tree decoration was the same as that in the temple of Solomon. The palm tree was a symbol of beauty (Song of Sol. 7:7); fruitfulness (Ps. 92:12-14); salvation and victory (Rev. 7:9); and regal glory (John 12:13). It is characteristic of the millennial age of which Solomon's reign was typical (I Kings 6:29, 32, 35; 7:36; II Chron. 3:5). Palm branches were used in the Feast of Tabernacles (Lev. 23:40; Neh. 8:15), a festival typical of the millennium also (Zech. 14:16 ff.).

THE OUTER AND INNER COURTS (40:17-37)

There is little in these verses that needs elaborate explanation. The pavement of verse 17 is probably a mosaic pavement (see II Chron. 7:3; Esther 1:6). The numbers 5, 20 and 50 are frequently used. The sanctuary formed a square of some five hundred cubits.

THE CHAMBERS FOR THE PRIESTS (40:38-47)

The matter of sacrifices in the kingdom has long been a crucial point of controversy. Certainly there will be offerings in the tribulation time (Dan. 9:27), a period that postdates the church age. The reiterated argument against millennial sacrifices is that it contradicts the truth of the epistle to the Hebrews. But does it? Hebrews is not speaking primarily nor specifically of the millennial era. Furthermore, sacrifices will have no more redemptive efficacy in the millennial period than they had in the ages before Calvary. Again, nothing and no sacrifice, before or after the work of Christ on the cross, invalidates or renders unnecessary that glorious work which we shall praise throughout the eternal ages. But just as the Lord's Supper now detracts not one iota from the glory of the work of Calvary, but rather has been a constant memorial of it for over nineteen hundred years, so the sacrifices of the millennial age will be powerless to diminish the worth of the Saviour's death on Calvary, but will rather be a continuous memorial of it for a thousand years, half the time allotted to us already for the memorial of the central fact of history. Recall that since Israel did not receive their Messiah in His first coming, they have never celebrated a memorial of His redeeming work. Need we begrudge them this in the light of the fact that the Scriptures are so clear that God has appointed the sacrifices for that age, and surely for their commemorative value?

Provision was made for leading the praises of Israel, just as in the temple of Solomon. The inner court, the court of Israel where they could bring their sacrifices and offerings, went around three sides of the sacred area, a breadth of about two hundred feet. But this court, exactly one hundred cubits square, with the altar in it, was in front of the temple. It was the priests' court and was referred to in connection with those who were in charge of the house, the altar and the service of music. In verse 45 the guide explained the building's purpose.

The mention of the sons of Zadok is an incidental indication of the historical ramifications of the passage. Proper names serve to tie the revelation to historic reality and validity, calling for literal interpretation. The Lord chose Zadok when He set aside the house of Eli at the time of Solomon, who deposed the family of Ithamar from the priesthood because Abiathar had joined the rebellion of Adonijah (see I Kings 1:7; 2:26-27). For other references to the sons of Zadok in this prophecy compare 43:19;

44:15; 48:11. This division of the chapter concludes with the altar, the actual center and focal point of the entire sanctuary, memorial of Christ's sacrifice.

THE PORCH (40:48-49)

Ezekiel continued to set forth detail after detail, making it increasingly difficult to interpret the whole in a figurative manner, in which case the abundance of minute details is worthless and meaningless. The intention appears to be to indicate that the porch of the sanctuary resembled that of the Solomonic temple. The pillars, too, corresponded to Jachin and Boaz of Solomon's temple (I Kings 7:21). There is no need to introduce here a thinly veiled paganism, as some seek to do, by relating these pillars to the obelisks which were placed before Egyptian temples.

THE WORTH OF THE WORK OF CHRIST

Throughout the Word of God it is revealed what infinite value God places on the work of His blessed Son. No detail is too much if it will serve to underscore the limitless worth of Christ's redemptive work. Why should this not be so in our thinking as well? Let us make much of Calvary.

41

APPOINTMENTS OF THE TEMPLE

BECAUSE IT IS INSTRUCTIVE and important to notice the differences between this sanctuary and Solomon's temple, this chapter should be studied in the light of I Kings 6-7. It is remarkable that silver and gold, which were so prominent in the tabernacle in the wilderness and in the Solomonic temple, should not be mentioned in chapters 40-48. If the previous chapter was difficult for an allegorizing interpretation because of the many details given, this one is no more encouraging. Yet one expositor declares that if this plan were meant to be implemented, it would have supplied us with more particulars. The record must be interpreted according to what is revealed, not what the prophet or reader may desire.

THE POSTS OF THE TEMPLE (41:1-4)

The dimensions for the inner sanctuary were the same as those for Solomon's temple and twice as much as those for the tabernacle in the wilderness. The name "tabernacle" in verse 1 is literally "tent," the name given the sanctuary before Solomon's temple was erected. When all the measurements of Ezekiel's temple and its surroundings are put together, the result is a square of a hundred cubits in breadth and a hundred cubits in length, apart from the porch (see 40:47). Ezekiel had entered the vestibule (40:48-49); here he was led to what may be called the nave, as distinct from the most holy place. The height of the temple was not indicated (cf. I Kings 6:3, 5).

It was not Ezekiel who went inward, but the Angel alone, toward the most holy place. One is reminded of an earlier economy indicated in Hebrews 9:8, 12 and 10:19. The mention of the most holy place in verse 4 shows the same two divisions which obtained in previous sanctuaries, namely, the holy place and the most holy. Apparently Ezekiel did not enter the second, though he was a priest. The most holy place was a square of twenty cubits. Holiness becomes God's dwelling place, and it is constantly emphasized throughout the Old and New Testament.

THE WALL AND SIDE CHAMBERS (41:5-11)

It will suffice to point out that Ezekiel was an eyewitness of the details of the future sanctuary. Visions of God they were, but they represented to Ezekiel, as they should to us, actualities and not fantasies or allegories. There was a sober and studied setting forth of the different features of the coming temple. When the details are pondered, it will be recognized that all was characterized by massiveness and spaciousness, features of Oriental structures, in addition to the impression of security and durability.

THE BUILDING BEFORE THE SEPARATE PLACE (41:12-14)

Along with the temple itself there was specified a building separate from the sanctuary proper, though the purpose of this building was not stated. Some relate this building that was before the separate place to the *parvarim* of II Kings 23:11, where horses were formerly kept that were held to be sacred to the sun god (see also I Chron. 26:18, ASV—called in this passage Parbar). The entire building covered a space of five hundred cubits square according to the calculation of the size of the surrounding wall (40:24-27).

THE GALLERIES ABOUT THE TEMPLE (41:15-20)

The galleries spoken of were terraced buildings with decorations described as cherubim and palm trees covering the walls from top to bottom. The cherubim were related to God's holiness (as seen in Gen. 3), and the palm trees were connected with righteousness and victory.

THE ALTAR OF INCENSE (41:21-26)

The altar of verse 22 was not the altar of sacrifice, nor the table of shewbread, but the altar of incense before the Lord (see Exodus 30:1-3; I Kings 7:48). It has been suggested that it was an altarlike table (cf. 44:16). The table of shewbread, candelabrum and other furniture of the temple were not mentioned. Each of the turning leaves (more fully described in I Kings 6:31-35) was constructed in two parts, each part having two folding leaves, making four leaves for each door. The palm trees were utilized for ornamentation on the exterior of the temple; cherubim were used for the holy place and the holy of holies. The dimensions of this temple were larger than those of Solomon's temple, evidently to accommodate a greater number of people. It is noteworthy that there was no reference to the ark of the covenant in the furnishings of the temple, which was in keeping with the prediction for the kingdom age already stated by

Jeremiah in his prophecy (3:16-17). All will be exactly as God has promised.

The Righteous in the Kingdom

The righteous will indeed flourish in the kingdom of Christ, for He will cast out all who do iniquity and offend. He cannot have in His presence those who do not stand in His righteousness alone. Having been declared righteous, let us live righteously to His praise.

42

MEASURING THE CHAMBERS OF
THE COURT

To THE CASUAL READER of Scripture this chapter can afford little of interest. In fact, the conclusion may even be that many details and features included are wholly unnecessary and without spiritual import. However, to one who has learned that God has not filled His Word with the irrelevant, inconsequential or trifling, the passage speaks clearly that our God is One of order, plan and decorum. Moreover, He has an abiding interest in all that pertains to proper worship of Him as Creator and Redeemer. If the Lord has gone to such lengths to give such minutiae, He does indeed seek worshipers who will approach Him in Spirit and in truth. Besides, we as New Testament priests may draw certain parallels relative to our worship today, even though it is not encompassed with so many earthly and carnal ordinances, which were anticipatory of the day of the realization of redemption through the coming Messiah of Israel.

THE INNER COURT OF THE CHAMBERS (42:1-12)

The same conducting and leading Agent seen in 40:1 is the One who revealed and demonstrated the future sanctuary and its manifold appointments to Ezekiel in this chapter. The accommodations were for the priests during the time of their service in one of the twenty-four courses (if we are to judge from the prototype indicated in I Chron.) in the holy place and at the altar (40:44). Here they were chambers specifically for the depositing of the sacrificial gifts and the official garments of the priests. It has been suggested that these accommodations for the priests speak of the mansions of John 14:1-3. The thought may be heartwarming to some, but there is no intended parallel or type of this character in the text. Even as an analogy it leaves much to be desired. From the precise measurements given in the early verses of this chapter it is clearly indicated that the building became narrower as it rose. Judging from the mention of pillars and courts, it is quite likely that there were cloisters inside the wall of the courts as in the temple after Ezekiel's time. The wall outside by the side of the chambers spoke of a screen wall at the eastern end of the chambers to screen the windows as the priests changed their garments. Thus every provision was made for beauty, order and decorum. The chambers on the south of the temple answered exactly to those on the north side.

The Priests' Use of the Chambers (42:13-14)

The uses of these chambers were twofold: (1) for the priests to eat the most holy things there, and (2) to keep there the sacred vestments when they put them off before going into the outer court to the people. What portions were theirs by right of the priesthood? They were entitled to the part of the meal offering not burned on the altar (Lev. 2:3, 10; 6:9-11; 10:12), the flesh of all the sin offerings and trespass offerings except the sin offerings offered for the high priest and the people, where the flesh was burned outside the camp (Lev. 6:19-23; 7:6). There was no mention of peace offerings, because the law did not require them to be eaten in a holy place.

The Measurement of the Outer Wall and the Whole Complex (42:15-20)

The angel first measured the height and thickness of the outside wall (40:5); then the outer court (40:6-27); next the inner court with the house and cells (40:28—42:14); finally, the extent of all the temple buildings outside. The buildings formed a square of five hundred cubits. Thus the total measurements of the temple were given in verses 15-20. The reference to the inner house was to all that had been measured, all within the wall of the outer court. The entire area was much too large for Mount Moriah where Solomon's and Zerubbabel's temples stood. The scheme requires a great change in the topography of the land which will occur as indicated in Zechariah 14:9-11, the very time which Ezekiel had in view.

As to the numbers in the text, from early times there has been a tendency to alter them (cf. the Septuagint and many modern commentators). In such cases what is the controlling factor to insure accuracy? In the last analysis the subjective opinion of the particular interpreter studying the passage provides the criteria. It is noteworthy that the angel, as seen by the Apostle John, measures the walls of the heavenly Jerusalem in the same order as here (cf. Rev. 21:13). The perfect cube may be emblematic of that which is both solid and unshakable. The terms "holy" and "common" in verse 20 (ASV) are used relatively (see 43:12; 45:4; 48:12). The wall was intended to protect the sanctity of the temple and its courts.

SEPARATING THE HOLY AND THE COMMON

Sin makes a separation from Eden to the lake of fire. God must make a separation between the sacred and the profane, for He can never be worshiped or have fellowship with those who are unlike His holy character and nature. What an incentive to holy living!

43

THE RETURN OF THE GLORY

In the earlier chapters of this prophecy much space and much emphasis were given to the departure of the Shekinah from the temple. Nothing was more heartbreaking than this for Ezekiel to record, for he realized that such removal symbolized the Lord's abandonment of His house and His people to their foes and ultimate destruction (see 10:19; 11:23). In a real sense the nation was in a Loammi ("not my people") position, set aside for the time from the protecting hand of their gracious God. But God had never meant for this condition to be permanent. At the end of the chastisement there was to be restoration and with it the return of the visible presence of the Lord in the cloud.

Glory Filling the House (43:1-5)

This chapter may be divided into three large divisions: (1) the Lord's entrance into the sanctuary (vv. 1-12); (2) the size of the altar of burnt offering (vv. 13-17); (3) the ceremonies in the dedication of the altar (vv. 18-27). For the purposes of exposition, however, a somewhat more detailed division is employed. Now that the temple had been described, it was necessary to signify that the building was accepted by God. This was accomplished by the manifestation of the glory of the Lord in the tabernacle (Exodus 40:34-35) and in Solomon's temple (I Kings 8:10-11; II Chron. 5:13-14; 7:1-3). The Shekinah glory is never mentioned in connection with the restoration (Zerubbabel's) temple, so that temple cannot be the fulfillment of what is predicted here. In a sense 43:1-7 was the climax and culmination of Ezekiel's prophecy. The Lord returned as the divine King to occupy the temple as the throne of His kingdom. Here is indicated that which alone could make valid and give efficacy to the structure, namely, the presence of God Himself.

Ezekiel was led from the west side of the temple outside the wall (42:19) to the east gate once more (42:15), and outside it to witness the Lord's reentry into the temple. The gate mentioned was the very one by which God had left the temple (cf. 10:19; 11:23). What blessedness that the Lord should return in His glory to His people and to His ap-

pointed temple! Ezekiel had to give some descriptive detail to this coming, so he described His voice and appearance. The voice like the sound
of many waters would appear to indicate both power and majesty; the
manifested glory was a slight foretaste of the exhibited excellence of the
Lord, which has been referred to in various parts of Scripture. The delineation is, under the direction of the Holy Spirit, the pattern for the
portrayal by John in Revelation 1:15 and 18:1. He who would discern
the meaning of the Revelation must pay close attention to the book of
Ezekiel (notice Ezekiel's influence on the Revelation: cf. Ezek. 1 with
Rev. 4; Ezek. 26-28 with Rev. 18; Ezek. 38-39 with Rev. 20:7-10; Ezek.
40-43 with Rev. 11:1-2).

Lest anyone misunderstand or misconstrue this appearance of God,
Ezekiel was quick to identify the present manifestation of the glory with
previous mentions, which serves to bind the book in a unity which belies
the dismembering process of divisive critics. The visions referred to are
those of chapters 1 and 10. Ezekiel spoke of his coming to destroy the
city of Jerusalem, referring to the transport in ecstasy to Jerusalem to
see the devastation of the city (see 8:4; 9:1 ff.). Here is one of the many
instances in the prophets where the complete identification of the prophet
with his message is evident. So controlled was the prophetic consciousness by the inditing Spirit, that Ezekiel said he had come to destroy when
he uttered forth the purpose of God to destroy Jerusalem. This phenomenon is never duplicated in actuality among any nations of the earth. It
is biblical and is at the heart of the Bible's insistence that the word uttered
or later written was and is in truth the very word of God.

The cloud of the Shekinah has been described as "simply the atmospheric clothing of the theophany." But however explained, it was only
the presence of the Lord which could make the building the house of
God. The mention of glory with regard to the consecration of the Mosaic
tabernacle or the Solomonic temple is not a part of the imagery of stage
setting. Rather it is the vital element which reveals the worthwhileness
of all that is set forth. Thus Ezekiel was expressly given the privilege by
the Spirit Himself of viewing the glorious return of the Lord to His
abode and His people. God's glory may always be depended upon to
fill His house; it has been so in the past and will be in the millennial era.

THE EXHORTATION TO PURITY (43:6-9)

The return of the glory of the Lord to His temple was graciously accompanied by a message from Him. The One who addressed Ezekiel
from the house was the Lord, as in 2:2 and 40:3, in the form of an angel,
that is, the Angel of the Lord. The content of the message immediately

reveals that a supernatural Person was speaking, not a mere man. God indicated that He was accepting the millennial temple as His very own, the place of His throne and His footstool, His abode and abiding place (see Isa. 66:1). The ark of the covenant was designated as the Lord's footstool (cf. I Chron. 28:2; Ps. 132:7). Since this was to be in the fullest sense the residence of the Lord, there had to be absolutely nothing that would defile. They would follow the pollution of idolatry no longer. The modern mind has no concept of the depths of degradation and filth to which the idolatry of that day led, unless one has read somewhat widely in extrabiblical sources.

The reference to the dead bodies of their kings in their high places has been differently explained. It is claimed, on the one side, that there is no reference to kings' burials in these places anywhere in the historical books of the Old Testament. Thus the mention must mean the pollutions of idolatry. The thought is that Ezekiel was speaking of the dead idols (see Lev. 26:30) for which the kings had built altars in the sanctuary.

On the other side, it is held that they were the graves of Israelite kings next to the sanctuary. This view is confirmed in verse 9. The Scriptures indicate that fourteen kings of Judah were interred in royal sepulchers in Jerusalem on the southeast hill, the city of David, where the temple and palace were located (cf. II Kings 21:18, 26). The Lord would brook no such defilements of the sacred precincts. Once the Lord's charge was followed, there was the promise of a lasting arrangement: He would dwell among them forever. This surely was the fulfillment of the very purpose for which God had earthly sanctuaries built among His people on earth. When idols were erected adjacent to God's temple, it was an affront and insult to the true and living God. As with Dagon of old, every idol had to be cast down in His presence. There was no proper reverence or respect for God's dwelling when only a wall existed between the royal tombs and the temple. Throughout the Bible, death—which came through man's sin—is seen as defiling.

"THE LAW OF THE HOUSE" (43:10-12)

The purpose for which the pattern of the house was shown to Ezekiel, and through him to the whole nation, was precisely to move them to repentance and a desire for the fellowship they had lost through their sins. Here is the key to the entire vision from chapter 40 on. A long and considered look at God's ideal and future plan would suffice to show them how much they had forfeited by their transgressions. The way of the transgressor is always hard, for only the obedient child of God finds His yoke light and His burden easy. The charge was that they were to follow the instructions given for their worship, thus manifesting their obedience to God. Minutely Ezekiel was to go over every feature of the temple, once the nation revealed genuine repentance for past deeds, so that every detail of the will of the Lord would be carried out forthrightly and joyously. The entire area of the temple was to be sacred territory. The economy of God's sanctuary was holiness and only that.

THE MEASUREMENTS OF THE ALTAR (43:13-17)

This is one of the main areas of the latter part of Ezekiel's prophecy which has presented (as noted earlier) much difficulty to expositors. One of the chief reasons for confusion is the abandonment of the literal interpretation of prophecy, which must be adhered to in keeping with the grammatical and historical approach to the Scriptures.

Another source of difficulty is a wrong view of the function of Old Testament sacrifices. They were never efficacious; they were never meant to be expiatory, that is, to care for the penalty of sin; they were never meant to be anything but symbolic of the forfeiture of life for sin (see Heb. 10:4); they never took away sin. Thus they are not meant to take away sin here, as though they are at long last invested with a power and adequacy which never inhered in them previously. Do not mistake it: this is not the golden altar of incense for prayer and intercession. It is unmistakably clear that Ezekiel was speaking of the altar of sacrifice. The offerings presented thereon were meant to be memorials, much as the Lord's Supper is no efficacious sacrifice but a memorial of a blessedly adequate and all-sufficient sacrifice for all time. Thus, whereas the sacrifices of the Old Testament economy were prospective, these are retrospective.

The question has sometimes been asked as to the necessity of such memorials with the Lord dwelling in the midst of His people. Remember that during the earthly ministry of Christ sacrifices were offered, and He was present then. And there were sacrifices still offered (see the epistle to the Hebrews) at the time of the Lord's forty-day resurrection ministry. We need to be reminded that not all people in the millennial kingdom of the Messiah will have experienced their resurrection bodies. Some will enter the kingdom directly from the tribulation period without experiencing either death or resurrection.

The word "bottom" of verse 13 is literally "bosom." Some have considered it a channel to carry off the blood of the sacrifices. It may have been a platform or base into which the square above seemed to sink as into a bosom. The upper altar (literally, *Harel* or "mount of God") may speak of the great security it will afford the people of Israel in that day.

The altar of the same verse (v. 15) is actually the lion of God, Ariel (Isa. 29:1). It will be a square like the altar of burnt offering (see Exodus 27:1; 38:1; also the altar of incense, Exodus 30:1-2). An interesting feature of this altar is that steps lead up to it. This was expressly forbidden in the Mosaic law (Exodus 20:26), but the height of this altar makes them necessary. Furthermore, Josephus[1], who claimed that a later altar had a ramp, said, "The figure it was built in was a square, and it had corners like horns; and the passage up to it was by an insensible acclivity." As in the tabernacle and the temple of Solomon, the priests would always face west in their ministering (unlike the idolaters who faced the sun and worshiped it, 8:16). Precaution must always be taken so that the pitfalls of former years may be avoided.

THE CONSECRATION OF THE ALTAR TO THE LORD (43:18-27)

A casual reading of the passage is sufficient to impress the mind with the importance with which the Holy Spirit has invested the altar of sacrifice. The consecration of the altar in the future will take seven days to celebrate (vv. 25-26). For the prominence of these services in the worship of Israel, see Exodus 29:37; Leviticus 8:11, 15, 19, 33; I Kings 8:62-66; and II Chronicles 7:4-10. Again it must be reiterated that throughout this portion the sacrifices are never intended to be propitiatory, but commemorative and retrospective. From verse 19 it is clear that the Levites of the sons of Zadok will stand in a position peculiarly near to the Lord. Why this is so is answered fully in chapter 44. The direct address in verses 20-21 indicates that the acts were to be performed by Ezekiel through the instrumentality of the priests, specifically those of the house of Zadok. Notice the variety of offerings: burnt offerings, sin offerings and peace offerings. Bullocks, goats and rams make up the list of animals to be presented. Crystal clear is the intention to show that the altar must be cleansed and purified through the application of shed blood, as in the case of the altar in the wilderness and in the Solomonic sanctuary.

The significance of the salt in the offering may be seen by referring to Leviticus 2:13. Israel was enjoined never to allow the salt of her covenant to be lacking. Eating bread with salt is common at every Orthodox Jewish meal today, and is equally well known throughout the Near East. Here the copious salting was probably meant to emphasize the force of the sacrifices. Though used with the meal offerings, salt was not mentioned elsewhere in the Old Testament with the burnt offering. God must always have the best, so no sacrifice may be offered which has any blem-

[1]Josephus, *Wars*. V. 5-6.

ish. If they are commemorative of Christ and His abiding sacrifice, and the author believes they are, then they must clearly symbolize His unblemished and untainted personality. The literal meaning of "consecrate" (v. 26) is to fill the hands, not from the idea of putting things offered into the hands of the priests (Lev. 8:25 ff.), which was probably the original literal meaning, but the later use of initiating or investing with office, as in the Assyrian language, where the statement is found: "The god Asshur filled his hand with an unrivalled kingdom."

Although all the offerings of Leviticus are not detailed here, it is considered by some that they are implied, and they may well be. Prospectively they all pointed to Christ, so this would be in keeping with that truth in the retrospective sense. After the rites of consecration are completed on the eighth day, the regular sacrifices will begin. The two main kinds of offerings are mentioned prominently (cf. 46:2, 12). The final word now is beautiful indeed. Ezekiel promised them that the Lord would accept not just their offerings, but their persons as well. This is indeed a bright prospect and comfort.

ACCEPTED OF GOD

Through the Levitical offerings the sacrifices of Israel and they themselves as well were accepted by the Lord. Thus Ezekiel is not presenting a new administrative principle with God, for acceptance with God is on the basis of sacrifice. Thank God for the efficacy of the work of Christ on Calvary.

44

UNGODLY AND GODLY PRIESTS

THE MAIN SUBJECT of this chapter is the regulations for the priests of the Lord who serve in the temple. Purity of worship is safeguarded and emphasized throughout, therefore attention is directed toward those having to do with introduction of pollutions in former times. Notice that all worship is carried on facing westward, as in the tabernacle of Moses and the temple of Solomon, to forestall any reenactment of the abominations of chapter 8. There will be no sun worship.

THE PRINCE IN THE GATE (44:1-3)

The chapter may be divided thus: (1) the place of the prince in the sanctuary (vv. 1-3); (2) the place of foreigners, Levites and priests in relation to the temple (vv. 4-16); and (3) the requirements of the priestly office and its privileges (vv. 17-31). When the Lord brought Ezekiel back through the outer gate of the sanctuary, it was the east gate. It is popularly believed that this gate is the present walled up Golden Gate in Jerusalem, but expositors of the prophecy do not make this identification, nor is it necessary for Ezekiel's purpose. The emphasis throughout this first section of the chapter is on the fact that the gate will be shut. The Lord Himself points this out to Ezekiel with the explanation for it: a special sacredness characterized it after God had entered it. As a mark of honor to an Eastern king, no person could enter the gate by which he entered (for a similar concept cf. Exodus 19:24, and the entire section, vv. 9-23). But there is one exception to the rule mentioned in verse 2. It is one called "the prince." It is important to determine at this point the identity of this personality.

Who is the prince who is prominently mentioned in this chapter and in every one through the remainder of the prophecy with the exception of chapter 47? The rabbis understood this to be a prediction of the Messiah, but there are cogent reasons why we cannot make this identification. The prince cannot be the Messiah, first, because he is distinguished throughout from a priest. He has no priestly rights, as some former kings exercised (see I Kings 8:22, 54; 9:25; 10:5; II Kings 16:12-13; II Chron. 26:16). On the other hand, the Scriptures are clear that the Messiah has definite priestly prerogatives in the millennium (cf. Ps. 110:4; Zech. 6:12-13). Second, the prince needs to offer a sin offering (45:22). There is no conceivable occasion upon which the stainless Messiah, Son of God, would need to offer a sin offering for Himself. Third, the prince has sons (46:16), which is unthinkable in the light of the person of the Lord Jesus Christ. Thus the Messiah is definitely ruled out as even a possibility for this role.

Who, then, is this important personage? Some think it is David himself, pointing to such passages as 34:23-24 and 37:24. But, as we have seen, these Scriptures foretell the Son of David, the Messiah. Though not impossible, such an identification with David is not probable in view of the broad context of prophecy concerning the kingdom. The author believes it is a future scion of David's dynasty who will represent the Messiah governmentally in the affairs of earth. He will have a representative position but not that of the high priest nor of the kings formerly in Israel. His will be an intermediate status between the priests and the people. He will be among the people in their worship seasons (46:10) but will not be permitted to enter the inner court, although he can approach nearer than the people (46:2). He will be obligated to provide the various festival offerings and the solemnities of Israel (45:13-22). He will have allotted to him a special portion of the land and will be forbidden to appropriate any inherited land of the people (45:7-8; 46:18; 48:21-22). His modified and intermediate status emphasizes the nature and importance of the theocracy in the millennial day, where high priestly and kingly rule will be combined in the King, the Lord Jesus Christ.

The prince, Messiah's representative in a special sense, will then have the privilege of sitting in the very gate where the Lord Himself will have entered. He will perform certain religious acts in the presence of the Lord, and have a particular ingress and egress to the house of God.

THE SANCTITY OF GOD'S HOUSE (44:4-8)

This portion of the chapter and indeed the remainder of the chapter have to do with the priesthood and its appointments together with its privileges. Once Ezekiel passed through the north gate, he saw the glory of the Lord fill His house. The sight was so glorious and awesome that Ezekiel fell prostrate on his face. It is interesting to compare the glory which characterized the dedication of the tabernacle of Moses and the temple of Solomon with that consummating glory of the returned Shekinah which here fills, never to be interrupted, the abode of the glorious God of heaven and earth. Twice Ezekiel was enjoined of the Lord to mark well the disclosure that was being granted him. He was to receive it in an audio-visual manner. It had exclusively to do with the going into and the coming out of the house of God. The hallowed dwelling place was to be guarded jealously, lest its purity be marred and its sanctity be compromised by the intrusion of any defiling person or act. In chapters 1-24 of the prophecy the term "rebellious," to characterize the spiritual condition and attitude of Israel, was employed repeatedly, but not after chapter 33 until this passage. In a sense God would remind them, in the midst of revelations of coming blessing and conversion, that their present condition was in great contrast to what awaited the nation in the hour of their regeneration and restoration to the Lord. The indictment concerned the nation's permission of foreigners to enter and profane the holiness of God's sanctuary, which was a clear violation by Israel of their covenant with the Lord. Foreigners or strangers were allowed to present offerings to the Lord (see Lev. 17:10, 12; Num. 15:14), but Ezekiel was denouncing their officiating in the sanctuary, which was an unauthorized practice. Some feel it was a desecration of the worship of the Lord to bring foreigners, uncircumcised in heart and flesh, into the sanctuary during the time of the offering of sacrifice, but the Mosaic regulations were in contrast to such a position. The Paschal meal was different, and purposely so (cf. Exodus 12:43-44). It has been suggested that the foreigners were originally prisoners of war given by Judean kings to the temple as slaves (see Ezra 8:20; Zech. 14:21; Joshua 9:23, 27—the case of the Gibeonites), but there is no evidence whereby this view can be authenticated. The difficulty throughout had been that Israel was more interested in what suited her purposes than in what conformed to her covenant with the holy God. As long as the officiating personnel met with her approval, she did not question the propriety of the selection.

THE JUDGMENT ON APOSTATE LEVITES (44:9-14)

Again the warning of God was issued that no uncircumcised in heart and flesh, and the order is significant, should be granted admission to the sanctuary of the Lord. The connection between verses 10 and 9 is this: just as the foreigners will be excluded from entrance into the sanctuary because of their unresponsive and stubborn hearts, so priests who are unfaithful to their sacred charge and vows will be placed on the same level and excluded as well. The reference is obviously to those priests who apostatized during all the periods when idolatry was rife in Israel. Such will be degraded because the millennial age is in question and righteousness will rule. Yet mercy is not lacking, for they will not be excluded from all types of priestly ministry. It is only that they will lose the dignity of the higher services of the priesthood, such as were performed in the holy place or the first compartment of the tabernacle and temple. Priestly acts carried out in the outer court will not be denied them, as they will still have charge of the gates of the house, and offer the sacrifices for the people. There is a difference here between the law of Moses and the revelation given Ezekiel. In Mosaic times and later the worshiper killed the victim himself; here the Levites will slay the private sacrifices of the people.

Because those who had come near to the Lord in His service, yet so forgot their high calling and privilege as to minister for the nation before idols— strengthening the nation in their inclination to apostatize from the Lord—God must manifest His righteous displeasure in forbidding such participants of the Levites from the higher areas of priestly ministry. Theirs will be an inferior phase and place of service. Finally, it is reiterated that they will be entrusted with the general oversight of the service of the sanctuary. The grace of God is to be found throughout the pages of the Old Testament, even if not to the degree manifested once the Messiah came to earth, ministered and died for man's sin.

THE MINISTRY OF THE ZADOKITE PRIESTS (44:15-27)

For a proper understanding of this portion of the prophecy it is necessary to consider as background material the facts recorded in I Samuel 2:35; II Samuel 15:24; and I Kings 2:26-35. Zadok was the son of Ahitub of the line of Eleazar (II Sam. 8:17; I Chron. 6:7-8). He was faithful to David during the insurrection of Absalom (II Sam. 15:24 ff.), and anointed Solomon as king after the abortive attempt of Adonijah to seize the throne (I Kings 1:32 ff.). The emphasis in the text is not upon lineal descent as the paramount feature, but fidelity to the Lord and His service. In every age the sovereign and gracious God has a remnant of those who cleave to Him in spite of adverse circumstances and the mounting pressures of the majority to conform. The Zadokite priests kept themselves from the idolatry of the nation, even though the other priests complied to the idolatrous desires of the disobedient people. For this faithfulness the reward from the Lord will be access to His presence, the privilege of ministering in any and all phases of priestly duty.

The table referred to in verse 16 is the altar of burnt offering (see 40:46; 41:22). Although the altar in the Old Testament is referred to as the table of the Lord, in the New Testament the Lord's table is never spoken of as His altar. In their ministry the priests will wear the appointed garments designated for them. The outward physical features often indicate the condition and state of the soul (cf. the garments in Exodus 28). It will be necessary that no wool be worn in order to avoid sweat (v. 18), which is considered uncleanness. Linen is preeminently the material for

the attire of the priests. The New Testament stresses the typical significance of this material (see Rev. 19:8). Moreover, the priests will not be
able to mingle among the people in their official robes in order not to
sanctify them in the Levitical sense (cf. Exodus 29:37; 30:29; Lev. 6:11).
Contact with holy things sanctifies.

In the matter of the hair the Zadokites must avoid extremes. Shaving
the head and allowing it to grow long were both signs of mourning (Lev.
10:6; 21:5, 10, ASV). The prohibition concerning drinking wine is in
agreement with Leviticus 10:9. What disastrous results such imbibing
can have is clear from the tragedy of Nadab and Abihu (see Acts 2:13,
15, 18 also, where godly joy and exultation were mistaken for drunken-
ness). The zeal of the priests, moreover, is to be holy and true, not in-
duced by outward carnal stimulants. Furthermore, if marriage be significant for the common people in Israel, it will be all the more so for
those who will minister in the immediate presence of the Lord in holy
things. Concerning marriage it is seen that the regulations which obtained for the high priest alone in the Mosaic economy, will be extended
to all priests (cf. Lev. 21:14). Ezekiel never mentioned a high priest, an
omission of significance, underscoring the prophecy of Zechariah 6:12-13.

Every feature of life was specified for the godly priests, but what will
be their principal duty? First, they will be the recognized and authorized
teachers of the people. They are to demonstrate to the people what is
pleasing to the Lord and what is not. Second, they are to serve in judicial
capacities also, with their decisions, based upon the revelation of God,
to be final for all who are obedient to the word of the Lord. Finally, it
will be their place to oversee the appointments for the feasts of the Lord,
that these appointed times of spiritual rendezvous may be conformable to
the law; the Sabbaths are to be kept from desecration as well. For the
general duties of the priests toward the people, see Leviticus 10:10 and
Malachi 2:7.

Since death is viewed in Scripture as Levitically defiling, bringing to
remembrance most forcefully the sin of Adam which introduced death
into the human family, priests will have to be careful in their contact with
the dead. They may attend the funerals of only the closest of kin. Will
there be death in the millennium? This passage is in a millennial setting,
so the meaning is clear that such will occur. Though death will be rare
in that age of righteousness, it will exist (Isa. 65:20). It is difficult for
many to differentiate between the perfect conditions of the eternal state,
when death will be abolished forever, and the less than perfect conditions
of the kingdom age with man's nature unchanged. The precise time of
absence of the priest from holy ministry was indicated, as was the offering

he will bring upon his reentry into priestly service. Our God is a God of order and consistency.

THE PORTION OF THE PRIESTS (44:28-31)

How blessed that twice over the Lord indicated that the priests will have their portion, inheritance and possession in Him. He is sufficient for any of His own. For the needs of everyday life they will be expected to live from the offerings of the people, even as now those who engage in the things of the Lord are entitled to be supported of the same. When this order is followed, it invariably results in blessing, spiritual and otherwise. But the offerer must be careful how he offers, for nothing less than the best is to be presented to a holy God. Under the Mosaic law this same restriction applied to all Israel (cf. Lev. 22:8; 17:15; Deut. 14:21).

GLORIOUS MINISTRY TO THE GLORIOUS GOD

That man is lost and estranged from God is sad enough in itself, for God is robbed of fellowship and love that belong to Him. But equally tragic is the fact that God is denied the glory and the service that should accrue to Him from redeemed souls who find in Him their inheritance. Let us render Him the service we owe Him with love and gratitude.

45

SACRED ARRANGEMENTS

THE STUDENT OF EZEKIEL'S PROPHECY is struck again and again with the mass of details and particulars that characterize the last nine chapters of the book. This is the strongest and most irrefutable argument against taking these chapters in an allegorical or symbolical or spiritualizing sense. Such a method of interpretation is a hermeneutical alchemy that puts to nought the plain text of the prophecy. Chapter 45 may be divided as follows: (1) the portion of the land for the Lord (vv. 1-8); (2) exhortations to righteousness (vv. 9-12); (3) the offerings of the people (vv. 13-17); (4) the sin offerings of the first month (vv. 18-20); and (5) the celebration of the Passover and Feast of Tabernacles (vv. 21-25).

THE HOLY PORTION OF THE LAND (45:1-8)

The first portion of the chapter concerns itself with the apportionment of the land for the priests and people. In Joshua's day the land was divided by lot; so will it be in a coming day (see Joshua 13:6; Prov. 16:33; cf. Acts 1:26). Before Pentecost casting lots was God's method for determining His will. Now it is by the Word and the leading of the Spirit. The first division is designated as an oblation to the Lord because it will be analogous to the sacrificial gifts which were lifted up before the Lord (see 48:8-22 for a more detailed and elaborate description of this portion). The provisions indicate God's ownership of the entire land. The holy portion of the land will cover a territory about eight miles square. A rectangle of 25,000 by 10,000 cubits in the middle of which will be the temple will be set aside for the priests. A similar rectangle north of it will be for the Levites. On the south a rectangle of 25,000 by 5,000 cubits will be reserved for the city itself. The temple was the heart and focal point of the national life in times past, and it will be in the millennial era as well. Notice the priests' area will be on the east and west, the Levites' portion on the north, and the prince's domain outside that of the priests; all in a sense protecting the sanctuary from profanation.

All the tribes will have the same extent of territory, for no preeminence of one over another will be recognized. Some deny Ezekiel's authorship of 45:1–46:18, but on no good or valid evidence.

The suburbs of verse 2 will be literally open spaces, so that the dwellings of the priests may not be too near the temple building. After the allotment of portions to each group there is the indication that the city proper will belong to all Israel, not to any tribe. It must be kept in mind that throughout this section the word "length" means from east to west (cf. 48:8). The word "breadth" refers to extent from north to south. The promise that the princes will no longer oppress the people is most welcome, for in former years without this provision set forth by Ezekiel there was always the temptation on the part of kings to obtain property by violence. The most notable case is found in I Kings 21 where Ahab confiscated the vineyard of Naboth (cf. also Num. 36:7-9; Isa. 5:8; Hosea 5:10, ASV; Micah 2:1-2). No one will be deprived of his rightful possession in that era of righteousness and justice under Messiah's benevolent reign.

THE CHARGE TO THE PRINCES OF ISRAEL (45:9-12)

In this section of the chapter Ezekiel reverted for the time to the day in which he lived in the sixth century B.C., and addressed his contemporaries. These conditions spoken of will not obtain in the era of glory and blessing for Israel. As ever, God is a God of equity and hates oppression and wrong dealing, whereby many are deprived of their rightful property and led into poverty. The exactions referred to are literally expulsions, indicating the unjust evictions of the helpless from their possessions. God regulates all, since nothing is beneath His notice and care.

The ephah was the dry measure equal to about eight or nine gallons or one bushel, divided into sixths for calculation purposes. The bath was a liquid measure equal to about nine gallons or ninety-one pints, divided into tenths. A hin was the sixth part of a bath. The Hebrews followed a decimal system. For the emphasis God places on proper weights and measures, see Proverbs 11:1; 20:10; Amos 8:4-7. Falsifying weights and measures is simply a form of robbery which can never be overlooked by God.

Verse 12 is admittedly very difficult. Most commentators, believing there is a corruption in the text, adopt the rendering of the Greek version which reads: "And the five shekels shall be five, and the ten shekels shall be ten, and fifty shekels shall be your maneh." It is acknowledged to be a conjecture, and it appears to be a quite colorless one, but it is certain that multiples of five are repeated. The maneh of gold seems to have been one hundred shekels (cf. I Kings 10:17 with II Chron. 9:16).

THE OFFERINGS FOR ISRAEL'S PRINCE (45:13-17)

There is not a great deal that calls for exposition or explanation in this portion. It is seen from verses 13-15 that there is a difference between the kind of offering and the quantity required. With wheat it is the sixth of a tenth; with oil it is a tenth of a tenth; with flocks one out of every two hundred. The setting is still the age of the millennium, for the prince is again mentioned in verse 16. Because of the dues paid him by the people, the prince is to provide the sacrifices for public worship. The feasts are the great pilgrimage festivals: Passover, Pentecost (not mentioned by Ezekiel) and the Feast of Tabernacles. All the appointed feasts embrace the entire festival calendar of Leviticus 23.

THE CLEANSING OF THE SANCTUARY (45:18-20)

It is indisputable that the ancient feasts of Israel will be celebrated in the millennium (see Zech. 14). Pentecost, for what reason it is not stated, is omitted. All are memorials. Then why not the sacrifices as well which formed a definite part of every feast? Compare Numbers 28:15 and 29:2-6 for the offerings for the new moon and particularly the new moon of the seventh month. Notice that there will be no waiting until the feast of the Day of Atonement in the seventh month for the purging and cleansing of the sanctuary (see Lev. 16). That will occur in the first month or Nisan.

The errors of verse 20 point to the sins which will be occasioned by the weakness of man for which a sin offering will have to be brought (cf. Lev. 4:2; Num. 15:22 ff.). The reference to simplicity is the folly of sin as so often stated in Proverbs (see Prov. 7:7). To make atonement for the house will be equivalent to the cleansing of the sanctuary (v. 18). Again, mark that the Day of Atonement is not mentioned.

THE FEAST OF PASSOVER AND THE FEAST OF TABERNACLES (45:21-25)

It is interesting to find that Passover and unleavened bread are combined, as in the New Testament and in rabbinic literature. Strangely, some hold the seven-day feast to be seven weeks in length, but the normal language of the passage will not allow this. At best it is highly questionable. The feast will cover, as in antiquity, a heptad of days. Of the three great or pilgrimage feasts, the feast of Pentecost is omitted. There is more than one possible explanation. The mention of the first and last feasts of the religious calendar of Israel may be taken representatively as including them all. Christ is designated the First and Last, the Alpha and

Omega, but these are not to be taken as excluding all the intervening factors. Furthermore, the feast of Pentecost is connected (Acts 2) with the church. The Holy Spirit came on this feast to baptize both believing Jew and Gentile into the body of Christ, creating a new entity or new man (see I Cor. 12:13; Eph. 2:15). This same program of uniting the two divisions of the human family will not be the order of the day in the millennium. It will be preeminently the age in which Israel, long the tail of the nations, will assume her promised place as leader and head of the nations. Actually, the millennial glories, though the church will enter into them as the bride of the King, were primarily, though not exclusively, promised to the people of Israel.

There are differences from the Mosaic legislation where for each of seven days two bullocks, one ram, seven lambs and an oblation of fine flour mingled with oil, were prescribed (see Num. 28:19-21). Here in Ezekiel seven bullocks and seven rams, and no lambs, will be required for each of the seven days. Other differences exist also. In general the offerings in the millennial temple will be much richer and more abundant than those under the law. The impression gained is that of the riches of the King and the fullness of the testimony that goes out concerning His person and finished work of redemption on Calvary. Here God finds all His delight for time and eternity. May it ever be true of us as well.

SACRIFICES INDISPENSABLE ALWAYS

If the Bible teaches any truth, it is the primacy of the need for sacrifice in order to effect fellowship with God. Both the Old and New Testament stress this basic requirement. To cut this element from the Bible, as some loudly suggest, is to excise the heart of the Scriptures and leave them worthless and useless. Let us emphasize what God does.

46

MILLENNIAL OFFERINGS AND SACRIFICES

LIBERAL COMMENTATORS on chapters 40-48 explain the interest of Ezekiel in the things priestly and Levitical as part of his priestly background, and partly from his intense desire to reinstate Israel's priestly order of service after the exile. But this facile explanation fails to take into account the fact of divine inspiration of his special message, and the substantiated position that he was speaking in these chapters of future, not merely ideal, conditions which will obtain in the earthly reign of the Messiah of Israel and King of all the earth. Moreover, any liberal who will not or cannot see the necessity of the sacrificial death of the Lord Jesus Christ, will naturally be unable to make much of the offerings and sacrifices which spoke of Him prospectively or will yet testify to Him retrospectively in a day yet future. If these principles be kept in mind, light will be shed upon a vast amount of theological writing and modern preaching.

OFFERINGS FOR THE SABBATH (46:1-5)

The emphasis here is unmistakably on the Sabbath and the new moon, which alone should indicate the Jewish setting of the passage, and that we are not here on Christian or New Testament ground. The broad context of the last chapters of Ezekiel, it cannot be repeated too often because so often ignored, is not treating Christian truth, though there are definite implications for such, of course. In short, the Sabbath of the Old Testament will be reinstituted for a restored and consecrated Israel. The Sabbath will be in force as soon as the church is translated because the end of Daniel's seventy weeks will occur on Jewish ground (Matt. 24:20). Then the Sabbath will continue on into Messiah's reign, for this is the consummation and culmination of Israel's, not the church's, history (study Isa. 66:23 and the broad context there). Notice here that legalizers and seventh-day observance advocates always fail to realize that the Sabbath consisted in more than just abstinence from labor on the seventh day of the week, important as that was for the commandment, but included also

267

specific sacrifices to be offered by an authorized priest in a designated place of God's choosing. It is folly and worse to take one part of the observance and wholly discard or disregard another, specifically that part which indicated how Sabbath rest was to be purchased for the believing soul through the coming sacrifice of the Davidic Messiah and Saviour. Now mark how the vital feature of sacrifices on the Sabbath carries over appropriately into the millennium to signify the millennial rest acquired for Israel and all at Calvary.

Notice how the spotlight is centered on the glory and sanctity of the Sabbath, for on that day of the week alone the gate of the inner court will be opened. It is by this gate that the prince will enter into the sanctuary to preside as the priests prepare the designated offerings which the prince himself will offer before the Lord. But this is no individual worship, for all the people will enter into the worship both on the Sabbaths and the new moons. It remains only to state that the burnt offering for the Sabbath will be enlarged considerably over that of the Mosaic law (cf. v. 4 with Num. 28:9).

Offerings for the New Moon (46:6-8)

Since Israel's calendar was a lunar one, the new moon had significance for them where it has not for us. Moreover, the feasts were reckoned in relation to the phases of the moon. The new moon in Old Testament times was heralded with ceremony, and even today in Orthodox Judaism certain prayers are recited at the appearance of the new moon. The sacrifices of the new moon (vv. 6-7) are reduced from the Mosaic requirements. What significance this has is difficult to determine.

Conduct During the Appointed Feasts (46:9-12)

The minute regulations concerning entrance and exit during the appointed feasts are given in order to prevent congestion and confusion, since all are to be present (see Deut. 16:16). God is concerned with proper decorum in His house, a fact that many need to learn today even in fundamental circles. It is heartwarming to witness the prince worshiping in the midst of the people, entering at either the north or south gate, and leaving at the opposite one. He thus sets a godly example of worship by his presence (cf. David's lament in I Sam. 26:19, the practice of the sons of Korah in Ps. 42:4, and David's godly resolve in Ps. 132:1-5). The emphasis in verse 12 is on the fact that the offering of the prince will be a freewill offering, given spontaneously by him. Notice that nowhere did Ezekiel speak of wine in the offerings.

THE DAILY SACRIFICES (46:13-15)

The uniform testimony of the Old Testament is to the effect that to remove the continual burnt offering meant an abolition of public worship (see Dan. 8:11-13; 11:31; 12:11; also I Macc. 1:45). In the Mosaic economy there was a burnt offering in the morning and evening (cf. Num. 28:3-4). Here there is no mention of such in the evening.

REGULATIONS CONCERNING THE PRINCE (46:16-18)

In the thousand-year reign of the Messiah there will be opportunity to celebrate twenty jubilee years. The suggestion has been made that the year of liberty referred to here is that of Jeremiah 34:14, the seventh year of release for Hebrew slaves. But a reading of this passage will immediately reveal that Ezekiel was not speaking of personal liberty for slaves (which incidentally also took place at the year of jubilee), but undoubtedly of the year of jubilee which concerned the reverting of property to its original owner. Israel will then fully understand the significance of the year of jubilee. The basis of the year was the truth of Leviticus 25:23, where God's inalienable ownership of the land is declared.

The prince will be married and have sons—a truth that makes it impossible for him to be the Messiah, as already noted—and it is natural that he will give them gifts, even of land. Whatever the prince gives them will remain theirs as an inheritance. A gift by the prince to any of his servants will be in another category, for it will be liable to revert to its original owner in the year of jubilee. But there is a prohibition now stated against violent seizure by the prince of the land of any of the people, for he is not to give gifts of land by confiscating the property and patrimony of others. He will have a portion of his own which he can distribute to his sons, but his family is not to be enriched through the impoverishment of others. This is in keeping with the strict righteousness of the age of justice.

THE SACRIFICIAL PLACES FOR THE OFFERINGS (46:19-24)

The millennial age will differ both from the present age and the eternal state, so to seek to make Ezekiel's arrangements conform to either period is to do violence to the plain meaning of the text, which is not ambiguous. The purpose of the regulations will be to inculcate a sense of the sanctity of the Lord's service, guarding against that familiarity which so often in the past led to gross defilements of the Lord's sanctuary. Special boiling places for the sacrifices, a practical provision indeed, will be appointed in order to avoid the ceremonial sanctification of the people, which would interrupt their ordinary course of life. The phrase "under the rows" (v. 23) means close to the ground, not on the stories above. The ministers of the house referred to in verse 24 are not the priests themselves apparently, but the temple servants.

THE NECESSITY FOR PRIESTHOOD

Whenever man denies the fall of man, he sees absolutely no need for a priest or intermediary between him and God. But if the Word of God teaches any truth, it is the crying need of all men for a priest. God has already pointed out His Priest, the Lord Jesus Christ, the great High Priest. Through Him we all have access to God.

47

THE WATERS OF THE LAND HEALED

THROUGHOUT THE PROPHETS of the Old Testament (see notably Zech. 14) there is a constant line of truth indicating that in the age of earth's climax amazing and far-reaching physical and geographical changes will take place in the earth, especially in the land of promise itself. This chapter deals mainly with changes in the water, concluding with instructions as to the division of the land among the twelve tribes in the kingdom age, a theme continued and completed in chapter 48. Chapter 47 may be divided as follows: (1) the origin of the river (vv. 1-2); (2) the river's increase (vv. 3-5); (3) the trees on its banks (vv. 6-7); (4) the emptying into the Arabah and the Dead Sea (vv. 8-12); and (5) the boundaries of the land divided among the tribes (vv. 13-23).

WATERS FROM THE HOUSE OF GOD (47:1-2)

The portion of verses 1-12 is sometimes called the vision of the living waters. Even many who take all from chapters 40-48 to be symbolical and figurative admit that this description is to be taken literally. However, this does not imply that the position is unanimous, for others still hold that the passage is to be interpreted spiritually, pointing especially to the picture in Revelation 22:1-5. But the Revelation text is not speaking of the same time as that of Ezekiel. Furthermore, where a prophet of the Old Testament speaks of the same era as Ezekiel does, there is harmony of presentation (cf., e.g., Joel 3:18; Zech. 14:8). One objection set forth is that, even supposing a change in the land, a stream rising on top of Mount Zion, of the magnitude seen in this vision of Ezekiel, would be entirely opposed to the known laws of the physical world. Such an objection is entirely beside the point and completely misses the emphasis of the entire description. If the passage teaches anything, it reveals that all this will be a result of the working of God's power; it is miraculous. Since when has God been confined to the laws which He Himself made in nature? He cannot and will not contravene His moral laws, but there is nothing inherently discrepant with His nature to alter any of His natural or physical laws.

271

The waters will issue from the entrance to the temple proper. All blessings, material and spiritual, will emanate from the presence of the Lord with His people. Evidently the Lord not only brought Ezekiel to see the source of the water supply, but its increase in volume and beneficial flow. Water-drawing on the Feast of Tabernacles (the basis of the words in John 7:37-39) owed much of its ceremonial symbolism to this passage. Some Christian writers have made Ezekiel's stream a figure of baptism, with which it has nothing to do. This is but one of the several hazards of an allegorizing of biblical interpretation.

THE MAN WITH THE MEASURING LINE (47:3-5)

The spiritualizing expositor is not convinced of the literal force of the scene by the description in these verses. To him it signifies the river or stream of life which comes from the presence and abode of God, regenerating by His word and grace a dead world, seen in the desert areas through which the water flows before it empties into the Dead Sea. The miraculous nature of the river is clearly presented because a natural river cannot increase to such an extent over such short distances, except there be other streams feeding into it, which is not the case here. Why was it necessary to bring Ezekiel through the waters in vision? The purpose was to reveal to him both the size and depth of the river. The trickle (the literal of "ran out" of v. 2 is "trickled forth") had become a veritable river during the measuring activity of the man in the vision.

THE HEALING OF THE WATERS (47:6-12)

If the early part of the chapter has been accorded fantastic interpretations by the allegorizers, this portion has fared no better. One suggestion is that all Christian history has been engaged in fulfilling and realizing this prophecy. In Christianity's spread it has increased its adherents, healed their spiritual illnesses and sweetened life's many bitter experiences. This may be allowed by way of application but will not stand for grammatico-historical interpretation. It has well been pointed out years ago that interpretation is one, whereas application is manifold. Since we do not treat historical accounts or doctrinal passages in this manner, let us not deal in this dual hermeneutic in the prophetic portions. Literally interpreted, they are full of blessing for Israel and the world.

The man with the measuring line directed Ezekiel's attention to the bank of the river, where the life-giving waters have been responsible for the lush growth of trees on both sides of the river. The deepest valley rift in the world is the Arabah in the Holy Land. The waters of the river will flow east through the Arabah into the Dead Sea. The immediate

effect of contact of the new waters with the waters of the Dead Sea will
be the healing of the latter. Nothing can live in the salty waters of the
Dead Sea, which is more than six times as salty as the ocean, but all
living things will revive and flourish with the infusion of the supernatural
waters. The rivers of verse 9 are literally two rivers, to bring out the
greatness of the river. Since it is increased with such speed, it has become
like rivers, though actually only one.

In order to manifest how thorough and genuine the healing of the salt
waters will be, Ezekiel added details to show how fishermen will find
the Dead Sea to be a choice spot for their trade and sport. Actual geographical sites are given, so there is no excuse for wild allegorizing, such
as that which makes the fishers those redeemed and made alive by the
Messiah's saving grace, and now become the heralds of the same good
news, making others alive to enter the kingdom of God and introducing
them into the church of Christ. This is not one whit behind the un-
restrained allegorizing of the rabbis and the Alexandrian philosophers
of the early Christian centuries. En-gedi is located at about the middle
of the west shore of the Dead Sea, whereas En-eglaim has not been
definitely identified. Some think it is Ein Feshkha near which are the
caves of the Dead Sea Scrolls. Thus En-gedi and En-eglaim may loosely
represent the two extremities of the Dead Sea. The sea in its entire
length will be completely changed.

What is the force of the statement that the marshes and the miry places
will be given over to salt? A study of the use of this expression throughout the Old Testament shows that it is employed not of blessing but of
judgment (cf. Deut. 29:23; Judges 9:45; Ps. 107:34, ASV; Jer. 17:6; Zeph.
2:9). Here the context is unmistakably one of blessing, so what is the
import of the prophecy? It has been suggested the salt will be needed
for food as heretofore. Another view claims that from this source of
supply would come salt for the temple service, as was the case in ancient
times. Even the Talmud pointed out that salt from the Dead Sea was
preferred above all other kinds because it was reputed to hasten the
burning of the sacrifices, as well as to minimize the unpleasant odors of
burning flesh.

THE METHOD OF DIVIDING THE LAND (47:13-14)

The picture through the entire passage is that of an enlarged Canaan
for all to inhabit. Verses 13-23 are related to chapter 48 since they treat
of the redistribution of the land among the tribes. The boundaries are
substantially those originally given to Moses in Numbers 34:1-15. In
Numbers the southern boundary is given first; here the reckoning is from

the north. Jordan is the eastern boundary, and the two and a half tribes, who had been settled in Transjordania, are in their original and intended place. All the tribes are located west of the Jordan. Mark how firm are the promises of God. The first statement on dividing the land, after the general comment that it will be in conformity with the twelve tribes, is that Joseph will be accorded two portions, which is in keeping with the ancient promise of Jacob to Joseph (Gen. 48:5-6, 22; 49:22-26). Joseph's sons inherited the birthright, always the double portion, lost by Reuben, because he had defiled his father's bed (Gen. 35:22; 49:3-4; I Chron. 5:1). The phrase "one as well as another" (v. 14) means equally. The twelve portions are to be exactly alike. It will be recalled that Levi was in antiquity given no tribal portion; the Lord was their inheritance, so they made their homes among the twelve (counting Ephraim and Manasseh) tribes.

THE BORDERS OF THE LAND (47:15-20)

As already indicated, these boundaries are to be studied in the light of Numbers 34:1-5, for they are practically those indicated there. Hethlon and Zedad (v. 15) are sites still unknown to us. So is Hazar-hatticon (v. 16). However, there has been an identification made of Zedad with Sadad, southeast of Homs between Riblah and Palmyra. Suffice it to say, the geographical locations are so exact that they cannot mean other than literal places. Meriboth-kadesh (v. 19, ASV) is called Kadesh-barnea in Numbers 34:4 (see also Num. 20:3-14). The brook of Egypt is not the Nile, which is not a brook in anyone's estimation, but the Wadi-el-'Arîsh in the land. Having thus defined the limits of the land to be divided, Ezekiel was ready to present the principles upon which the area is to be divided.

INSTRUCTIONS ON THE DIVISION OF THE LAND (47:21-23)

Those who feel Ezekiel is cold and formal must have overlooked or failed to consider this small paragraph which occupies itself with the fortunes of the stranger in Israel. The stranger will not be excluded in millennial Israel, which is in keeping with the beautiful reminder in Leviticus 19:34. However, the Mosaic law did not permit them the right of acquisition of land, as is granted them here. The right is extended only to those who had settled permanently in the land of promise, begetting children there. There is no condition attached to the promise that they are to become proselytes. Of course, all who enter the kingdom will be righteous, but procreation then does not guarantee saved children any more than in any age. Apart from other considerations such strangers will be vouchsafed the right of full inheritance. Permanence of residence is the sole condition.

PROMISED HEIRS

How many times the godly in Israel in ancient times pondered these passages and their future inheritance, we cannot tell. But we have some concept of how the godly in Christ turn again and again to the promises concerning our heavenly inheritance laid up for us (I Peter 1:4 ff.). It is a grief that carnal believers make little of this inheritance and do not live in the light of it. By example let us provoke them to good works.

48

THE CITY OF THE LORD'S PRESENCE

THE FINAL CHAPTER of this surpassingly important prophecy concerns the distribution of the promised land for the millennial age. Events on earth are always riveted into the twin considerations of time and place; history and geography are ever vital. The great redemption events took place at a certain time ("the fulness of time") and in a certain place ("a place called Golgotha"). Thus the material before us is not of secondary significance. Compare for a parallel Revelation 21 where the emphasis is again on a city and a place. As a proper background for study of the chapter see Genesis 15:7, 18-21; 17:8 concerning the territory God unconditionally promised to Abraham. The chapter may be divided thus: (1) the territory of the seven tribes from the northern boundary to the center of the land (vv. 1-7); (2) the sanctuary, the land of priests and Levites, and the prince's land (vv. 8-22); (3) the territory of the other five tribes from the last mentioned point to the southern boundary (vv. 23-29); (4) the size, gates and name of the city (vv. 30-35).

INHERITANCE OF SEVEN TRIBES (48:1-7)

This division of the land differs from that in Joshua's time in these ways: (1) All the tribal portions extend across the breadth of the land from the eastern boundary to the Mediterranean, making parallel tracts of land. The seven tribes inherit areas in the northern part of the land, running from east to west. (2) All the tribes are west of the Jordan, whereas the two and a half tribes in Joshua's day were east of the Jordan. (3) There is a central tract of land, about a fifth of the whole, which is separated for the holy oblation (sanctuary), city and prince's land. The distribution is to be by lot (cf. 47:22 with Prov. 16:33). Notice that the tribes who are descendants of Leah and Rachel are nearest the temple; tribes who are descendants of Bilhah and Zilpah, the farthest. Because of the territory designated as oblation, and the division of the land to all twelve tribes, each tribe will receive somewhat less than two-thirds of that allocated formerly by Joshua.

"THE OBLATION OF THE LAND" (48:8-12)

It is immediately evident that Judah and Benjamin, the tribes which remained faithful to the Davidic dynasty, will be honored by proximity to the center of the millennial kingdom. A certain area in the heart of the land will be set aside for the sanctuary, pointing up its central importance in the life of the redeemed nation. The distinction made in chapter 44 regarding the sons of Zadok is repeated here, showing how God delights to dwell at length on the fidelity and faithfulness of His servants. Evidently Levites were more involved in apostasy and idolatry than the priests, which is confirmed by the fact that at the time of the return from Babylonian exile there were less than 400 Levites and an equal number of Nethinim who returned (see Ezra 2:40-58; Neh. 7:43-60). At the same time there were 4,289 priests.

THE BORDERS OF THE LEVITES (48:13-14)

South of the territory of Judah and north of the sanctuary a strip of land running east and west will be allotted to the Levites, an arrangement totally different from that which obtained in the Mosaic regime. Again and again it was stated there that the Levites were to have no special territory distributed to them. Because of their firm and courageous stand for the Lord at the time of the golden calf at Sinai (Exodus 32:25-29), when they regarded no blood or family tie (Deut. 33:8-11), the Lord canceled the curse of Jacob (Gen. 49:5-7) by overruling the scattering of Levi for blessing instead of judgment as with Simeon. Thus throughout Israel's settlement in the land of promise the Levites were to be found among all the tribes of the land.

THE EXTENT OF THE CITY (48:15-20)

To the south of the sanctuary will lie the great King's resplendent city with its thousand suburbs. The city will belong to all the tribes, so each will assume its proper responsibilities. Since there is nothing inherently sinful in labor, for Adam before the fall was charged to till the soil, laborers from all the tribes will till the soil of the city. Notice once again the great minuteness of detail. This is more than strange, it is inexplicable, if all the statements are to be taken symbolically. As far as we are aware, no such abundance of details occurs anywhere else in Scripture outside the instructions for the construction of the tabernacle and its priestly service, which no orthodox expositor feels called upon to interpret other than with strict literalness. Then it is only consistent to do the same here. No commanding considerations indicate otherwise.

THE PORTION OF THE PRINCE (48:21-22)

Flanking the sanctuary and the holy city, the land of the prince will occupy a strategic position in order to administer governmentally the affairs committed to him by the ruling King. Again his portion will be contiguous to that of the tribes of Judah and Benjamin, so that conceivably he will be able to utilize their services in governing the land. Their former loyalty in this area during the defection from the Davidic dynasty will fit them peculiarly for this service. It is another instance of what is called poetic justice, but in biblical terms it may be referred to as committing much to those who have been faithful in little.

THE INHERITANCE OF THE REMAINING FIVE TRIBES (48:23-29)

The enumeration of the portions of the tribes, begun in verse 1 with Dan, is now resumed in order to complete the division to all the tribes. It must not be overlooked that the first tribe mentioned, Dan, was omitted by John in his listing of the 144,000 in Revelation 7. The reason cannot be dogmatically stated, although it has been suggested that it was because Dan as a tribe was the first to go into idolatry in ancient times (cf. Gen. 49:16-17 with Judges 17-18). But mark how the grace of God wipes out the past, for Dan is mentioned first in the distribution of inheritances in the millennial age. The five remaining tribes will inherit land south of the city of Jerusalem. As for the overall picture it is to be recalled that the Levites will not be numbered among the tribes for purposes of land inheritance. Joseph's portion will be divided between Ephraim and Manasseh as in ancient times. Notice also the uniformity of statement, almost monotonous but purposeful, concerning the distribution of the territory. It should make for ease in uniform and equitable administration in the age of the kingdom of righteousness and peace.

THE GATES OF THE RESTORED AND GLORIFIED CITY (48:30-35)

The egresses of the city have reference to the extremities of a tract of land. When the names of the gates of the millennial city are enumerated, Reuben, Judah and Levi are at the head of the list. These three sons of Leah, the unloved wife of Jacob, stand first also in Moses' blessing in Deuteronomy 33:6-8: the firstborn in age, the first in patriarchal blessing, and the one serving God in place of every firstborn in Israel (see Exodus 13). The fact that the names of all the tribes will appear on the gates of the glorious city is harmonious with the statement of our Lord Jesus Christ concerning the rule in the kingdom (Matt. 19:28), and beautifully symbolizes at the same time in visible form the unity and harmony in the nation so long divided. All the ancient rivalries, contentions and jealousies will be gone, and blessed unity will prevail.

The final verse of the book provides the crown and consummation of all Israel's history. The measurement of 18,000 reeds calls for a circumference somewhat less than six miles. Jerusalem in Josephus' day (first century, A.D.) was about four miles.[1] A new name meant in biblical thought and usage a new characteristic or character to correspond to it. The presence of the Lord God of Israel will be the chief glory of Jerusalem. The day referred to is that of the coming fulfillment of prophecy, indicating incidentally that Ezekiel was not thinking in ideal terms of the future nor was he referring to conditions in his own day. The city's name will be Adonai (for the unpronounceable Tetragrammaton) Shammah ("The Lord Is There"). The rabbis of the third century A.D. said: "Three were called after the name of God; the righteous (Isa. 43:7), and the Messiah (Jer. 23:6), and Jerusalem (Ezek. 48:35)"[2] (cf. Rev. 21:3 for a parallel truth). Ezekiel saw the glory of the Lord depart (chap. 11), return (chap. 43), and abide forever (chap. 48). This is God's objective in Israel gloriously fulfilled.

ICHABOD OR CHABOD

This incomparable prophecy began with a vision of the glory of God and concludes with a description of the glory of the Lord in the glorified city of Jerusalem. Ezekiel concluded, as John in the Revelation, with God dwelling with man in holiness and glory. Beyond this there is no greater goal of history and God's dealings with man.

Just as the glory of God departed temporarily from the children of Israel (Ichabod), so it may temporarily depart from the life of a Christian. It is pertinent to ask at the conclusion of this study of Ezekiel whether or not our lives are characterized by the glory of God (Chabod) and whether or not they are bringing glory to His name. The people of God have just as much responsibility to honor and glorify Him today as did Israel in Old Testament times and as will millennial saints of the future.

---

[1]See Josephus, *Wars of the Jews.* V. 4. 3.
[2]See Babylonian Talmud, *Baba Bathra,* 75 b.

SELECTED BIBLIOGRAPHY

NOTE: Ezekiel's prophecy, though not treated often enough, has been commented upon in expositions that cover the entire Bible. The serious student will have to utilize works in foreign languages, for some of the more substantial contributions are in the European languages. The best bibliography through the nineteenth century can be found in *Lange's Commentary*, and the most helpful for this century is found in Peter R. Ackroyd, "Commentaries on Ezekiel," *Theology*, LXII (1959), 97-100. The critical questions of Ezekiel are treated in both liberal and conservative introductions to the book. Probably the most extreme positions are those found in C. C. Torrey, *Pseudo-Ezekiel and the Original Prophecy*. New Haven: Yale Oriental Series Researches, 1930; and W. Irwin, *The Problem of Ezekiel*. Chicago: U. Chicago, 1943. The aim of this annotated bibliography is to give the prophecy student a cross section of the available literature without attempting to be exhaustive.

Beasley-Murray, G. R. "Ezekiel," *The New Bible Commentary*. Eds. F. Davidson, Alan M. Stibbs and Ernest F. Kevan. London: Inter-Varsity, 1953. The comments are reverent and useful but necessarily short, for the entire prophecy is treated in less than two dozen pages.

Bewer, Julius A. *The Book of Ezekiel*. 2 vols. New York: Harper, 1954. The notes are extremely brief. Good use is made of parallel passages. Unfortunately, textual changes rest almost solely on the Septuagint. Too much transposition of the Masoretic text is suggested.

Calvin, John. *Commentaries on the First Twenty Chapters of the Book of the Prophet Ezekiel*. 2 vols. Grand Rapids: Eerdmans, 1948 reprint. Calvin displays exceptional exegetical skill but does not see distinctions between the church and Israel nor certain eschatological details. He deals with the first twenty chapters only, but at the end of Vol. II he has a full outline of the entire prophecy along with his own translation of the first twenty chapters. The material is translated from the original Latin and compared with the French version.

Cooke, George A. *A Critical and Exegetical Commentary on the Book of Ezekiel* in *The International Critical Commentary*. Eds. S. R. Driver, A. Plummer and C. A. Briggs. Edinburgh: T. & T. Clark, 1936. The writer's theological stand is moderately critical. He makes good use of the versions, although in the matter of the text he allows greater activity to an editor than is warranted. The work lacks a cohesive principle and does not underline the original character of the prophet's thought. A bibliography is lacking although he includes three figures of the predicted temple of chapters 40-48.

Davidson, A. B. *The Book of the Prophet Ezekiel* in *The Cambridge Bible for Schools and Colleges*. Cambridge: U. Press, 1892. This work was revised by A. W. Streane in 1916. The prophecy is outlined in detail, and help is given on practically every verse of the text. Although certain expressions in the commentary are too critical of Ezekiel's method and message, in the main there is a faithful exposition of the meaning of the prophecy.

Ellison, Henry L. *Ezekiel: The Man and His Message*. Grand Rapids: Eerdmans, 1956. This work is too brief to allow more than a general overall view of the prophecy. The last nine chapters of the prophecy are treated in less than eight pages. The theological perspective is moderately premillennial.

Erdman, Charles R. *The Book of Ezekiel: An Exposition*. Westwood, N.J.: Revell, 1956. This short volume is helpful for a panoramic view of the book.

Fausset, A. R.; Brown, David and Jamieson, Robert. "Ezekiel," Vol. IV, *A Commentary Critical, Experimental and Practical on the Old and New Testaments*. Grand Rapids: Eerdmans, 1945 reprint. This six-volume commentary must take its place among the best in the English language. Based on the original language, it uses parallel passages well, clearly expounds the text and always gives spiritual applications of value. It should be the first among the commentary tools of any student of the Scriptures.

Feinberg, Paul D. "A Study of Ezekiel's Temple Vision." Unpublished Bachelor of Divinity thesis, Talbot Theological Seminary, 1963. A fine treatment of the interpretive principles underlying chapters 40-48.

Flack, Elmer E. "The Book of Ezekiel," *Old Testament Commentary*. Eds. Herbert C. Alleman and Elmer E. Flack. Philadelphia: Muhlenberg, 1948. Necessarily brief in a one-volume commentary on the whole Old Testament, the commentator does not reveal confidence in the integrity of the text. Comments on eschatological portions reveal a nonmillenarian outlook. Historical portions are treated in a more helpful manner.

Gaebelein, A. C. *The Prophet Ezekiel, An Analytical Exposition*. New York: Our Hope, 1918. The author's position, apart from minor details, is that of the present work. He deals with the prophecy more briefly in his *Annotated Bible* (1921), but from the same doctrinal position.

Gardiner, F. "Ezekiel," Vol. V, *Ellicott's Commentary on the Whole Bible*. Ed. C. J. Ellicott. Grand Rapids: Zondervan, 1954 reprint. This work labors under limitations of space but is helpful throughout with the exception of the exposition of the last nine chapters.

Grant, Frederick W. "Ezekiel," *The Numerical Bible*. New York: Loizeaux, 1889-1903. The author manifests an awareness of the chief emphases of the prophecy, and is conversant with prophetic details. From the same doctrinal viewpoint, but presenting a comprehensive picture, is J. N. Darby, *Synopsis of the Books of the Bible*. Vol. II. New York: Loizeaux, 1942 reprint.

Gray, James M. *Christian Workers' Commentary on the Old and New Testaments*. New York: Revell, 1915. Gray combines splendid insight with a preciseness of expression for the busy pastor or missionary with limited library facilities. The work is premillennial and dispensational, sane in all its remarks. Questions help the student working on his own.

Guthrie, Thomas. *The Gospel in Ezekiel Illustrated in a Series of Discourses*. New York: Carter, 1862. Twenty-two discourses are given on chapter 36 alone. It is a fine example of how the prophecy may be applied today for the spiritual uplift of God's people.

Henderson, Ebenezer. *The Book of the Prophet Ezekiel*. London: Hamilton, Adams, 1855. The author was an accurate expositor.

Hengstenberg, E. W. *Christology of the Old Testament*. Vol. III. Edinburgh: T. & T. Clark, 1875. A translation from the original German, this book is a classic on the doctrine of Christ in the Old Testament. Since it treats only the Messianic passages, it is limited in its treatment. But the prophecies of the Messiah are treated with reverence, insight, fullness (sometimes perhaps overly so) and warmth.

Ironside, Henry A. *Expository Notes on Ezekiel, the Prophet*. New York: Loizeaux, 1959. The writer has presented his public addresses on Ezekiel, a good example of how Bible books can be made to live through continuous expository preaching of an entire book.

Keil, Carl F. *Biblical Commentary on Ezekiel*. 2 vols. Grand Rapids: Eerdmans, n.d. Keil is unmatched in his use of the original, the rabbinic sources and a full treatment of the text. His outlook is always spiritual.

Kelly, William. *Notes on Ezekiel*. London: Moorish, 1876. What this volume loses by brevity, it gains by its broad sweep of the prophecy. The author always sees the main emphases and interrelationships of Ezekiel.

May, H. G. "Ezekiel," *The Interpreter's Bible*. Vol. VI. Ed. George A. Buttrick. Nashville: Abingdon, 1956. Good for bibliographic material, cultural backgrounds, cognate languages, the ancient versions and certain spiritual applications, this work has a moderately liberal approach to the authenticity of the text and handles the text too freely. A good example of a modern treatment of Ezekiel.

Pearson, Anton T. "Ezekiel," *The Wycliffe Bible Commentary*. Eds. Charles F. Pfeiffer and Everett F. Harrison. Chicago: Moody, 1962. Because of its brevity many problems in Ezekiel are not treated. It has a fine, full outline of the prophecy, and good use is made of the original language. In the highly eschatological portions much time is spent refuting the literal interpretation.

Plumptre, E. H. *Ezekiel* in *The Pulpit Commentary*. Eds. Spence, H. D. M. and Exell, Joseph S. Grand Rapids: Eerdmans, 1950 reprint. Much help is offered on specific passages in the prophecy, but in detailedly eschatological portions the method of interpretation is nonliteral.

Schröder, F. W. J. *Ezekiel* in *A Commentary on the Holy Scriptures* (Lange's Commentary). Trans.-ed. Philip Schaff. New York: Scribner, 1873. This commentary is among the finest on Ezekiel and fully treats the book's problems from practically all angles. It reveals breadth of research, acquaintance with the literature on the subject and an adherence to the original text. The last nine chapters are treated seriously and with fullness, but the outlook, like Keil, is the nonliteral.

Skinner, John. "The Book of Ezekiel," in *The Expositor's Bible*. Ed. W. Robertson Nicoll. New York: Armstrong, 1896. The author's expository method is smooth and yields many insights, but he does not see the correlation of the book's parts, nor does he give sufficient force to Ezekiel's dominant themes.

Wardle, W. Lansdell. "Ezekiel," *The Abingdon Bible Commentary*. Eds. Frederick C. Eiselen, Edwin Lewis and David G. Downey. Nashville: Abingdon-Cokesbury, 1942. This one-volume Methodist commentary is far too sketchy. It is moderately liberal, casts doubt on the integrity of the text, and offers little in the way of a coherent commentary. Chapters 33-48 are treated in fifteen columns of material. It suffers, as do all one-volume Bible commentaries, from too great a brevity which does not allow the message to be properly treated.

INDEX